TRIUMPH THROUGH TRIALS

TRIUMPH
THROUGH
TRIALS

The Epistle of James

David R. Anderson, Ph.D.

I would like to dedicate this book to Jimmy.

TABLE OF CONTENTS

"GOD'S UNIVERSITY"

James 1:1-4

In some respects this life is a university. In order to graduate with honors in any given major a student needs to take both elective courses and required courses. Some required courses are not much fun and we may question the point.

How well I remember orientation week at Rice University in August of 1963. We were asked to choose a course of study. Most of my family is in medicine and that is the direction I intended to go. I had never really cared much for school, but had done well in math and science, so medicine seemed a good route. In the commons at Baker College, one of four men's residential colleges at Rice, I approached a guidance counselor to discuss the courses for first year students who wished to pursue medicine.

I listened as he began listing the first semester courses. Biology—good. Chemistry—good. Calculus—good. History—what? English—seriously? It had only been three or four years since Rice had been called Rice Institute of Technology (RIT), like MIT. It was a research institute turned university. "What's with this history and English stuff?" I wondered. I hated English. I was going into medicine. Why would I need to deal with the humanities? The guidance counselor explained that since Rice was now a university they intended to graduate more wellrounded students. Things like history, English, and philosophy were all required. I had no choice. Take the required courses or don't graduate. So I hunkered down and did it. The rigorous math and science courses were easy next to these others, which I had no interest in taking. They were the real grind.

The Christian life is like a university. Graduation day is when Jesus comes for His bride, the church. The nice thing about God's University is that no one can flunk out. My entering class of 1963 had 450 students, but only 250 graduated four years later: some transferred, some flunked out, and six committed suicide. Not so in God's University. If you matriculate, you graduate. If you have received Christ as your personal Savior, you are guaranteed to graduate. Your job after graduation depends on how you respond to the courses God wants you to take while in His University. Do you hunker down and take the required courses? Even those you have no interest in taking?

Many high school graduates head off to college with lofty dreams and high hopes of how their education will provide them a successful and productive life after graduation, only to find the rigors of the university more than they can endure, so they drop out. Others have the wherewithal to graduate, but they find the required courses for their intended line of study more than they can bear, so they switch majors (maybe several times) always looking for the easiest way out. Yet, the greatest rewards go to the university student who commits himself to the course of study that fits his gifts and passions and who endures the required courses which will best equip him for his future career.

Fortunately, God has appointed a Guidance Counselor to help us navigate the curriculum and overcome trials. The Holy Spirit is the Guidance Counselor our Father has provided to walk us through our time at the university, course by course. He has employed professors to assist us as well, which is good because we need all the help we can get.

We can't do this alone. We need help. James is one of the professors God has chosen to help us get through the required courses. But who is James? We'll cover that, but first let's establish the thread that connects James' letter to the early church to our lives as Christians today.

Notice James 1:2-3, which urges us toward endurance in our trials. Now look at 5:10-11, which emphasizes patience during affliction. From beginning to end, James is a book about having the right attitude toward trials or required courses. The picture painted upon the canvas of this book is set against a stormy horizon, heavy with the rain and hail that pours down on us in life. James depicts how we should respond when the hail begins to fall. That is the thread that ties the book together, a thread we will develop passage by passage. Perhaps the hail has been falling on your life for some time now. Perhaps it's pelting your home or business or your own body right now. This may not be a course you want to take or ever thought you'd sign up for, but trials are a requirement of this life. Let's listen to what Professor James has to teach us.

The Salutation (Hello)

Jas 1:1   James, a bondservant of God and of the Lord Jesus Christ,

To the twelve tribes which are scattered abroad: Greetings.[1]

The Author

According to the course catalogue, the professor listed is just James. Nothing more, other than that he was a servant of God and of the Lord Jesus Christ. Was this James the brother of John? Not likely, since Acts 12:2 speaks of the early martyrdom of that James. The only other likely candidate would be James, the brother of our Lord Jesus Christ. You might say, "But I thought Jesus' brothers and sisters didn't believe in Him." True, until the resurrection. We are told in the gospels that there was strife and perhaps jealousy between Jesus and his younger siblings. They taunted Him with dares to prove His claim to be God. They entertained the popular rumor that His birth was illegitimate and they let Him know it. James especially might have thrown verbal

---

[1]   *The New King James Version.* 1982 (Jas 1:1). Nashville: Thomas Nelson.

darts at Jesus, as the oldest of Jesus' brothers and sisters. If Jesus had been illegitimate, then the birthright of the firstborn would go to James. Even if Jesus was a legitimate son, James, the second born, would have competed with Jesus for the attention of his mother and father.

Can you imagine what it would have been like to have Jesus as an older brother? Scripture says Jesus grew up like any other child as he developed physically, intellectually, and socially (Lk 2:52). But there was one exception —Jesus never sinned. Jesus always did what His mother told him—the first time. He always picked up His dirty clothes, always brushed His teeth, always did His homework, and always washed out the ring around the tub. He always did everything right. How could a parent avoid favoring such a child? And how could a bit of jealous sibling rivalry fail to develop between Jesus and James? Undoubtedly, His brother and sisters began to resent Him. And when He began His ministry and claimed to be God, they even thought He was insane. They tried at one point to get Him out of the public eye (Matt 12:47-50). He was a constant source of embarrassment to the family. His brothers and sisters wanted nothing to do with Him.

1 Corinthians 15:7 shines a hopeful sidelight on this rather dismal domestic situation. Jesus made a special post-resurrection appearance to James, His oldest brother. And James recognized Him. How emotion-packed that moment must have been. Now James, who had grown up with Jesus, knew what Emmanuel really meant—God with us. He received his own brother as his Savior and Lord. James went on to become the head of the church at Jerusalem. It was he who gave Paul his stamp of approval after Saul of Tarsus had been converted, and it was James who defended Paul's ministry twice at a later date.

This, then, is the professor who will help us deal with some of the required courses of life. You might say, "Well, why didn't he just say so? Why did he merely identify himself as a servant of Jesus? Just say you are Jesus' brother. What a way to gain an audience. If ever there was justification for name dropping, this would be it." Why didn't he? I think you know. Here was a man who had been ashamed of his older brother all the time they were both alive. James possibly delighted within himself when Jesus was nailed to a cross between two thieves. "Finally," he might have said in his bitter heart. "Finally, he's gone. Good riddance. What a trial he's been for our family. What an ordeal for our mother." But then to meet his risen brother face to face as his Lord and Savior! Oh, the shame, the regrets, the humiliation. I don't think James ever forgot the ill treatment he had given Jesus in those years growing up. He hadn't claimed Jesus as his brother when it might have dishonored his reputation—nor would he now claim Him as his brother when it might enhance it. In sincere humility, James says, I'm just a voluntary slave to God and the Lord Jesus Christ. I will ever bend the knee before, not my brother, but my king.

In fact, James did so much knee-bending in prayer before Jesus' throne of grace that they nicknamed him "Camel-knees" in the early church. Indeed, his letter says much about prayer. James was also known as "The Just" by the early church, which could hint to his understanding of justification in James 2. Finally, tradition tells us that James was martyred by being thrown from the top of the temple and then stoned beyond description or recognition.

The Readers

Now who are the readers or recipients of this letter? The text says "the twelve tribes, which are scattered abroad." The Greek word here is *diaspora*, which means "sown throughout." These people are Jewish Christians who, like seed from the sower, were sown throughout the world of that day as the cycle of persecution swept through early Christendom. Originally, the early Christians were all centered in and around Jerusalem. When persecution against them began, it did not begin in Rome. It began in Jerusalem with the stoning of Stephen. To avoid being killed, thousands of these Jews who had been part of the Jerusalem church got out of Dodge, and they were scattered around the Mediterranean world.

These believers were the first to learn something of what our Lord meant when He said, "If they hated Me, they will hate you. The servant is not greater than his master." They were hated by Gentiles simply because they were Jews. They were hated by Jews because they had become Christians. They knew something about hatred and grief. People would throw tomatoes at their shop windows. Their businesses were boycotted. Their children were snubbed and spat upon. Some Jewish schools even shut their doors on them. Old family members were incommunicado—no letters from home. Yet in the midst of these trials they received a letter, not from home, but from James, their former pastor. In the midst of their troubles they unravel the parchment paper on which this letter was written, and what do they read: "Greetings."

To translate the Greek word *charein* as "greeting" loses some of the force of the word. It is the only time we find this opening to a book in the entire Word of God. Essentially, it is a command to rejoice or to be satisfied. Surely, they almost dropped the scroll in disbelief. "Rejoice." That's like saying, "Good morning!" to someone who has just received news of a death in the family. Good morning—what's good about it? Rejoice—what do you mean, rejoice? Are you mocking us, James? And yet, wrapped up in that one word is James' entire message. He tips his hand right in his salutation. He sets the tone for the letter. He knew what kind of effect that word would have on his readers. He knew it sounded like just another prescription promoting the power of positive thinking. You know the kind: "Jaws just swam by and chomped off one of my legs, yet I managed to escape. And as I pulled my exhausted, bleeding body out of the surf onto the beach, a lifeguard comes and offers me a hand saying, 'Think positive thoughts.' Think positive? What is this, some kind of joke? Don't you see my leg has been ripped off? Rejoice? I am in pain!" They must have wondered what James could possibly have been trying to say. Did he just want them to forget or ignore their troubles? No way.

James knew what they were thinking. He knew their pain. So in the next verses he gives some reasons why these Jewish Christians should have genuine joy in the midst of their trials. In fact, the first twelve verses compare the blessings that accrue from trials to interest in a bank account. Is this psych-out joy? Is James trying to get them to overlook their trouble? Not on your life. Christianity is not a psych-out. In fact, Christianity offers the only realistic approach to facing trials, which moves us into the introduction of James' letter.

Introduction (1:2-18)—The Value of Trials[2]

In the introduction to the body of the letter James gives three positive values that trials add to our lives: needed endurance, needed wisdom, and a great quality of life. In verses 2-4 he writes about endurance, which I suggest is the most needed virtue in the Christian life. Because without endurance, we will not hang in there long enough to develop the kind of faith that moves mountains; without endurance, we will not be around long enough to develop *agape* love; and without endurance, we will not grow to the point that our hope lies not in this world but in the next. We can view needed endurance from the perspective of: Responding to Trials (2), the Reason for Trials (3), and the Results of Trials (4).

Responding to Trials (2)

My brethren, count it all joy when you fall into various trials.

That the joyous Christian life is no delusion becomes evident from the main verb of verse two: "count it." It is the word *hegeomai*, one of four words in the Greek language for coming to a conclusion: two are based on feelings and two are based on facts. This is a conclusion based on facts. It says, "Let's be objective. Don't let your feelings throw you in the midst of your trial. Let's get some perspective on the situation. Let's look at the facts." And, oh, how I like that word, my Christian friends. It tells me that my feelings don't have to dictate joy.

---

[2] The outline I am using for the exposition of James is one I picked up from Zane Hodges in class at Dallas Theological Seminary in the spring of 1970.

The facts do. Sometimes when that trial comes knocking at our door, we innocently open the door, and whammy; the intruder punches us in the stomach. Do you ever feel this way when a trial hits? I do. I feel it physically. My insides feel all discombobulated, and it seems like my cheek muscles would have to lift a hundred pounds for me to even manage a smile. I do not *feel* joyful.

But this word, *hegeomai*, tells me I can arrive at genuine joy by seeking an objective view of the entire situation. In fact, the root of this word means, "to lead." It suggests that a careful consideration of everything involved will lead to a joyous conclusion. This is important to me. It tells me that when a trial knocks the wind out of me, although my initial response is not joy, gaining an eternal perspective on the situation will lead me to genuine joy.

One more angle to this word—it is in the aorist tense, which, in this context, suggests point in time action. This means that, in the darkness of my trial when I am groping frantically in the closet of my mind for something to hold on to, I reach up to heaven and my hand finds the string to the closet light. I pull that string and—instantly—there is light where there was darkness. I once was blind and now I see. God's light shines in the midst of darkness. *Count it* true joy. That happens at a point in time, in an instant. So much meaning is wrapped up in this one word. Let me summarize its impact. It says that when a trial hits, my initial response will be a feeling, and that feeling will not be joy. But as I objectively review the situation and seek God's point of view on my predicament, I can find facts that will turn a light on in that dark hour, enabling me to find genuine joy.

I say "genuine joy," which is true; but the text actually says, "all joy." The thrust of that statement is pure joy—unmixed joy—unadulterated by depression or self-pity. Total joy. There was a song many years ago that said, "Look for the silver lining when'er dark clouds appear in the sky." We can all probably buy the silver lining philosophy. If I look hard enough at the storm clouds, I can probably find something to be happy about, a streak of light perhaps. But James is not presenting a silver lining philosophy of troubles. He doesn't say to count it just a little bit joy when you fall into various trials or count it mostly joy when you fall into various trials. He says to count it *all* joy. That's a powerful statement. "Count it an unmixed pleasure; count it a pure joy." It's *all* silver when we see it from God's perspective.

James mentions "various" trials. This word is *poikilois* in the original. We get the term polka-dotted from it. It often meant "many-colored, variegated." Trials come in all different sizes, shapes, shades, and hues. In another song from yesteryear the singer pined to be painted blue, red, or even black, according to her mood. One trial might say, "Color me light." Another might say, "Color me dark." But this text says, "Whatever the color of your trial—no matter what its character, shape, description, size, or hue—count it an unmixed blessing from God."

Notice another important word in this opening advice. James doesn't say, "Count it all joy *if* you fall into various trials." He says, "Count is all joy **when** you fall into various trials." Trials are not optional; they are inevitable. Peter writes, "Beloved, do not think it strange concerning the firey trial which is to try you, as though some strange thing happened to you; but rejoice to the extent that you partake of Christ's sufferings, that when His glory is revealed, you may also be glad with exceeding joy" (1 Pet 4:12-13). Trials are a normal part of God's process of bringing us to glory. It isn't something strange, but rather something inevitable.

Recently I read a story about a man who was riding on the subway in New York. It was quite crowded, and he had to face the door. He was prone to motion sickness and began to get quite sick. The train raced into the station, the door opened, and, becoming violently ill, the man vomited. The doors quickly closed, and the train sped on into the night. There happened to be another man who had been standing on the platform waiting to get on the train at this particular door. In utter dismay he turns to a man standing behind him, with his suit bearing the evidence of his trial, and asks, "Why me?" I think that's the way we feel sometimes when trials hit. "Why me, Lord?" But we shouldn't be surprised, as if there were some way to live this life that does not involve hard times and struggles. Trials are to be expected. It's the normal Christian life.

Yet, if this were all I had to go on, just this snippet of the introduction to the Book of James, I would be frustrated indeed. This reads no differently than all the humanistic literature about positive thinking. Rejoice! Count it all joy! "Why?" my spirit cries out. Now James gives us a reason for our trials.

Reason for Trials (1:3)

. . . knowing that the testing of your faith produces patience.

Here we get a tangible reason for rejoicing, some perspective that helps us turn on the light. It says, "because you know or we know." And this word for knowing means, "to know by experience." This is not an armchair theologian speaking. James has been on the playing field. He didn't get this knowledge at seminary. He learned it from some of the horse-collar tackles and crack-back blocks of life. He says without wavering that we can count it all joy because past experience has shown us something. What? It has shown us a divine purpose behind trials.

This intent shines forth in verses three and four. The trying or testing of our faith results in endurance. It's from this word "trying," *dokimion*, that we get the classic picture of purifying metals. Our faith enters a fiery furnace ignited by the trials of life. The purpose of this searing process is the trying or testing of our faith, in hopes that any remaining impurities will smolder and burn away. In the furnace our faith endures. That is exactly what verse three is saying. The result of testing our faith is that we gain endurance, *hupomonēn*.

The NKJ translators tell us that our faith produces "patience." But the word for patience in the NT Greek is not *hupomonēn*. It is *macrothumia*, which is a fruit of the Spirit in Galatians 5:22. This word *hupomonēn* is made up of two Greek words: *hupo + moneō*. The first means "under," like a hypodermic needle goes under the skin. The second word means, "to remain." Christian endurance is to "remain under" God's revealed desire for our lives. It is as though He is holding a protective umbrella over us to shield us from the worst effects of our trials. We stop enduring when we step out from under His umbrella to try to handle things on our own or simply to follow the flesh. When we are under His umbrella nothing can harm us eternally. The storms will come but they will not touch us. The most severe hailstorm cannot pummel us; the most devastating tornado cannot funnel us away. And to me, that's what this word *hupomonēn* means: to stay under God's umbrella when the storms come. To trust Him and submit to Him during the most threatening and ominous storms—that is endurance. But once I step out from under the umbrella, I leave God's protection. It's then that I'm exposed to the elements of the storm. It's then that endurance has disappeared. But God wants to hold that umbrella over our heads while He guides us to the warm hearth of our heavenly home.

Endurance entails more than just our protection. It also produces in us maturity. In verse two we read about Responding to Trial, and in verse three we discovered the Reason for Trials. Now in verse four, James reveals the Results of Trials.

Results of Trials (4)

But let patience have *its* perfect work, that you may be perfect and complete, lacking nothing.

The word for "perfect," *teleios*, means "complete, finished, mature." We find an excellent parallel in Paul's writings when he asks the Galatians in 3:3, "Having begun in the Spirit, are you now being made perfect by the flesh?" Or, as he says in Colossians 1:28, "Him we preach, warning every man and teaching every man in all wisdom, that we may present every man perfect in Christ Jesus." It is the goal of the Christian life to become mature.

The Greek word for "complete" is another compound word: *holo* + *klēros*. The first word means "whole" and calls to mind a soldier fully equipped for battle or a ship decked out for a voyage. A Christian needs all the weaponry and armor he can get lest he retreat from battle. He needs to be thoroughly decked out for the voyage, lest his ship be whipped onto the ragged rocks by the lashing waves and the fierce winds. The second part of this compound means, "lot," as in our lot in life. God has a great purpose for each of us. This word speaks of getting the full benefit from the circumstances allotted to us.

Verse four is actually something of a caution from James. An illustration of this truth comes from my own experience as a student. In my first year of seminary I took a course in what was called "Baby Greek." It was for those who had had no prior exposure to the language. In this course the professor gave us a quiz every morning over the homework. I found that my grades on these daily quizzes were directly related to how I did my homework. If I went home and did the assignment with a flea comb, searching for every detail I might glean from the assignment, then the quiz was no problem. But sometimes I would go home and do the assignment rather rapidly. And then before the quiz I would look over the assignment again, somewhat hastily. I would say to myself, "Oh, think I know that, and I don't need to spend any more time on that." Then I would close the book. But when the quiz was given, invariably I would wish I had done the assignment much more thoroughly.

Most of us tend to be hasty students, especially in times of trouble. We say, "Oh, yes, Lord, now I see what you're trying to teach me. But now let's close the book and get on to something else. Let's get over this difficulty. I've learned my lesson." Many times when trouble comes we recognize the basic lesson that God designed it to teach, so we rush through it without allowing it proper time to nurture and cultivate that which God intended.

This fourth verse is a warning from James about running through the lesson too rapidly. "But," he says, "let endurance have its complete work. Be sure," James says, "you reap all the benefits from the test God designed for you to reap. Be sure you lack nothing the test can furnish you." This requires an additional measure of endurance, so I say to myself, "I think I see what God is trying to do with me in this test, but maybe there is a little bit more I can learn, and therefore I will allow Him to determine the time when the test will be terminated." I think that's precisely what James is emphasizing. Be sure, he says, that you get the full benefit. Use the flea comb.

Now we can have genuine joy. We can survey the wreckage of our trial and overcome the initial punch in the stomach with true rejoicing. Why? Because verses three and four give us that eternal perspective. God uses trials in our lives to fit us out for a journey which *will* have some rough spots. He is equipping us with armor to win battles against spiritual forces. He wants to develop us into mature soldiers who can stand with His Son in the final day when He calls for a volunteer army to defeat His foe (Ps 110:3).

Therefore, my brethren, count it all joy when you fall into trials of various colors and shades. This is not false joy; it is genuine joy stemming from a mental journey from earth to heaven to survey the eternal horizon and search for God's point of view. Sometimes the eternal perspective will be seen immediately. Sometimes it may take years. And still, in other cases, we may never know the eternal reason for our trial until the next life.

Years ago I watched the film version of Corrie ten Boom's life, *The Hiding Place.* Like so many of the Dutch who were inspired by King Christian, Corrie and her older sister Betsie resisted the Nazi regime by hiding Jews from the Gestapo, but they were caught and sent to a Nazi concentration camp. Betsie ten Boom's bright smile and encouraging words from Scripture became stars of hope for numerous prisoners. She said, "Be thankful for everything. God doesn't make mistakes." Corrie stabbed a dagger of doubt into Betsie's faith when she pointed to all the lice crawling in their hair and on their mats. A few moments later they overheard another prisoner say, "Thank God for the lice. Not one of the male soldiers will set foot in here while the lice prevail." There was Betsie's answer. The light bulb went on. Those lice would protect them from the advances and intrusions of Nazi solders while they had Bible studies inside. She gained the eternal perspective almost immediately.

But Corrie never did see the light bulb go on while she was at Dachau. She left—questions still burning in her bitter heart about why her family had to die in that ghost hole while only she was discharged. Why Dachau for her? Why all that suffering? Why that trial? And why did she escape death instead of Betsie? She never grasped the eternal perspective while in the concentration camp. Only years later, after God had sent her to sixty-two foreign countries sharing the love of Christ and how He sustained her and turned her bitterness to love for the German people, not until then did she fully see God's hand at work. And what about Betsie? It's unlikely she ever saw the eternal purpose for Dachau during her life on earth. She died imprisoned. But in heaven, by Jesus' side, she can see the divine purpose in all of her suffering. It had all been to inspire her more hearty and healthy younger sister to carry the message of God's love to the world.

Sometimes the light bulb will come on almost immediately. Other times it takes years. Sometimes we will be in the dark until the next life. But there is a purpose we can see right now regardless of when the picture becomes complete. God has a university. Every one of His children gets a full scholarship to this university. In it, God prepares each one according to his gifts and talents for a useful place in His eternal future and to further His kingdom work on earth right now. Some of the courses at this university are fun—the electives. Some are very difficult but are required for us to become all we can be. And for those who don't drop out, graduation day will be the happiest day of their lives. That's when we find out just what all those required courses were about. That's when we stand before Him at the Judgment Seat of Christ to learn about the exciting place He has prepared for us to serve and glorify Him forever.

Ever since I can remember, I looked forward to being a father. I can remember having fun playing with little kids even as a fifth grader. Of course, as I grew older I found there were things I'd learned over the years both in sports and the classroom that I wanted to pass along to my children one day, like I was collecting wisdom just for them. And

I never really had a gender preference. Like many parents I thought either a boy or a girl would be equally great.

When our firstborn came along I ran all the way from Baylor Hospital in Dallas to our apartment to call my parents and tell them we had a new baby boy. We called him Jimmy. Everything seemed wonderful until around Jimmy's first birthday. My wife Betty thought there might be something wrong with our son. She was the oldest of six sisters, so she had a pretty good feel for babies, having been a big help to her mom with all of those younger siblings. But I had my doubts. *My* boy? What could be wrong with *my* boy?

Then when Jimmy learned to walk we let him play with other seminary children at the seminary playground. We began to notice strange, small incidents when Jimmy would play. If he fell down, he would get up and find the nearest kid and push him down, even if the kid was ten feet away. In his mind, I suppose, if he had fallen, someone had pushed him down. So he'd find the nearest kid to punish—search and destroy. Of course, I just thought that this kid was going to make an incredible linebacker.

A couple of years later we were in our first pastorate and we continued to notice odd things. When I began tossing a Nerf ball to Jimmy, he couldn't catch it. When he tried to throw the ball, it would just hit his feet. Then we noticed when it came time for Jimmy to learn to read he had trouble making his eyes travel across the page. At this point we took him to be diagnosed by a leading expert in Houston. She came up with twenty-two neurological observations that basically told us something had happened to our son during the birth process that had impaired various neurological functions. For instance, he could hop on his left foot, but not his right. He could touch his fingers to his thumb on his left hand but not on his right.

When Jimmy was six, he wanted to play t-ball with his friends. I thought, well, the ball is sitting there, not moving. Maybe he could do that. There were twenty-six kids on that team, but my son was the worst. Baseball had been my best sport growing up, so I hurt for him. What made matters worse was the fact that his coach had been a professional football player for the old Los Angeles Rams and he couldn't relate to a kid with gross motor problems. One day I was watching practice and the coach began making fun of Jimmy. Though I am a pastor, I am also a parent. I felt the anger rising up from my feet to my neck. I wanted to march out there and strangle that coach.

However, being a pastor in a small town, I could see the headlines the next day: "Local Pastor Kills Local Football Hero." Then I realized that he had been a professional football player and how much worse the headlines would look if they read, "Local Football Hero Kills Local Pastor." So I swallowed my anger. Jimmy walked over to where I was standing just outside the fence, crying his eyes out.

"Why can't I do it, Daddy?" I didn't know how to answer. I thought a moment and said, "Well, Jimmy, God made some people good at some things and other people good at others. We just need to find what you are good at." He looked down at his feet, still crying, and back up at me with his big blue eyes, and said, "But, Daddy, God didn't make me good at anything." Now I had my own tears. I couldn't argue with him.

Though Jimmy did not have some of the abilities the world holds dear, of our four children, he had the earliest hunger for spiritual things. He had seen my wife give a flannel graph presentation of the gospel through Child Evangelism when he was just three. That night he got on all fours while supposedly going to sleep in his bed and just chanted, "I want a white heart, . . . I want a white heart, . . . I want a white heart," while rocking back and forth banging his head on the wall. Betty and I could hear him, of course, but we thought he was too young to understand spiritual things. Finally, as we realized he was close to knocking a hole in the wall of our rented home, we looked at each other and said, "Let's go talk to him."

"So, Jimmy, why do you want a white heart?"

"Cause mine is black."

"Why is your heart black?"

"Because I have sinned."

"How have you sinned?"

"I pulled Christie's hair" (his little sister).

"What do you think will make your heart white?"

"The blood of Jesus, you stupid preacher, don't you know anything?"

(Okay no, he just said the first part about the blood of Jesus)

Betty and I looked at each other and sort of shrugged, admitting, "Who are we...?" So Jimmy trusted Christ that night and was a different person. His disabilities did not disappear, but he had a joy that was new and a great spiritual curiosity. On one evening with a beautiful full moon in the sky, we were driving out to the lake when Jimmy asked, "Dad, do you see that moon?" "Yes, son." "Well, that's God's eye. He's watching you." I promptly slowed down (radar in the sky, you know). And so it went. He seemed to have a direct line into heaven.

We worked with Jimmy through the years and actually found a couple of sports he could do well at—swimming and football. He never became a great student, but he was a hard worker and became an A- student in high school and a B student in college. It took him more years than most, but he wound up with a couple of bachelor degrees and he became a Microsoft Certified Engineer and a manager for Singular. Then, at around age thirty, he came to me and said, "Dad, I think I have proved that with hard work I can make it in the world, but I don't find it fulfilling. I'd like to give the rest of my life to serving the Lord on the mission field." Wow. So he entered seminary and soon after found a girl that was willing to join him. He was going to introduce her to us on February 23, 2003, a day I will never forget.

We got the call at about 4:30 in the morning. Ben Taub, the county hospital, was calling to ask us to come down to identify the body of our son Jimmy. He had been walking across the street to his car on Saturday night when a woman in a Ram truck, who had been to eight bars that night and who already had a DWI conviction, hit Jimmy and killed him. A hit and run. But upon impact, the license plate fell off her truck and the police found her an hour later, still at .22 blood alcohol content, a nearly toxic level.

Why? No parent wants that phone call. No parent expects that phone call. You just never dream while you are raising your kids that you might outlive them. Yes, it's a very real possibility, but it just never enters your mind, unless you are sending them off to Vietnam, Iraq, or Afghanistan—to war. You don't expect it like this.

It was almost ten years ago that this particular trial knocked on our door. It is still with us. Statistics say that eighty percent of parents who experience the death of a child end up in divorce. Yet, by His grace Betty and I are closer to each other and to the Lord than ever before. People along the way have asked what sustained us. Of course, we point heavenward. That's the short answer. This book is the long answer. There are other passages outside of James that would complete the picture. Maybe that's for another book. But James is an excellent place to start. "Count it *all* joy **when** you fall into various trials." So read on.

"THE OPTICAL ILLUSION"

James 1:5-12

Optical illusions can play tricks with our eyes. Optical illusions can also play tricks with our lives. The Mueller-Lyer illusion is familiar to many as an example of *apparent* movement: <--------> >--------<. Not only does one line appear longer than the other, we can also watch the shorter line grow. This is caused by a shift of images on the retina over a very short period of time. The line does not actually get any longer. It just appears to be getting longer. To give you another example of apparent movement, take a pencil and hold it at arms length. Now alternatively open and shut one eye after the other. The pencil will appear to be moving back and forth, but you and I know it really isn't. The amount of motion depends on which eye is opening at a given time. The dominant eye tends to produce the greater shift in the pencil. Another optical trick played on us is called gamma movement. When you are sitting in a room with the main light source in the center of the ceiling, turn the light on and off. The light will not disappear from your vision immediately. It disappears at the bulb last and first leaves the field of vision from the outside. In reality, we know the light disappears first from its source, the bulb, but our eyes do not see it that way.

The point is very simple. **We can't always trust what our senses tell us.** Optical illusions can play tricks with our eyes. Optical illusions can also play tricks with our lives. As James becomes our optician, let's see how he can help distinguish between illusion and reality.

In James 1:1-4 we began studying a letter about triumph in trials. From the beginning to the end the picture painted upon the canvas of this book is set against a stormy horizon, heavy with the rain and hail that pours down on us in life. Going further into the letter, the body of the Book of James teaches how to respond when the hail begins to fall. Perhaps the hail has been falling on your life for some time now—on your home, your business, your health, your dating relationship. If it hasn't been, it will. We learned in our first lesson that trials are not optional in the Christian life; they are inevitable. And God directs or allows these trials to occur to help build the kind of endurance that will keep us going while He is developing other virtues and qualities in us that we will need both in this life and in the life to come. Endurance is the theme; the benefit of trials brings us to maturity in Christ. If we truly let endurance have a complete work in our lives, then God will have time to thoroughly equip and furnish us for His chosen task. We will lack nothing.

In verse five James gives an example of something that may be lacking in our lives, something trials may provide—wisdom. In this section we look at 1:5-11, the Value of Testing in Providing Needed Wisdom. Here is what our outline of the book looks like so far:

JAMES

"TRIUMPH THROUGH TRIALS"

Salutation (1:1)

Introduction (1:2-18)—The Value of Trials

A.	*Trials Can Produce Endurance*	*2–4*
B.	*Trials Can Produce Wisdom*	*5–11*
	1. Prayer for Wisdom	5-8
	a. Requirement	5
	b. Restriction	6a
	c. Reasons	6b-8
	2. Example of Wisdom	9-11
C.	*Trials Can Produce Happiness*	*12–18*

Trials can produce wisdom. In 1:5-11 we will look at a Prayer for Wisdom (5-8) and an Example of Wisdom (9-11). Examining the prayer first, there is a requirement, a restriction, and reasons.

Prayer for Wisdom (5-8)

Requirement (5)

If any of you lacks wisdom, let him ask of God, who gives to all liberally and without reproach, and it will be given to him.

If we lack wisdom, **just ask** God for it. Asking is the requirement. Later in this book James will say, "You have not because you ask not" (4:2). So if we need wisdom, we must ask for it. But what is wisdom, anyway? Coleridge said, "Common sense in an uncommon degree is what the world calls wisdom."[3] That's pretty close to biblical wisdom. A man may have a great deal of knowledge, but very little common sense as to how to use that knowledge. Spurgeon put it this way: "Wisdom is the right use of knowledge. To know is not to be wise. Many men know a great deal and are all the greater fools for it. There is no fool so great as a knowing fool. But to know how to use knowledge is to have wisdom."[4] That hits it on the nose. Wisdom is the ability to apply knowledge to experience. And in times of trial, this may be precisely what we are lacking. "What should I do?" is the most frequently asked question by persons in the midst of trials. In other words, "How should I respond?" There are so many options. Which one is best? What that person needs, what he lacks, is wisdom—how to apply knowledge to that particular situation. James says, "In such a situation that man should ask God."

I used to think this verse meant a light bulb experience like

---

[3] Samuel Taylor Coleridge, http://www.quotedb.com/quotes/1493.

[4] Charles H. Spurgeon, http://thinkexist.com/quotation/wisdom_is_the_right_use_of_knowledge-to_know_is/13014.html.

the one we discussed in verse 2. I thought in the midst of my trial I needed to get down on my knees before the Lord and pray for wisdom. Suddenly, there would be a flash of lightning and an angel would appear with a package on a silver platter all gift-wrapped and labeled "Wisdom." That wouldn't be an optical illusion, by the way. That would be a hallucination. This verse isn't talking about a light bulb experience. Joy comes that way. But wisdom—not necessarily so. The light bulb experience came from the point-in-time action of the aorist tense; but the word James uses for asking is not in the aorist tense. It is in the present tense. It isn't just an immediate, point-in-time action. It means *now*, repeatedly knocking on the door, asking over and over, continual petition. Thus, the wisdom we receive from a trial does not necessarily come from one prayer, but from repeated prayer throughout the experience. In fact, the wisdom may come long after the trial is over. It's the old adage, "Experience is the best teacher."

Someone may say, "Well, if that's the case, why pray at all? Anyone can learn by experience, God or no God." Yes, I agree—anyone but a fool. Proverbs 17:10 says, "A reproof enters more into a wise man than an hundred stripes into a fool." The point is that every trial contains a message from God. The wise man reads and heeds it well. The fool never bothers to open the envelope. He throws it in the trash like another advertisement. I heard a friend once say these words and they have always impressed me. He said, "When we fall into a trial, we usually pray: Lord, deliver me from this miserable situation. Rather, we should be praying: Lord, teach me what you want me to learn in this miserable situation." God's purpose is not always to deliver us; it may well be to give us wisdom.

James tells us that when we go to God seeking wisdom, it shall be given to us. And the giver is none other than the God who gives to **all** men **liberally** and who does not **reproach**. What a beautifully encouraging statement about God this is. Three items impress me here. First of all, it says God gives wisdom to all persons who seek Him. That's a wonderful promise, isn't it? He doesn't say God only gives wisdom to those who go to Sunday School and church, or only to those who keep the Ten Commandments, or only to those who give a lot to Him in the offering plate. James simply states that God gives wisdom to all men who ask Him. God isn't prejudiced. James goes on to put some candy on the apple. God is a generous giver. The adverb used to describe God's giving certainly doesn't depict Him as stingy; He doesn't give a lot to Bob and only a little to Sally. He gives to all men unbegrudgingly and openheartedly. This word communicates that God gives generously to any who would ask and He does so without bargaining with us.

Not only does God not bargain with us, the text also says He doesn't reproach us. This means He does not insult or make fun of us. I think if we're to understand what James is getting at here, we must remind ourselves that one's prayer life depends directly on one's concept of God. Most people visualize God much as they visualize their human father. I've heard one woman say she couldn't believe God loved her. Why? Because her earthly father didn't. Another said she couldn't pray because God seemed so distant, cold, detached and far away. Why? Because that's how she saw her earthly father. So why does James include this statement about God not reproaching, criticizing or embarrassing one of His children when he or she comes before Him with a request? Simply because so many fathers on earth do exactly that.

Once there was a boy named Billy who wanted to learn how to tie his shoes. So he said, "Daddy, will you teach me how to tie my shoes?" "Sure, son," was the happy response of a father glad to be relieved of this onerous responsibility. The next day his son was back again and said, "Daddy, will you show me how to do it again. I forgot." His father obliged. But day after day it was the same request. Finally, Billy's father became quite annoyed and said, "What's the matter with you, son? You got rocks in your head? Can't you remember anything?" Billy never asked his father for help again. James is assuring us our heavenly Father is not like that. How elementary some of our questions must seem to Him; how easy for Him to say, "Now why do you ask me a simple question like that? Don't you read the Bible? How many times have you heard a sermon on that and you still haven't learned the lesson? You got rocks in your head? Can't you learn anything?" And yet the lovely thing about this text is that James says this is precisely what God doesn't do. If any man lacks wisdom, let him ask of God who gives to all men liberally and does not make fun, and it shall be given him. That's a wonderful thought about God. We can come to Him with our childish, foolish, simple, easy questions to get the wisdom we need in our hour of trial. It is a lovely concept, I think, about a giving God. No respecter of persons, generous, who doesn't make fun or get annoyed at our repeated requests. Yet, there is one restriction on this promise.

Restriction (6a)

But let him ask in faith, with no doubting.

No doubting. That's the restriction, or qualification if you will, for our prayer to be admitted to the throne room of the Generous Giver. It must be ushered in by faith. Faith, you know, is just another word for trust. In the midst of our trial, if we would receive any help or wisdom from God, we must be willing to trust in Him, not ourselves. That would seem to go without saying, yet the phrase points to a very real pitfall we encounter when faced with a trial. The text says, "not doubting," but the Greek word here, *diakrinomenos*, has another, more appropriate meaning, for the situation at hand. It means "to debate."

We might translate it this way: "If any man lacks wisdom, let him . . . debating nothing." The picture is this: we are faced with a problem. We go to the Lord for wisdom. But as soon as we are up off our knees then we begin tossing around in our mind the solution to our problem. Shall I do this about it, or shall I do that? We are as furiously debating our problem *after* we have asked God for wisdom as we were *before* we asked Him. And I think what James is saying here is very simply this. If you're going to turn to God for wisdom, stop your own inner, raging debate. This paints a fuller picture than just "to doubt." For what good would it do to tell the doubter that he'll receive nothing from the Lord? He didn't expect anything anyway. It's the man who is debating the options vociferously within himself who is told not to expect anything. Additionally, there are more reasons James lists regarding why one shouldn't inwardly debate.

Reasons (6b-8)

For he who doubts is like a wave of the sea driven and tossed by the wind. For let not that man suppose that he will receive anything from the Lord; he is a double-minded man, unstable in all his ways.

Not receiving anything from the Lord would be reason enough to stop the internal debate, but James also says this man who continues to debate his options is "like a wave." He is up and down; an emotional train wreck. He cannot decide. He can't make up his mind. He is going two directions at once and doesn't know which way to turn. That is why he is like a wave. Whichever way the winds of circumstances are blowing at the moment, that is the way he's moving, because he's constantly wrestling with the problem in his own mind. I like to explain it this way since the imagery here is the picture of a stormy sea. What James is really saying to us is:

Sail the ship of your mind into the safe harbor of God's wisdom;

Drop the anchor of your thoughts into the quiet depths of His infinite understanding.

That is what we should do when we come to God for wisdom. It doesn't mean we stop thinking about the trial completely. It means we put to rest the furious debate that goes on in our hearts. We turn our problem over to him and wait for His insight. Nothing is lovelier than the calm, unruffled soul who waits upon God and His wisdom in the midst of adversity.

Let's flesh this out by taking an example James provides. That is one of the great things about reading the Book of James. He often follows one of his principles with an example or illustration. We have seen the prayer for wisdom (5-8). Now here is an example of wisdom.

Example of Wisdom (9-11)

Let the lowly brother glory in his exaltation, but the rich in his humiliation, because as a flower of the field he will pass away. For no sooner has the sun risen with a burning heat than it withers the grass; its flower falls, and its beautiful appearance perishes. So the rich man also will fade away in his pursuits.

James started his letter by talking about joy, which can come from realizing that God may be trying to teach us something through trials (2-4). Then James said that what God may be trying to teach us is wisdom (5-8). Now he gives an example: a problem area in which an eternal perspective is needed, a trial in which divine wisdom can be lacking—personal finances. The Jewish Christians reading this letter had been facing economic persecution. Many of them were scraping the bottom of the barrel. Questions arose. How should we feel about this situation of economic persecution? What should our attitude be toward money? Verses 9-11 address these questions.

James told his audience to count it all joy when they fall into trials and now he gets specific. He says if you're a lowly brother, and by this he must mean poverty stricken because this brother is contrasted to the rich man, then take this particular attitude toward your trial. If you happen to be a rich man, then take this other attitude toward your trial. The lowly brother is to exult in his exaltation. The rich brother is to exult in his humiliation.

A chapter in the Apocrypha (Sirach 2:1-5) parallels this admonition. It says:

My son, if you come forward to serve the Lord, prepare yourself for trials. Get your heart right and be steadfast and do not be hasty in time of calamity. Cleave to him and do not depart that you may be honored at the end of your life. Accept what is brought upon you and in changes that humble you, be patient. For gold is tested in the fire and acceptable men in the furnace of humiliation.

Sirach and James both recognize two things to be inherent in trials. First, testing brings a man low, often bringing him way down to the bottom. That's humiliation. But, according to James, testing is also designed to lift a man up. Tests ultimately make him the kind of man he ought to be, a man capable (according to v. 12) of receiving the garland of life. So there are always two facets in trials or testing: there is the lowliness, which is our experience, and then there is the exaltation, which is to be the result.

What James is saying here is extremely interesting. The man who is already lowly is to focus upon the exaltation part of the test. And the man who already has the high station in life is to focus on the fact that he is brought low. James is saying that every man should react to trials according to his own individual need during that hour of trial. Here is a poor man who is constantly experiencing neglect, deprivation, and so on. What can a trial really mean to him? How exactly is it valuable and profitable? It will mean that God is paying attention to him, and that God is trying to make him and mold him and lift him up. God wants to bring him to a place where He can honor the poor man and reward him. That would be a very meaningful thing for a man who lives in poverty.

But to the man who is already on top of the world and has all he needs, the old saying, "What can you give to a man who has everything?" comes to mind. God says, "I'll give him a trial," in order to bring that man to a realization of what he really is in this world, to realize that he is just a blade of grass. There is something about trials that do that. We see ourselves as being secure, even those of us who are not considered rich. We have a house to live in, a car to ride around in, a guaranteed income perhaps. The moment one of these things is plucked from us, the plank of security on which we are so eager to rest is swept away. And we are brought face to face with the fact that we are very transient, fading, mortal individuals, thoroughly touched by trials.

I teach a Bible study every Wednesday during lunch at the Petroleum Club in Midland, Texas. Many of the men who attend have done very well in the oil business. After one particular luncheon I was walking out with the man who sponsors the luncheon. He asked me to look at a wall with about thirty pictures of oil field luminaries from years past. "Do you know any of those men?" he asked me. "No." "Well," he said, "unless I do something with all that God has given me that goes beyond just me and my family, someday I'll just be a picture on a wall that only a few people ever knew." As James mentions later in this book (Jas 4:14), life is just a vapor, a drop of water on hot pavement—unless we find a deeper meaning, a higher purpose, a transcendent cause.

I really think in verses 9-11 James is saying that in our trials we ought to find the thing best suited for our psychological/spiritual needs. If we really believe God designs trials to meet our needs, then that means in each test there is something hand chosen by God to meet our soul's needs. There is something designed for the psychology of the lowly man; there is something designed for the psychology of the rich man; there is something designed for your personal makeup, as well as for mine.

As we look back at these eleven verses, it seems there is one key James applies to discovering genuine joy. That key is this: this world is an optical illusion. As our five senses perceive this world, it appears to be something that will last forever. It seems to be the only thing worth living for. Eternity and spiritual beings like angels, a resurrected Christ and the Holy Spirit, all of these seem so remote in comparison to this tangible world of air, earth, fire and water that we can touch, taste, hear, see, and smell. This world seems so solid, so permanent, when actually it is crumbling, degenerating, and ephemeral. Even science teaches us this with the Second Law of Thermodynamics and the principle of entropy. Yet the future world, which seems so unreal, without substance, and something we can't put our hands on, that is the only world that truly has permanence and eternality. It's really the only solid rock we have to stand upon. This is what the writer to the Hebrews (12:26-28) is trying to teach us when he says that someday the world we can see will be shaken and will disappear. Then the world that cannot be shaken (the spiritual world) will be seen. Right now it is invisible to the physical eye, but it is the only permanent world. This one is passing away, as is the lust thereof (1 Jn 2:15:17). That is what James is trying to say. This is wisdom.

This is the eternal perspective that secures genuine joy. Applied to life, this insight can bring happiness, as we shall see in verse 12. When the rich man is tried, he is reminded of what this world has to offer—only impermanence, since it is all passing away. When the poor man is tried, he too can be happy, for in the world to come his lowly attitude and riches in faith (2:5) will yield an eternal exaltation.

We can live this life in one of two ways. We can live for the present world or we can live for the future world. If we live for the present world, then ultimately our life will yield sadness, grief, loss, and disappointment. For this world is passing away and the lust thereof. But if we live for the future world, no present loss or disappointment can permanently damage or daunt our enthusiasm for life. Why? Because we know the present world is passing away and we have oriented our activities, our goals, our hopes, and our dreams toward a future world where there will be no more death or sorrow, no more crying and no more pain, because this world will have passed away.

Oh, my Christian friends, don't let your senses fool you. This world is an optical illusion. It is impermanent and passing away. Why invest your love and your life in something passing away? I see our existence in three stages. In the first stage we are in total darkness— for approximately nine months. During this stage God is at work. He is making eyes, but we cannot see the world yet. He is making ears, but we do not hear very much. He is making olfactory nerves, but we need not smell anything, yet. And so on. Why does God do this? Is it a waste of time?

We know the answer. The five senses are developed in stage one for use in stage two. This second stage of our existence is another time of development for those who have become a part of God's forever family. It is much longer than the first stage (eighty years versus nine months). In this stage God develops the spiritual senses: spiritual ears to hear His still, small voice; spiritual eyes to see His handiwork; spiritual taste buds to taste that His Word is good; spiritual touch to be sensitive to the needs of others; and a spiritual sense of smell to appreciate the sweet aroma of suffering for His cause.

The spiritual senses are only enjoyed in a glimpsing way during the second stage. They are being developed primarily for use in the third stage of our existence. The spiritual senses will be used on a full time basis in the third stage. This stage is much longer than the second stage, just as the second stage was longer than the first. Additionally, there is one important difference between the first and second stages other than their duration. In the first stage, a baby cannot place the growth process on hold, but in the second stage he can. Yes, a baby Christian can even abort the work of the Spirit. He can quench the Spirit; he can grieve the Spirit; and he can resist the Spirit. But no one in his right mind wants to be a spiritual abortion.

Hence, if I choose to be as wise as James would have us be, then I will assist in God's work to develop those spiritual senses. I do not chafe under His hand. I yield; I cooperate. He wants to make you and me into sweet wine, so He plucks the grape and squeezes it between His fingers. If we become unyielding and resist His fingers, then He cannot do His work. But if we yield, He makes us into sweet wine.

The problem is we don't like the fingers God uses. Do you realize the people who are squeezing you right now, the circumstances pressing on you, are the fingers of God? They are simply extensions of God's hand. That is why Peter (1 Pet 5:6) says, "Humble yourselves under the mighty hand of God that he might exalt you in due time." God is behind those fingers. The same hand that squeezes us will also strengthen us. As the Psalmist (20:6) has said, "Now know I that the

Lord saves His anointed; He will hear him from His holy heaven with the saving strength of His right hand." And again (138:7-8), "Though I walk in the midst of trouble . . . your right hand shall save me—the Lord will perfect that which concerns me." Let us humble ourselves under that mighty hand. Let us see that hand which squeezes us as that hand which strengthens us, and all of it in order to perfect God's work in us.

J. Lanier Burns and I became Christians at the same high school, The McCallie School in Chattanooga, Tennessee. Then, it was a semi-boarding school of about four hundred students. Its most famous graduate is probably Ted Turner. I was from Nashville and Lanier hailed from Knoxville. After high school, Lanier went off to Davidson College and I left for Rice University in Houston. We both wound up at Dallas Theological Seminary in the late sixties. Lanier and I became best buds, playing racket ball once a week and having a weekly in-depth Bible study. Then we each started a family and began having children. Each of us had four children with Lanier's staggered about six months behind mine. Our firstborns were both boys.

Lanier's father had done quite well in business, owning the largest independent insurance company in the South. Lanier grew up on a beautiful bluff overlooking the Tennessee River, right next to the country club where he had became an accomplished junior tennis player. Unlike most of us seminary students who had to scratch and claw for a living while going to school full time, thanks to a generous trust fund from his father, Lanier did not have to work. He was an excellent student, ended up earning two PhD's, and became the head of the Systematic Theology Department at DTS. He seemed to have the perfect life—a beautiful and godly wife, a growing family, lovely home, plenty of money, academic excellence, athletic ability, and so on.

Then lightening struck. Lanier's firstborn was developing a growth in his tongue, which was enlarging and protruding from his mouth.

It was a benign tumor, but its growth could not be stopped. The only recourse was surgery. With ample means available, Lanier could search the world for the most competent surgeon for his child, yet his search yielded a surgeon right there in Dallas. Little John almost died on the operating table three different times. He underwent many surgeries over a period of ten years. The tumor brought this great surgeon to his knees because he could not permanently excise the thing; it just kept coming back. Of course, John had trouble talking with his tongue so large and protruding. We all know kids can be mean—they called him "dirty mouth."

After one of the surgeries I met Lanier as he was coming down the hall. He grabbed me by the neck, held on, and said, "I've never known what it was like to suffer." Most parents will agree that some of the most painful suffering is to watch your children suffer. Lanier would later say that he learned more about endurance in the Christian life through the years of watching his son suffer than all of the training he got in seminary. Likewise, James says in this passage that suffering and endurance can work together. We must first know the Scriptures—what God has to say on a matter. Then we must remember that the wisdom verse five calls for is an understanding of how to apply spiritual knowledge to the difficulties of life. Together, biblical knowledge and the trials of life forge the Christian character that guides our ship safely to shore.

It would be incomplete to share this example without "the rest of the story," as Paul Harvey would say. After a decade of surgeries the tumor was finally gone for good. John developed into a good student like his father. He went to Vanderbilt with the dream of becoming a plastic surgeon like the doctor who had helped him. He wanted to help as he had been helped. He did not receive immediate entrance to medical school, but he kept taking graduate courses until he finally was accepted. Today, Dr. John Burns is an accomplished plastic surgeon practicing in Dallas, Texas.

Without doubting, in faith we can ask our generous God for wisdom to see His long-term perspective in our particular trials.

"GOT ZOT-ROT?"

James 1:12-18

One day a loving, thoughtful Christian brother came into my office and said he'd been thinking about me. I tried to express my appreciation and then I asked if his thoughts had been good or bad. Laughing, he pulled out a clipping from "The Wizard of Id" and said it reminded him of me. In the cartoon, the Wizard of Id is looking up at God in a plaintive repose as he says, "I have tried to show them the way, but they are dumb, ignorant clods." Next section: "If you want me to go on . . . give me a sign." Never one to frustrate the fervent prayer of a righteous man, God sends His sign—a bolt of lightning which hits the Wizard of Id with a loud ZOT and reduces him to an ash heap. Next pane—in reflecting on his experience, the Wizard allows that a mere clap of thunder would have been a sufficient sign from God that he should continue his ministry.

Now, I'm not sure which part of this cartoon reminded my friend of me. I certainly hoped I had not given my parishioners the impression that I considered them to be dumb, ignorant clods. If they were coming to hear me, obviously they were people of great intelligence and discernment! What really captured my attention in this cartoon was not the disdainful attitude of the Wizard toward people, but the center section with the big ZOT. I really think this is the inner, albeit unexpressed, attitude many of us have toward God. You know, He's just sort of up there with a quiver full of lightning bolts on His back and one in His hand. He's all poised, with arm cocked, just waiting

33

for an opportunity to hit us with a big ZOT. Obviously, that imagery borders on the ludicrous, but I don't think it is too far removed from the concept of God hidden in the back of many minds. We sometimes suffer from a spiritual malady I would dub as ZOT-ROT. Time after time we go to the Lord for help in an area and next thing we know that area of our lives is blowing up in our faces. Whatever we pray about turns out just the opposite of what we asked.

Little kids grow up with the dinnertime prayer, "God is great, God is good. Let us thank Him for our food." But the child soon grows up and begins to realize that the great and good God who filled his tummy when he was little is not filling the tummies of millions of starving children in Africa, India, and Asia. As she grows she begins to wonder if God is so great and so good after all. Yet even though she's been made aware of the reality of this type of suffering, it is so far removed from the average American living room that she can easily block it out, change channels, ignore it.

It is in that moment of apathy and comfort the big ZOT strikes my life. I can no longer ignore suffering because the very thing that never happens to anyone I know just happened to me. I pray for faith, so I lose my job. The housewife prays for patience with her kids, so they go wild. The disciple prays for better priorities, so his golf clubs get stolen. And after a series of such episodes, as in the life of Job, we are temped, perhaps, to curse God and die, depending on how big the lightning bolts have been.

ZOT-ROT sets in. We become afraid to pray because we're afraid of what God's answer may be. We become spiritual jackrabbits, evermore hopping around trying to avoid God's gunshot. In short, we lose awareness of His love and respond to Him only in fear. We become gun shy and harbor a lingering fear in the back of our minds, anxiously wondering what He may do to us next. We might think we are now paying for past mistakes and wonder if God will be disciplining us because of them for the rest of our lives. This is ZOT-ROT, a serious disease that rots away our spiritual vitality and zeal. If it doesn't cause us to drop out of the Christian life altogether, it may leave us sitting on the pew with a glum look just going through the motions. We're afraid to serve lest we get a divine slap in the face. This is a disease doctor James tries to nip in the bud with a bit of preventative medicine in James 1:12-18.

This then is the third value of trials found in the introduction to James. First, we saw that trials can produce endurance (2-4), then that trials can produce wisdom (5-11), and in this final section of the prologue we learn that trials can actually produce happiness (12-18). After shockingly making the claim that trials can make us happy (12), James tells us what God does not do (13-15) and then what God does do (16-18). So let's begin by seeing how trials can make us happy (12).

James is a book on how to respond to the trials that bombard our lives. In verse 12 James summarizes verses 2-11 by saying that these trials are not given by God to make us miserable; rather, they are given to make us happy, happier than we could ever dream possible. Through these trials God wants to provide for us an abundant life. And that is exactly what we hope to establish in verses 12-18.

> **Blessed *is* the man who endures temptation; for when he has been approved, he will receive the crown of life which the Lord has promised to those who love Him (1:12).**

This verse serves as a swing verse in that it looks both backward and forward. It looks back to the ground already covered in 2-11 and looks forward to what James is about to say in 13-18.

The word "blessed" is *makarias*, the same word Jesus used in the Sermon on the Mount for His beatitudes, or what some have called His "behappitudes". And the word "temptation" in the NKJ is the same word as in verse 2, *peirasmos*. It can mean temptation or trial, depending on the context. Here the context calls for "trial." At first blush it doesn't make sense to say that trials can bring happiness, but just like in the Sermon on the Mount (which the Book of James parallels in many ways) there are many counter-intuitive statements. Fortunately, James gives us an explanation for this claim when he says "for." This word introduces the reason for his bold claim about trials.

The word "approved," *dokimos*, can be found on the bottom of thousands of pieces of pottery archaeologists have unearthed in the

Middle East. It was a predecessor of sorts to our Good Housekeeping seal of approval. It was placed on pottery that passed through the furnace intact. But if the pot cracked in the firing they would inscribe "disapproved," *adokimos*, on the bottom and it would go on the discount shelf. Golfers know that manufacturers of golf balls will still sell those that came through the line with a minor defect, but they stamp the cover of the ball with xxx and sell it at a discount. James is saying if we endure our trial, then we receive God's Good Housekeeping seal of approval, *dokimos*. The result, says James, will be happiness because we will receive a "crown of life." This crown is usually explained as something a faithful believer receives after this life is over at the Judgment Seat of Christ. But if we look carefully, the text says we get this crown after we have endured the trial and come out without cracks—approved. That happens in this life.

The crown given here refers to the garland wreath given to the victorious Olympic runner or to the conquering general in battle. The man who endures a trial has won a battle or an Olympic contest with spiritual forces in high places (Eph 6:10ff). This victorious adornment is similar to Paul's statement in Romans 5:17 that through Christ we shall reign in life—this life! It is God's intent to equip us to live in the midst of a world filled with pressure and problems and stress as victors rather than victims. We need never be overwhelmed by any circumstance because we have an infinite Lord who is ready for anything and who amply equips us. When we have laid hold of our Lord we will discover He is adequate for anything. Through Him we are victors in battle and we can wear the crown of life. I really think this crown of life is true happiness. It isn't just a laugh or a smile. It's deep inner peace, that bubbling of living waters springing up within. It is the deep satisfaction of having finished a difficult task, of having finished the race.

A friend of mine, in his mid-thirties at the time, wanted to run a marathon. We used to spend time together in the Scriptures and then go for a run. I would only go five miles since I wasn't interested in training for a marathon. As the great day approached, this Annapolis grad and fighter pilot from the Vietnam War looked very determined but also a shade concerned. He was afraid of not finishing and he asked me if I would run the last half with him. I'd never run thirteen miles but figured he'd be so tired by the last half that I might be able to keep up with him. It was a good thing I went. Three times during the last half of the race he became so disoriented he began running the wrong direction (possible since the race was an eight mile loop around White Rock Lake in Dallas and we were always being passed by people going the opposite direction). So I would turn him around and keep him going in the right direction. When he hit the proverbial wall the look of pain on his face was excruciating. But he finished, and I had never seen such a look of happiness on his face. Was there pain along the way? You bet. But somehow the joy and happiness he experienced upon finishing a race that truly tested his mettle and endurance outweighed the pain, so much so that it spurred him on to continue running marathons into his forties. That is the garland of life, which comes at the end of the trial.

James winds up verse 12 by saying the Lord promises this crown of life to those who love Him. I wonder what a statement like that is doing at the end of a section about the testing of our faith. Could James be giving us the key to victory here? A trial is not only a test of our faith, it is also a test of our love. Deep love for God will carry us through when a trial begins to dampen our faith. In the dark moments of my life, when it is difficult for me to trust that the hand of God is at work in my life, it is precisely then that my love for God enables me to endure. The trial reveals whom or what I love the most: God, the world, or myself. If we endure, then God knows we really love Him.

This is what Moses (Deut 8:2) was trying to tell the people before they crossed the Jordan: "And you shall remember that the Lord your God led you all the way these forty years in the wilderness, to humble you *and* **test** you, to know what *was* in your heart, whether you would keep His commandments or not." And again (Deut 13:3-4): "The Lord your God is **testing** you to know whether you **love** the Lord your God with all your heart and with all your soul. You shall walk after the Lord your God and fear Him, and keep His commandments and obey His voice; you shall serve Him and hold fast to Him." Our reward for holding fast will be a crown of life—a more abundant, joyful, happy, fulfilled, and peaceful life here and now, which will also accrue dividends in the world to come.

At this point James anticipates an objection. His Jewish Christian reader might be sitting on the floor of his den where the La-Z boy recliner used to be before he had to hock it. Instead of reading by the light of the floor lamp, James' letter is illuminated by a candle because the electric company has cut the juice. He comes to verse 12 and says, "Wait a minute, brother James. You call this an abundant life? You've got to be kidding. And talk about loving God, I'm getting downright bitter about all of this. He's responsible for all my problems! If I hadn't become a Christian, none of this would be happening. It's His fault. How can I love that kind of God? After all, what have I done to deserve this?"

In order to deal with this ZOT-ROT, which he must have anticipated, James pens verses 13-18. He writes to tell us what God does not do in verses 13-15, and then in verses 16-18 he shares what it is God does do.

What God Doesn't Do (13-15)

> Let no one say when he is tempted, "I am tempted by God"; for God cannot be tempted by evil, nor does He Himself tempt anyone. But each one is tempted when he is drawn away by his own desires and enticed. Then, when desire has conceived, it gives birth to sin; and sin, when it is full-grown, brings forth death.

This passage will confuse us if we do not realize that the word for testing in the original Greek language is the same as the word for tempting. The word *peirasmos* is like a coin with two sides: testing and tempting. The problem arises when we confuse the testing of God with the tempting of God. If God were the one who tempted me, I would be justified in blaming Him for my sinful failures: "If you hadn't put that woman before me . . ." In verses 2-12 James uses this word in the sense of a trial or test. But in verses 13-18 he makes a word play and emphasizes the other meaning, which is temptation to evil. The word has a good meaning and a bad meaning.

Here are some of the passages outside of James where *peirasmos* (noun) or *peirazō* (verb) means something good. Jesus tests Philip's faith at the feeding of the 5,000 (Jn 6:6); God tests Abraham's faith by instructing him to sacrifice Isaac (Heb 11:17); the nations were left in Israel to see if God's people would keep His way or not (Judges 2:25); and we have already seen Deuteronomy 8:2. In all of these examples God tests His people to develop their devotion and loyalty to Himself. And that's good.

But the word *peirazō* can also mean, "to entice to evil." For example, in Galatians 6:1, spiritual brothers are instructed to watch their attitudes while correcting a sinning brother lest they too are tempted. Satan is called the tempter in 1 Thessalonians 3:5 who might tempt us. In 1 Corinthians 7:5 a married couple is cautioned against a prolonged period of abstinence lest they be tempted to infidelity. We can also recall that in the wilderness the devil tempted Jesus to do evil. So James is saying one type of trial, or *peirasmos,* is from God and is good and beneficial. But the other type is from Satan and is evil. God, says James, has nothing to do with the latter. So when one is temped to do evil, let him not accuse God of tempting him in that way.

What James is getting at is this: every temptation or trial or test of a general nature contains in it a possible solicitation to evil. If I lose my job—that's a test. But having lost my job, I may be tempted to steal—that's a temptation issuing out of my trying situation. **God may be responsible for the test but never for the temptation.**

Since Job is clearly in the back of James' mind (5:11), his life is illustrative. Job is a real hero in James' eyes when it comes to enduring trials. The similarity between 1:12 and 5:11 suggests that Job may have been in the back of James' mind when he wrote the section of his letter we are studying now. First of all, Job was greeted by trials at his door (*peirasmois*) in the most general sense. And when the thunder and lightning struck—when the Sabbeans took away his oxen and donkeys, when fire came from heaven to consume his sheep and servants, when the Chaldeans took his camels, and when wind blew down the house of his sons and daughters, killing them—that was *peirasmos* in the broadest sense. This was obviously a trial, but latent behind the trial was a temptation to curse God, to blame God, to resist God in this test. In Job 1 the general sense of testing is in the foreground and the temptation is latent. But in Job 2 the temptation to evil becomes explicit. When Job is further smitten and his body is covered with boils, his wife says to him, "Why do you maintain your integrity? Curse God and die." That is solicitation to evil, pure and simple. Here we have both sides of the *peirasmos* coin. We have the calamities of life. But along with them and in them and as a part of them is the temptation to respond in a sinful way.

James is saying, when calamities come our way, let us not blame God for the temptations that accompany them. The test may be from God, but the temptation is from Satan. Job saw the difference. He said, "Should I receive good at the hands of God and not calamity or adversity also" (2:10). He saw the test as from God, but when his wife was used by Satan to tempt him to evil, he said, "You speak as the foolish women speak," (2:10). It would be easy for us to say, "Well, this trouble has come to me from God, and since the trouble comes from God, the opportunity to rebel against it or to respond sinfully also comes from God. He brought the trouble; He also brought the opportunity to sin." But James is saying here, "No, that is untrue. If I am tempted to evil in the midst of trouble, that solicitation comes from within me and not from God."

Several years ago at the Air Force Academy there was a scandal. The Academy worked on an honor system. I suppose it was assumed that an Academy man would conduct himself with honor. It was discovered, however, that a rather large number of cadets were availing themselves of copies of the examinations before they were given. Copies of the exams were circulating among the cadets. When it was discovered the cadets were expelled, and in a certain sense it was a disgrace to the Academy. It would have been easy for one of the cadets to have said, "Well, really the Academy is responsible for this because they put the exams within our reach. They didn't lock them up in a safe. Therefore, they tempted us to cheat." And yet, you and I realize, the honor system is no temptation to anyone who has a completely honest nature. It's only when there is a trace of dishonesty or a possible trace of dishonesty within a person that the honor system affords temptation.

For example, I might drive my car down to Wal-Mart and in my haste jump out and leave the keys in the ignition. While I'm in the store, someone might come by and say, "My, I'd like to have that car." He sees the keys in the ignition and, unable to resist the temptation, jumps in and drives away. As he's driving away, he says to himself, "That man shouldn't have tempted me to steal his car." Well, I don't think I tempted him. The keys in the ignition would be no temptation to a perfectly honest man. They would only be a temptation to a thief, or a man who already had the inclination. This is James' point. If in our trouble we feel a solicitation to evil within us, the only reason it's there is because there is something corrupt within us, namely, our lust. We cannot blame this part of the *peirasmos* on God. It is something that originates within us.

Now, in describing lust's effects on our lives, James has drawn a clear, graphic picture. His imagery is impressive. As I see it, he depicts lust as a woman of the streets with whom our heart has an illicit relationship. This woman, Madam Lust, becomes pregnant with sin. When the sin grows to the point it can no longer be contained, Madam Lust gives birth to it. No longer just a thought nestled within the womb of my mind, sin now takes up residence in my home, involving itself in my life and actions. This newborn baby Sin is capable of so much growth. By repetition and by persistence (bottle feeding, if you will) it gains strength; it gains maturity. And when the little baby Sin that Madam Lust gave birth to is fully grown, it becomes capable of producing its own offspring. And this offspring is Death.

So we may say from the imagery of James that Lust is the grandmother of Death: Lust produces Sin, and Sin gives birth to

Death. This is easily illustrated. Here's a person who comes from a poor, economically deprived situation. All the time he is surrounded by the superior possessions of other people. And there is born in his heart a desire for those possessions, however he might get them. The more he sees them, the greater his desire to have them, until one day, in his school room perhaps, he sees an unattended twenty dollar bill lying unprotected on a desk. He snatches it away. At that point, the sin, conceived by lust in his mind, has grown so big that it is born into action. But this was just a tiny sin. Having become a thief once, however, he goes on to bigger and better things and eventually becomes an armed robber, holding up liquor stores and gas stations and drive-ins. In one of the hold-ups, a storeowner shoots and kills him. That's just one illustration of what James is talking about, this time involving death of a violent nature. There are others. But I think the point James is making (and the point the Bible as a whole makes) is that any sin leads to some form of death. It can literally shorten life. The Proverbs say, "The fear of the Lord prolongs days, but the years of the wicked shall be shortened," (10:27). Sin can also lead to misery, depression, and defeat—all of which Paul calls death (Rom 6:23; 7:24; 8:6). Righteousness tends to life; wickedness tends to death. They that pursue it follow it, the Bible says, to their own death.

In the light of the imagery James has employed here, it seems to me we could say this: in this context and in this context alone, abortion and infanticide are much to be desired. While Lust is conceiving and before Sin has been brought forth, that is the time to stop the growth, so that Sin is never born. The more we toy with something in our mind, the harder it becomes to resist it. The more we allow it to remain there, the longer we allow our minds to feed on it, the stronger it becomes, until finally birth is inevitable. We need to cut if off while there is opportunity to cut it off. And then if Sin is born as a result of Lust, kill it while it is still an infant. Repent of it, turn aside from it before it can become mature and fully developed.

We have seen what God does not do. He does not tempt us. But what does God do? James tells us in 1:16-18.

What God Does Do (16-18)

Do not be deceived, my beloved brethren. Every good gift and every perfect gift is from above, and comes down from the Father of lights, with whom there is no variation or shadow of turning. Of His own will He brought us forth by the word of truth, that we might be a kind of first fruits of His creatures.

What does God do? He gives us good and perfect gifts. James says the only thing our God ever gives is something good. He never gives us anything evil. Some scholars see a significance to the two different words used for "gift" in this verse, *dosis* and *dōrēma*, but most see hexameter and the use of different words to accomplish the hexameter, which simply means James may be quoting a verse of poetry. If so, there is no substantive difference in the meaning of the two different words for "gift." The emphasis here is on the quality of God's gifts—good and perfect.

The word for "good" means useful or beneficial. The word for "perfect" suggests a gift "without defect or want." James' point is simply this: God's gifts always meet the need completely, fully—what a contrast to the gifts we give. Not only does God give what is needed and what fully meets our needs, but only He gives gifts in this way. We always faced a yearly dilemma when my father's birthday rolled around. My wife Betty would usually handle buying gifts for our relatives, but it is hard to shop for some people. So Betty was stumped one year and called me at my office from the store where she was shopping. I thought very deeply for a moment and came up with an incredible solution: get him a tie. Of course, he probably didn't need a tie. But even if he did, we would probably send him one he couldn't use. We might send him a blue polka dotted tie when he really needed a solid brown one. God's gifts are never like this. They always meet a need because God knows exactly what we need. His gifts are without defect. They never wear out and never need to be sent back for an exchange or repair.

Someone says, "Yeah, but it seems to me God is kind of moody.

Sometimes He's nice to me and sometimes He's mean. If the God of the OT and the God of the NT are the same God, then surely this is a fickle, moody, capricious God. One day He gives me soft, delicious saltwater taffy and the next He hands me a popcorn ball with razor blades in it."

Not so, says James. God is a Father who consistently gives good and perfect gifts to His children. After all, He's the Father of lights with whom there is no variableness or shadow of turning. These are all astronomical terms. God is compared to the sun, moon, or stars here. He doesn't move from one side of the horizon to the other. He's not a full moon today and a half moon tomorrow. He never shifts positions. He never changes. Nor is there ever a shadow cast over our lives because He has turned His back on us. God doesn't rotate. If a shadow does indeed darken our day, it is only because we have turned our back on Him. Men change. God doesn't. The only gift which ever comes down from heaven is a good, necessary gift, which is without want or defect. All of His gifts appreciate in value. They never fade or depreciate.

A perfect example of just such a gift is found in verse 18. "Of His own will He begot us." The word "begot" is the same as in verse 15. Sin begets death; God begets life. James illustrates God's capacity to be the ultimate giver of good and perfect gifts by His gift of the new birth. Likewise, 1 Peter 1:23 says, "Being born again not of corruptible seed, but of incorruptible, by the Word of God, which lives and abides forever." It is the gospel message that Jesus, the Son of God, died to pay the auction price to get us off the slave block of sin and death, thereby giving us the new birth. Contrary to the opinion of many who think James teaches salvation by works, James teaches that salvation is an absolutely free gift from above. He almost sounds like John, who said, "Marvel not that I say unto you, you must be born *from above*," in John 3:7. *Anōthen* is usually translated "again," but there is even more support for translating it "from above." John and James are saying the same thing. Salvation, eternal life, is one of God's good and perfect gifts. It comes from above.

Notice as well that it says, "Of His own will He begot us." Nowhere is the absolute sovereignty of God in the giving of new birth more clearly stated than here. There's no place for works. Salvation is God's gift. It never fades in value. It is a complete package. And guess what? God never takes this gift back again. There are those who think we can lose our salvation of our own free will, just as we got it that way, who have said, "Yes, salvation is a free gift from God. But I must receive it. And after I choose to receive it, I, at some later date, can choose to reject it or to give the gift back to God." No way. Romans 11:29 clearly states that the gifts and calling of God are something about which He does not change His mind. Once you receive the gift of life from above, it is forever yours. You couldn't give it back to Him if you wanted. Such are God's gifts—good, useful, complete, and permanent. What a beautiful picture of a loving God.

At this point we must address an important side note. Because of the controversy surrounding James 2:14-26 on the relationship between faith and works, some theologians want to maintain that James is addressing a mixed audience of believers and unbelievers. They want to maintain that faith that does not produce works is not "saving faith." They are assuming, as did Martin Luther, that the passage in question deals with who gets to go to heaven after death and who doesn't. With that understanding these scholars would say that James is assuring his believing brothers that their works give solid evidence that they have saving faith, but those who do not have these works are just fooling themselves.

Faith without works is dead, which they claim means that there is either fake faith or insufficient faith to open the gates of heaven. In order to maintain that argument they have to maintain that James is addressing two groups: those who really possess Christ and those who merely profess Christ but do not possess him. In this case, they claim, James is warning these professing Christians by telling them if they do not have the proper works to accompany their profession of faith, then they are merely *professors* and not genuine possessors. This is a common argument stemming from Reformed theology, which is based on Augustine's theology. They would say that salvation is by faith alone, but saving faith is never alone. Subtly, they have injected works into the salvation formula.

We will address that passage directly in due time, but at this point we can state one fact with certainty: James is not addressing a mixed audience. I am not claiming that there are no unbelievers in any given congregation. I am simply claiming that James is not addressing them here. How do we know? Read 1:16-18 again. Who is James addressing? "My beloved brethren." And who is the "us" of verse 18? Obviously, it is the beloved brethren, but it also includes someone else: us. "Us" has to include James, doesn't it? God brought **us** forth. That is a birthing term, as we have seen. Who has received the new birth? According to James it is the beloved brethren, including James himself. His letter is not an evangelistic message. It is about God's children becoming victors in their trials instead of victims.

I once had a conversation with a highly published New Testament professor about this very fact. To his credit he said, "I'm about to agree with you." To which I responded, "If you agree with me on just this one point, your entire system of theology falls." He replied, "I know, but I'm too far gone the other way." My, my. As we shall see, many passages in James addressed to the "beloved brethren" or to the "brothers" would have to be interpreted differently if we assumed the word "brother" doesn't necessarily mean "brother." As just discussed, verses 16-18 disagree. By the Word of Truth God "begot" James *and* his readers ("us"). In James, a brother is a brother.

I believe James wrote these words as a dose of preventative medicine to keep us from getting ZOT-ROT. God is not up there in heaven waiting for the first opportunity to throw a lightning bolt our way. The only thing coming from his hand is a needed and perfect gift. He gives trials, yes, but temptations, no. He may give us a trial because we need something it can impart to us.

The suffering that enters my life from a trial I can accept with joy because I know it is something designed to help me develop in some way. It is undeserved suffering such as Job endured. However, there is another type of suffering for which we cannot blame God: deserved suffering. These verses explain an important principle, one we might call "sin suffering." The principle of sin suffering simply says that a great deal of the suffering we face comes upon us totally apart from God. We bring it upon ourselves by our own foolishness or sin.

Remember, the offspring of fully developed sin is death. A man drinks and drinks and drinks. He becomes an alcoholic. He loses his job. He loses his family. He gets sclerosis of the liver. He is suffering. He is in misery, but he cannot blame God. God is not responsible for his suffering; sin is, sin conceived by his illicit relationship with lust in his own heart.

Most of the suffering I have experienced I brought upon myself through foolishness or sin. I cannot blame God for it. Unchecked sin can bring an avalanche of suffering crashing down into my life and it is only the grace of God that can break the boulders up before I am killed. A man has been nurturing his sin for years. Suddenly his wife decides to call it quits. In desperation, he turns to Christ and says, "Bail me out." Christ can forgive his sins and give him eternal life. But if his marriage does not mend, he cannot blame Christ. His long habit of sin, which is almost fully grown now, is merely running its course. Only God's grace can stop the growth of sin and unchain us from our bondage to it. That is the good news James 5:20 tells us. God's amazing grace can interrupt the cycle of sin and even restore the years the locusts have eaten. But even if God does not intervene and prevent the consequences of our sin, there is no excuse for ZOT-ROT in the life of God's children.

In these verses James has corrected a possible misunderstanding. We can never blame God for the temptations we face, nor can we blame Him when suffering and misery knock on our door, or when we invite Lust and Sin into our hearts and homes. Don't be deceived, brethren. God is not a sovereign sadist. He doesn't have a quiver of lightening bolts, nor is he a fickle fan—one day treating us and the next day tricking us. The only things God will ever send us from heaven are gifts, good and perfect gifts. Or as Jesus put it (Matt 7:9-11), "What man is there among you who, if his son asks for bread, will give him a stone? Or if he asks for a fish, will he give him a serpent? If you then, being evil, know how to give good gifts to your children, how much more will your Father who is in heaven give good things to those who ask Him!"

Rick Wallace developed a severe case of ZOT-ROT. He had been a faithful husband and father, a successful homebuilder, and an eager servant at his church. Then all of a sudden he disappeared. I contacted his wife and discovered Rick had moved out and was having an affair. After about three months it was over, but Rick and his wife had not reconciled and he certainly was not back in church. When I finally tracked him down he told me this story.

> As a homebuilder we almost always have people making changes to the plans or asking for extras, which were not in the original bid. Sometimes a lot of our profit comes from these change orders. Well, the buyer's wife started getting really friendly with me. She would show up at the site alone while her husband was at work. Finally, she offered me certain favors in exchange for doing some extras on her new house with no charge. The temptation was strong. At last, I agreed to meet her at the site at 5PM for a romantic rendezvous. I arrived early, about 4:30, and began to pray.
>
> I said, "Lord, I know this is not right. I have never been unfaithful to my wife. But I am weak. I know you are strong, Lord, so I am counting on you to stop this lady from coming." I waited nervously and prayed again at 4:45. I said, "Lord, you have fifteen minutes left to keep this from happening. I know you have the power to do this." With five minutes to go, I prayed again. But right on time she showed up and I succumbed. Now I know I can't count on God in a tight spot. He really let me down.

Rick was embarrassed and humiliated. But he also had ZOT-ROT. He blamed God for his failure. He blamed God for not answering his prayer to stop the temptation. I counseled this couple off and on for a couple of years. The marriage was saved. It took another year for Rick's ZOT-ROT to go away. I am happy to say that Rick has been faithful to his wife and to his church and to the Lord for the last thirty-five years, but there was a time he almost lost it all when he blamed God for his own sin and allowed himself to sink into ZOT-ROT. "Let no one say when he is tempted, 'I am tempted by God'; for God cannot be tempted by evil, nor does He Himself tempt anyone."

"THE ART OF BEING A GOOD LISTENER"

James 1:19-27

God does not speak in an earthquake; He speaks in a still, small voice. It stands to reason that we must listen very carefully. Unfortunately, few of us are good listeners. A professor Matson from Drew University in Madison, New Jersey, once tried to prove that most people are poor listeners. He was being honored at a faculty reception one evening and because his work was in the realm of communication, he decided to try an experiment. As he was standing in a long line of other faculty members, waiting for people to come through the line to congratulate him or to speak with him, he planned to say one sentence to each individual and to say it very clearly. The sentence was this: "My grandmother died last night." That wasn't true; it was just a statement to see what the response would be. As a result of his experiment, Professor Matson stated, "Don't worry about what people think. The large majority doesn't. It is rare even to find a person who really listens to what you are saying. As I said to each one, 'My grandmother died last night,' I had such replies as, 'Congratulations, Dr. Matson.' 'Nice to see you here this evening.' 'Wonderful to have you with us.'"

We are not good listeners. Most of us spend our time with people talking, and even when we are supposed to be listening to someone, we are busy thinking about what we're going to say next.

I learned the power and the importance of being a listener when I was dating my current and only wife. It didn't take a drop of brilliance on my part to realize Betty wasn't just another pretty face. She was a dean's list student, interested in medicine (my chosen field at the time), she was a Christian, and most important of all, she laughed at my corny jokes. So I said to myself, "Hmmm, I've got to get to know this girl a little better." I needed to figure out how to make her like me. Normally, I would try to impress a girl with one of my great accomplishments, like the time I locked myself in the bathroom—what a classic—or perhaps some equally impressive feat. This time, however, I decided to try a new tactic.

I had recently read Dale Carnegie's book, *How to Win Friends and Influence People*. One chapter was about how to be a good listener, and one of the keys was to find out what the other person was interested in and start asking questions. So I decided to do precisely that. I would just find out what she was interested in and then listen while she talked. I soon discovered her interests were a little different from mine—numbers one and two on the list were sewing and knitting. So she started talking about what she was sewing at present. With all the enthusiasm I could muster, I said, "Fantastic, tell me more." Months later after we were engaged, I asked her what it was that first caused her to take a deeper interest in me. Without hesitation, she said, "You were the first guy I'd ever dated who was willing to listen to what I had to say about what I was interested in. All the other guys I dated just wanted to talk about themselves." Single guys—write this down. It really works.

But it is true, isn't it? We love to talk about ourselves. And the time we crave an audience the most is when we are in the midst of a trial. What do I want to do first when I have a problem? Tell someone about it. Unload my troubles. I want to tell them what a problem I am facing—what difficulties I am going through. **It is very easy to be talkative in time of trial.** But the first thing we learn from James 1:19-27 is that while we are talking, we ought to be listening.

We are in a book that deals with Christians and their trials. In the introduction we learned that trials can be valuable. They can produce endurance, a much needed quality in the life of any servant of God; they provide wisdom to the Christian who will ask God for it; and they promise a crown of abundant living to those who endure. Having finished his general overview on the value of being tested, James moves into the body of his letter. At the outset he gives us a thematic statement hinging on the little Greek word *hōste*, which begins verse 19. Many Greek manuscripts start with a different word here, but I believe *hōste* is the preferred reading. It also makes more sense as the transition from the introduction to the body of the letter. *Hōste* means "therefore, wherefore, so then." The connection is this: if you want the rewards of trials, then you need these three traits— quick to hear, slow to speak, and slow to wrath. Wherefore, seeing that every Christian will be faced with trials and since these trials can have such a positive effect on our lives, here is how we should respond when trials hit. We should be quick to hear, slow to speak, and slow to wrath.

Those three responses give us a thematic breakdown for the body of the letter. Here is our outline so far:

JAMES

"TRIUMPH THROUGH TRIALS"

Salutation (1:1)

Introduction (1:2-18)—The Value of Trials

Theme (1:19-20)—Qualities Needed

Body (1:21-5:6)—Qualities Developed

    I.   In Regard to Hearing (1:21-2:26)

    II. In Regard to Speaking (3:1-18)

    III. In Regard to Fighting (4:1-5:6)

The first major section after the introduction (1:21-2:26) deals with being quick to hear, a good listener. Chapter 3 addresses being slow to speak. And finally, 4:1-5:6 speaks to being slow to wrath. These, James teaches us, are the qualities we need in the midst of a trial. Rather than rushing out to tell the world about our problems, the first thing we should do is simply listen—listen for that still, small voice from God so that we might know what to do. Instead of hearing Him, we too often hear ourselves talking. God made us with two ears and one mouth. The law of proportions suggests we ought to spend twice as much time listening as talking. In fact, our troubles can often be compounded by what we say in the midst of them.

I think Job stumbled here. Has it ever occur to you how little of the Book of Job we would have to read if Job had never opened his mouth? The answer is only the first two chapters and a portion of chapter 42! Job's verbosity is to blame for the rest of the book. Remember the three friends who came to sit and observe Job in silence? They were too stunned by his suffering to say anything. Then Job opened his mouth and cursed his day. And then they were off! One speech leads to a rebuttal followed by more speeches and further rebuttal. On and on it goes until out of a whirlwind God interjects and demands to know, "Who is this that darkens counsel by words without knowledge?" Or in other words, "Job, you talk too much. You are obscuring the whole issue by talking too much." Job could have been a bigger hero if he had kept quiet. Our opinion of Job was wonderful when we got to the end of chapter one, but it's somewhat lowered when we get to the end of the book. In fact, Job's own opinion of himself is lowered—"I repent in dust and ashes," he says (Job 42:6). Too much talking. That's the danger in times of testing, when above all we need to open our ears to God. "Lord, what are you trying to say to me?"

There is a story about a young man who came to Socrates to learn how to speak. He was a voluble young man. As the story goes, before Socrates could get a word in edgewise, his prospective student had poured out a whole volume of material on why he wanted to learn to speak. Finally, when he had paused for a breath, I suppose, Socrates said, "Fine. I'll be happy to teach you to speak, but for you the price will be double." The young man was incensed: "Why would you charge me double?" "Well," replied Socrates, "because I'm going to have to teach you two lessons. First I am going to have to teach you how to be silent. Then I'm going to have to teach you how to speak." Often in times of testing God must first teach us to be silent so that

He can speak and be heard. God does not speak in an earthquake, but in a still, small voice.

James wants us to learn to be good listeners in 1:21-2:26. He approaches being quick to hear from three angles: 1) It is more than just listening (1:21-27); 2) it is more than just morality (2:1-13); and 3) it is more than just faith (2:14-26). In this section,1:21-27, we learn that being quick to hear means more than simply listening. In these verses James presents the preparation, the potential, the precaution, and the practice of being a good listener.

Preparation for Being a Good Listener (19-21a)

So then, my beloved brethren, let every man be swift to hear, slow to speak, slow to wrath; for the wrath of man does not produce the righteousness of God.

In order to hear the still, small voice of God we need not only a listening ear, but also a calm, quieted spirit. We need to be slow to wrath, because the wrath of man does not result in the righteousness of God. This is why arguments are no good. Communication does not take place in the midst of an argument. Usually one or both parties are angry while arguing. An angry person cannot hear what the other is saying. He is too bent out of shape, emotionally. The picture at the end of verse 19 and in verse 20 is one of agitation. We cannot hear God's voice when our spirits are agitated and bent out of shape. Similarly, when a seed goes into the ground, it cannot grow if disturbed. It needs water, warmth, and quietness.

I wonder what kind of preparation we make within our soul when we want to hear a word from God. Verses 19-20 are about the first step to being a good listener, preparation, which in this regard means to open one's ears, close one's mouth, and quiet one's spirit.

What kind of preparation do we make in order to hear God's voice in church? I have been privileged to pastor independent, Bible-teaching churches for many decades. These are churches with a lot of joy. When people walk into the sanctuary they often hear a lot of noise because the people inside are so glad to see their friends and are socializing. I've often wondered if it wouldn't be better to have some quiet moments before the service begins to calm our spirits and prepare our hearts to hear His voice. For some of us He would have to speak out of an earthquake to get our attention. Don't get me wrong. The church sanctuary is not designed to be a tomb and neither is it to be a morgue. Rather, the sanctuary is designed to be a place where we can hear God speak. James suggests that a little calming of the spirit, a little quietness is good preparation to be able to listen to Him.

In verse 21a, though this is where the first section of the body begins, James is still talking about preparing to hear God. He says,

Therefore lay aside all filthiness and overflow of wickedness, and receive with meekness the implanted word.

The first step of the preparation process is to quiet one's mouth and calm one's spirit. Here in the first clause of verse 21 is another step of preparation. The word for filthiness here is especially illustrative. It is a word that literally means wax in your ears. In this context it points to the dirt in our lives or hearts, as does "overflow of wickedness." But the imagery is significant. Not until we clean out our ears will we be able to hear distinctly the small voice of God.

And so that you might not misunderstand what I am saying, I think the second step in preparation is to clean up one's life and heart, primarily through confession. When I desire to know what God wants to tell me, I must first calm my spirit. I set aside any cares or concerns of this world. Then I cleanse my heart by confessing any filthiness, evil thoughts, or known sin in my life. Whether it is my private devotional time or at an hour of worship, I can never expect to hear God's voice if I have wax in my ears. Preparation is so important. No wonder my prayer communication can seem so unproductive. No wonder Bible reading can feel so dull. No wonder church is so boring—we'll never hear what God is saying without proper preparation.

How well I remember my early days as a pastor. My salary was $800 per month. However, we were a two-car family. One car cost me $100 and the other $200. The paint on one had become an eye sore, so I researched the cost of a paint job from Earl Schwab. $100. Well,

I could do better than that myself. My wife had purchased a trusty Kirby vacuum cleaner with a spray gun for painting. I could buy the paint for $20. I asked around and was told the most important step is preparation. I went and bought some paint and read the instructions, which said to sand down the car first. Great, I thought. My wife's Kirby cleaner also had a sander, which I thought would come in handy.

I hitched up the circular sander and got after it. The only thing was, I thought I was supposed to remove all the old paint right down to the metal. Do you know how much work that is? Also, I was informed later, a circular sander makes what painters call spider webs on the car, which show up after the new paint job is finished. Never mind—ignorance is bliss. I worked for about three weeks sanding the car down. Then I primed it and was ready to paint, or so I thought. Of course, I didn't see anything wrong with doing all this in our front yard as long as it was a nice day. So I cranked everything up and began to paint.

The first sign of trouble came from the spray gun. What I was using was closer to a squirt gun than a spray gun. It didn't spray; it squirted and sometimes even coughed. So after I had coughed paint all over the car, the second sign of trouble came. Bugs. I didn't realize how much bugs and spiders like paint. My car might as well have been a skating rink for insects as they left their tracks all over it. As if this weren't enough, the coup d' etat came from God. He forgot to write my paint job down on his schedule. The clouds rolled in and the paint rolled off. What a mess. A perfect case of poor preparation. And like the paint, God's Word will never stick without the right preparation.

There is a third step in preparing for God's message. "Meekness." This lovely word speaks of gentleness and humility; it's talking about a teachable person. The next word is "receive," but that doesn't match the strength of the original word, which is actually a word for hospitality. It means, "Welcome the Word with open arms." This is the third step of preparation. It is like a person who isn't a finicky eater. He doesn't care who prepares the meal. He is teachable, open to anything, because he loves the Provider who gives him what he needs to survive.

When I was in seminary, I had the privilege of listening to many fine preachers. I had my favorites. Yet, I learned that just listening to a man talk, no matter how much I liked him, yielded nothing if I missed the still, small voice of God. If God has something to say, He can say it through a flute or a trumpet, a violin or a trombone. It is not the music we are listening for; its God's still, small voice. A teachable, humble attitude listens for God's voice. It may come through the Scripture reading; it may come through a song; it may come in the middle of the message; it may come at the end; but it will never come if we are simply listening to the voice of a man.

Early in my marriage my wife was amazed at my stomach. She learned it had an enormous capacity to hold food, and just like Jaws, it wasn't particular about what it ate or how the food was cooked, just so there was a lot of it. There is a reason for this. I was raised in a fairly large family, and we had a nickname for finicky eaters. The nickname was "hungry." If you didn't like the way the meal was cooked, you simply passed it up until the next meal came along. You ate what was served or you went hungry. We quickly learned that being a finicky eater didn't promote survival.

But many Christians aren't like that. Are you particular about who prepares your food? Many Christians are. They want it served with finesse or on the same serving pieces—similar to what they are accustomed to. When they get it, they smell it, suspiciously. Ever smell your food? As a little boy I used to smell my food. "Is this good, mom?" "No, son, it's terrible. It'll kill you. It'll destroy you." It was a habit I had to get out of. There are Christians who smell their food. "Hmm, I don't like that. I don't like the way he says, 'Gawwd.'" Or, "I don't like that. I've never had that before. Don't know if it'll digest." That's a finicky eater. Ladies, have you ever served a finicky eater? Don't you just want to mash the plate in their face sometimes? Instead of "finicky," God says "with meekness." Take what is served to you. He says, "I provided it for you. It has the vitamins and protein I know you need. This guy's only the cook. Forget about him. Don't be finicky. Welcome whatever is set before you. Be teachable. Humble. Meek."

When I was a young preacher I helped a new church get started. We didn't have that many people, so while preaching I could see everyone's face. After awhile there was one person I just couldn't look at or I would have quit the ministry. She was one of the pillars of our church and a fine Bible teacher. That being said, this woman would sit on the third row giving me that "teach me something new" look, that "oh, I already know that" look. Her body language couldn't hide what see was thinking. She would glance at me, make a disdainful face, hyperventilate, cross her legs, and look askance. It all said she had never been so bored in her life. It was most discouraging to a guy who had never planned to be a preacher—ever. I was struggling for my homiletical life, barely keeping my head above water. Her lack of humility and unteachable attitude did not help. It's ironic how some of the most difficult people to teach the Bible to are Bible teachers themselves. Knowledge puffs up.

· James tells us that without adequate preparation, we will not hear God's voice. We may be talking when we should be listening. We may be listening but have wax in our ears so we miss the message. We may be listening but not like the sound of what we hear. These things need to be corrected in order to become good listeners. Having educated us on the preparation for being a good listener, James now talks about the potential of being a good listener.

Potential of Being a Good Listener (1:21b)

Which is able to save your souls.

If we listen well to God's voice, it can "save our souls." There is more behind that expression than getting to heaven some day. In fact, I don't think that is what it is talking about at all. If it is, then we get to heaven by works. Why? Because we were just told we have to clean up our act and be teachable, humble Bible students in order to "get saved." That is exactly what verse 21 teaches, but based on other Bible passages we do not believe works are a requirement to go to heaven. So when we find a passage that would seem to contradict the clear truth of something like Ephesians 2:8-9 (for by grace are you saved through faith), we must look for a way to harmonize the unclear passage with the clear passage.

The first thing we observe is that James is instructing the "beloved brethren" of verse 19. We spent some time in verses 16-18 establishing that these beloved brethren are born again. It would be gratuitous for James to tell people who are born again how to be born again. We can look around to see if this phrase "save the soul" is found elsewhere in the NT. Well, guess what? Jesus, the half-brother of James, taught this concept clearly to his disciples in Matthew 16:24-27. That the passage in Matthew is not a Go-To-Heaven passage is clear from verse 27, which says Jesus will come back someday and "reward" each man according to his deeds. It is about rewards, not getting to heaven. In fact, there are few passages on how to get to heaven in Matthew, Mark, or Luke (the Synoptics).

What about the word "soul"? Surely saving a soul must refer to evangelism. Well, it could in the right context, but James is talking to people who already have their tickets to heaven. The issue for them is what portion of their remaining time on earth, before death or the Rapture, will be rewarded at the Judgment Seat of Christ. And sure enough, a concordance study on this word for "soul" (*psychē*) reveals that only five out of the 105 times the word is used in the NT does it mean what we think of when we say "soul." Of the remaining uses, about half of them refer to our inner personality (mind, emotions, will—our psyche); the other half refer to our time on earth—our lives.

If I were to ask you what you are going to do with your life, you would know that by "life" I mean the rest of your time on earth. Once we are born again, the countdown begins. The issue becomes whether we will "save" our time on earth (our lives) for our own selfish purposes or if we will dedicate our time on earth (our lives) to seeking first the kingdom of God. That was the issue at hand in Matthew 16. Peter felt the sting of rebuke from the Lord who had said, "Get behind me, Satan," and he never forgot this lesson about saving his life for eternity. In fact, he wrote a whole letter about this theme (see 1 Peter 1:9). Now because James grew up with Jesus, he probably would have used words in a similar way. Most likely Peter would have as well, since they were both from Galilee and because he sat under the teaching of Jesus directly.

So coming out of the woods of research, we propose that a better translation for "soul" here would be "life." James wants his readers to save their lives for eternal purposes, thereby increasing their rewards at the Judgment Seat of Christ. We will see that this concept is of great concern to James and understanding it will help solve a number of the difficult passages in his letter. Some books are about the Way; others are about the Walk. From James 1:2-4 we know this book is about the Walk. It is about how a Christian can benefit from trials in his life—Triumph through Trials. Therefore, we shouldn't expect to find a lot of teaching in this book about the Way because it's clearly about the Walk. James wants these people to "save their lives" from the trials they are experiencing today, not from the fires of hell tomorrow, because their eternal tomorrow has already been settled. This is the potential benefit of being a good listener. In the midst of trials, God's wisdom could deliver them from the devastation of trials and thus save their lives (their time on earth) for eternal purposes.

Some years ago the little church we started had a tennis tournament. I didn't know how to play tennis, but I'd played other sports through the years in high school and college, so I went out and bought a bunch of books on how to play tennis. The tournament was months away in April. This was December. So I read and practiced; read and practiced. When the tournament came, I was able to get to the finals (small church), but then lost to a sixteen year old who was on the high school tennis team. He beat me 6-2, 6-2.

Well, after the defeat, a guy who was watching came over, introduced himself, and asked me if I would like to learn to play tennis. My inner thought was, "Well, just who are you? Don't you realize that I just reached the finals of the All-World Church league?" But I just said, "And you are?" He said he was a touring tennis pro who had just left the European tour to work for Rod Laver and Roy Emerson. He had started attending our church and would like to teach me how to play tennis for free. Wow! How could I turn that down? There was just one catch. "I want you to teach me the Bible." Turned out he had been a believer for about a year and had a hunger to grow. Of course, I bargained with him for a while, but when we struck a deal (to my advantage, I believe) our relationship began. He said that his life goal up to that point had been to be the best tennis player in the world. He'd recently had a match against Bjorn Borg.

"Wow," I said, "did you really play Bjorn Borg?"

He had a low, guttural laugh as he responded, "Not very long."

We spent three years together. I did my best to learn tennis, but alas, my athletic abilities are limited. On the other hand, this guy's hunger for the Scriptures was insatiable. I'll never forget the turning point in his life. It was when he understood the concept we are covering right now. "You mean there is more to it than just going to heaven when you die?" Much more. In fact, this concept of "saving your life" deals with finding the very reason God made you—your purpose in life. Miss this and you miss your uniqueness—why God made you the way you are. My friend wound up leaving the tennis world to become one of the finest Bible teachers I know. Why? Because he learned that the Word of God could save his life. And it can save yours, too. That's the awesome potential of being a good listener.

In this section about the Art of Being a Good Listener, we've covered its preparation and its potential. Now we dive into a Precaution in 1:22-24.

Precaution in Being a Good Listener (1:22-24)

> But be doers of the word, and not hearers only, deceiving yourselves. For if anyone is a hearer of the word and not a doer, he is like a man observing his natural face in a mirror; for he observes himself, goes away, and immediately forgets what kind of man he was.

In these verses James contrasts a Poor Listener (22-24) to a Good Listener (25). The Poor Listener is found in 1:22-24. In verse 22 there is a word of caution: be a doer of the word, not a hearer only, or you deceive yourself. To understand this word of caution we must understand two meanings of the Greek word *akouō* translated here as "hear." In Greek it can mean to "audit" or to "hearken." It meant just what it means today. An academic auditor is someone who audits a course at the university. You remember the characteristics of an auditor? He is the most relaxed one there. Why? Because all he is doing is filling his notebook with notes. There are no assignments, no homework, no papers, and no tests. He just takes in the information.

Churches are filled with auditors coming to class Sunday after Sunday. They fill notebooks with information about Christianity, but they never do anything about it. They would be hard pressed to show God, their family, or close friends any significant change in their lives since they started the course. How about it? Is there any significant change you can point to in your life to prove that you are any more than just an auditor? Howard Hendricks used to say, "The Word of God is alive and powerful. When you back into 300,000 volts of electricity, you don't just sit there; you move!" That is, unless you are just an auditor.

The other meaning of *akouō* is "to hearken." "Hearken unto the voice of the Lord." In other words, **obey** the voice of the Lord. This is the way James uses *akouō*. He who has ears to hear, let him hear. James says if you listen to God's still, small voice, do something about what you have heard, or else you are just auditing the course. He illustrates the auditor in verses 23 and 24. The Word of God (as it is in 1 Corinthians 13 and 2 Corinthians 3) is like a mirror. This auditor sees the face of his birth in the mirror. But as soon as he steps away, he forgets what the face of his birth looks like.

Usually this is interpreted to mean that a man looks in the Word of God and sees his sinful nature, but turns away without doing anything about it. If that's your understanding, fine. However, I think the context of the passage supports a slightly different interpretation. There is nothing here about our physical birth. Verse 18 is referencing our spiritual birth. So I would suggest the possibility that this forgetful hearer is one who looks into the mirror of God's Word and sees the reflection of his new birth; he sees all he is in Christ; he sees all he could become through Christ; but then he turns away and lives as though he had never been born again. He lives just as he used to. "I'm not any different from the way I ever was," he says to himself. This is James' precautionary illustration.

We have studied the preparation, the potential, and the precaution in being a good listener. Now let's dig into a good example, a contrast to the poor listener of verses 22-24. Let's look at the practice of being a good listener in 1:25-27.

Practice of Being a Good Listener (1:25-27)

> But he who looks into the perfect law of liberty and continues *in it,* and is not a forgetful hearer but a doer of the work, this one will be blessed in what he does. If anyone among you thinks he is religious, and does not bridle his tongue but deceives his own heart, this one's religion *is* useless. Pure and undefiled religion before God and the Father is this: to visit orphans and widows in their trouble, *and* to keep oneself unspotted from the world.

The hearkener, the good listener, is in verse 25. This man stoops down closely to look into the mirror. That is the meaning of the Greek here. He studies closely the face of his new birth. He sees what he can become in Christ. He sees the law of liberty—freedom—free from his old hang-ups and sinful ways. And this listener does not turn away; he abides therein. He gazes at what he can become. He keeps his eyes on his position in Christ rather than his condition on earth—and what happens? He becomes a doer of the word. I like that word "becomes." It reminds me of 2 Corinthians 3:18 where the Holy Spirit molds us into the image of Christ as we think about Christ. That's what we have here. As he becomes a hearkener rather than an auditor, he, in the midst of his trials, becomes a happy person.

In verses 26-27 James makes an application. He says, "Let me be clear about what I am saying. Do you think you are pretty religious? You go to church every Sunday? Take communion? Been baptized? Sing in the choir, perhaps? Let me tell you something. If you do all that and cannot even saddle that bucking bronco in your mouth, it is all useless. Forget it. Don't bother. God doesn't need more auditors."

But if you have the real disease, then here are the genuine germs in verse 27. Notice he says "before God." Ha! James could not care less about what kind of religious parody we display before men. God knows where the action is and it is two-fold. Do something about the affliction of others—the widows and the orphans. And do something about the leprosy in your life. Don't be a forgetful hearer. Be an effective doer.

That's the thing about James. He gets down and dirty—right where we live. On the one hand it is an exciting adventure, this Book of James; on the other hand, it is a painful encounter. The book hurts; it cuts; it stings; it stabs. It won't simply rebuke you—it attacks and assaults your life where it is out of kilter or out of balance with the standard of truth. But when we line up with the truth, and become hearkeners instead of just auditors, we reap true happiness. That is what the word "blessed" means, *makarios*. It's the same word found in 1:12. Happiness doesn't come from just believing. It comes from believing and doing. That is why Jesus said in John 13:17, "If you know these things, happy are you if you do them."

To visit someone who can do nothing for you in return brings happiness. It's being a doer of the Word, not just a hearer—a hearkener, not just an auditor. Want to get out of the depression that has lowered around you like a dark cloud because of the trials you are facing? Then do something, especially for someone in greater distress than you. It will transform your depression into happiness. As a pastor, I have made quite a few hospital visits over the years. I've rarely left the hospital without saying, "Thank you, Lord." No matter what distress I might be in before I walk in, it pales in comparison to the suffering of some of the people in there. And it always brings me a measure of happiness to bring a smile to a face in there, or a little more peace and rest.

The art of being a good listener involves preparation. We cannot hear God's voice if we're talking, or if we're angry or finicky, or if we have wax in our ears. But once we have heard God's voice, it means little unless we hearken unto it. And **the one who hearkens is the one who is happy.**

A wealthy man lived in Paris. Though he had everything he needed, he was bored and disgusted with his debauched life. So he went out to the Seine River to commit suicide. It was twilight, however, not dark yet, so he decided to walk around a bit until it got dark. While he was walking near the River, he happened to reach into his pocket and discover a bag of gold coins, which they used for money in those days. He thought to himself; "Well, these gold coins won't do anybody any good if I jump in the river with them. I'll look around for someone who is poor and needs them." He began to search the area and before long spied a house, the exterior of which spoke of poverty. He went in. He found a mother lying sick on the bed with six little kids in rags around the bed crying out for food. So he went up to them and presented the bag of gold. Immediately their tears of sorrow turned into tears of joy, and they thanked him profusely. He was so filled with satisfaction that he changed his mind about committing suicide. He decided to devote the rest of his life to doing good and he made this comment: "I never realized doing good could make me so happy."

That is precisely what James says at the end of verse 25. It's what he illustrates in verses 26 and 27. The secret to happiness is to find people you can help. If we are eaten up with ourselves and our own concerns and problems, we will eventually become depressed and disappointed. It is essential that we learn the art of being a good listener. Are you prepared to listen to what God says to you? Are you going to act on what He says? Remember, God does not speak in an earthquake, but in a still, small voice. He who has ears to hear, let him hear, then be a doer.

Paul Holloway was a fun-loving, guitar-playing, girl-chasing high school kid when I met him. He was a regular at the new Young Life Club in town, which, with three hundred kids coming, became the largest in Texas. Paul was a believer, but he never let that get in the way of having fun. He went off to school at Texas A&M. Then, the summer after his freshman year, Paul asked me to teach him how to study the Bible. He was a good student and became what James would call a "good listener." He suddenly saw that Christianity was more than just going to heaven. It was a revelation to him to discover that the Scriptures could "save his life" on earth for eternity—that each day could count for God's glory.

The truth of being a good listener hit Paul like 300,000 volts of electricity. He said, "I've got to transfer to a school where I can learn Greek and Hebrew." So he went to UT in Austin and took all the Greek and Hebrew they could offer an undergraduate. He then went to Dallas Seminary, but because he already knew most of what they were offering, he only stayed a couple of years. He helped start a church in Galveston, which reached out to the medical community from UT Medical School. Simultaneously, he enrolled in a masters program at Rice.

After Rice, Paul entered a very special program at the University of Chicago, which only took two new students per year to develop into New Testament scholars. He got his Ph.D. under Hans Dieter Betz and won the largest scholarship in the nation for his last year of study. Some years later I was asked to present a paper before forty NT scholars in Marburg, Germany, where Rudolph Bultmann, a renowned NT scholar of the twentieth century, did his work. I went into the NT library to browse around, and to my surprise and delight I just happened to see a copy of Paul Holloway's dissertation in the stacks.

Paul went on to become a professor of the NT at Samford University, then the University of Glasgow, and currently the University of the South. He has been published by at least ten of the top scholarly theological journals in the world, and he is writing a commentary on Philippians for the *Hermenia* series. What changed the direction of his life? It was when he became a good listener.

"THE UGLY DUCKLING"

James 2:1-13

When I was growing up my parents took me to see a musical about the Dutch storyteller Hans Christian Andersen, staring Danny Kaye. He told a number of stories I've never forgotten, but perhaps the one that moved me the most began when a flock of children gathered around Hans to hear a story, all except a little boy whose head was shaved. He stood off by himself looking very dejected and lonely. The other kids laughed and made fun of him. They would not include him in their group or games. Hans addresses the boy when the children leave and asks if he wants to hear a story. He tells him about the Ugly Duckling. In the Hollywood version, the words go something like this:

> There once was an ugly duckling
> > with feathers all shabby and brown
> And the other birds in so many words
> > Said "Scat, get out of town.
> Scat, get out . . . Scat, scat, get out, . . .
> > Scat, scat, get out of town."
> And he went with a quack and a waddle
> > And a quack and a very unhappy tear.

Although the ugly duckling had been rejected by his own kind because he didn't look right to them, over the wintertime as he hid himself away, a fantastic transformation took place in his life. He turned into one of the most beautiful birds of all, a swan. No longer an ugly duckling, he became one of God's loveliest creatures, the envy of every eye on the pond.

Undoubtedly Andersen tells the story in the musical to encourage the little boy. In addition to being encouraging, it also illustrates a certain lack of perspective in Christian circles. The other birds, in so many words, were making a value judgment of this ugly little duckling that was entirely false. The reason for their mistake was that they looked only at his outward appearance. If only they could have looked on the inside, they would have seen a marvelous process of transformation, which would one day turn him into the loveliest bird on the lake, a swan.

This gets right to the heart of a problem we have, a problem that must be solved; or, otherwise, we who pride ourselves on our plumes and feathers may turn into very ugly ducklings indeed. This problem isn't new to Christians, for it is the very same problem James was trying to solve as he moved into the second chapter of his letter. Toward the end of James 1, he tells his readers something positive and something negative. On the positive side, he defines pure and undefiled religion before God as visiting widows and orphans in their affliction. On the negative side, he warns us to keep "unspotted from the world." The spot he refers to is illustrated in chapter two, where James condemns the shallow, worldly attitude (spot) that has tainted the church, an attitude which prevents us from being good listeners.

We want to have triumph through our trials. To do that we need to be quick to hear, slow to speak, slow to wrath. We are right in the middle of the first section of the body of this letter, a section on being quick to hear. In 1:21-27 James teaches that being quick to hear is more than just listening, it is also hearkening. It is hearing and obeying. In this section he tells us that true hearing is more than just morality (2:1-13). James looks beyond our actions into our attitudes. For example, maybe you have not committed adultery, which is an *action*, but if you have a judgmental *attitude* you have still broken the royal law of love.

We want to look first at the Problem (2:1), then the Illustration

(2:2-4), and finally the Inconsistencies associated with this problem (2:5-13).

The Problem: *A Shallow, Worldly Attitude (2:1)*

My brethren, do not hold the faith of our Lord Jesus Christ, *the Lord* of glory, with partiality.

Notice from the outset that James is presenting family truth: "My brethren." It is not a book about the Way; it is a book about the Walk. Then he puts his finger right on top of a spot from the world that can keep our religious practice from being pure. In Greek it is the word *prosōpolēpsiais*, which is made up of two words: the face + to receive = to receive the face, or to take things at face value, as we say today. It's interesting that this Greek word is only found in Jewish and Christian literature. Apparently, *prosōpolēpsiais* is a problem prevalent among religious people. We must understand that God never receives things at face value. The word is used in one form or another in four other places outside of James. In each case it says in effect, God is not a respecter of persons, which means that God does not accept people or things at face value. He does not look at the external (Rom 2:11; Eph 6:9; Col 3:25; Acts 10:34).

There is a good example of this in 1 Samuel 16 when Samuel is looking for a new king. God has rejected Saul as king and has commissioned Samuel, as high priest, to go out to anoint a successor. Samuel was led by the Lord to the family of Jesse. As he is looking at Jesse's sons, his eyes light on the oldest, Eliab. He must have been a tall, impressive, handsome young man because Samuel thought, "Surely this must be the Lord's choice. He has all the marks of kingship about him." Samuel should have known, based on Saul, that impressive physical characteristics do not make a good king. But the Lord said to Samuel, "Don't judge this man on the basis of his appearance and stature, because I have rejected him. God does not see as man does; man looks on the outward appearance, but God looks on the heart."

You see, God doesn't draw people who are tall, dark, and handsome, necessarily. Many of them are short, shot, and shapeless.

He is not impressed by external features and factors, but by the heart. To be swayed by the external is a hindrance to hearing. God says, "In Christ there is neither Jew nor Greek, there is neither bond nor free, there is neither male nor female: for you are all one in Christ Jesus." Yet, our eyes too often carry more weight than our ears. We look at people—we look at the externals—and we start drawing distinctions and making judgments at face value. Having identified this bad attitude, James illustrates it in 2:2-4.

The Illustration (2:2-4)

> For if there should come into your assembly a man with gold rings, in fine apparel, and there should also come in a poor man in filthy clothes, and you pay attention to the one wearing the fine clothes and say to him, "You sit here in a good place," and say to the poor man, "You stand there," or, "Sit here at my footstool," have you not shown partiality among yourselves, and become judges with evil thoughts?

James says, "Here is a good example to illustrate my point. Take the rich man and the poor man." The first guy to walk in is Goldfinger, straight from the 1964 Bond film. He is ushered right up to one of the choice seats. Shortly after him entereth the Ugly Duckling with feathers all shabby and brown. The near-sighted usher probably thought he was being very loving in his attitude toward the Ugly Duckling. He probably thought, "This miserable wretch. Well, I must show him Christian love, so we will put him in the standing room only section. Oh, I know what! I will really go the extra mile. I will let him sit by me—at my footstool, of course, the place for servants, slaves, and conquered enemies. I must be careful not to cause a stir by letting this duck perch wherever he wants. Can you imagine what Mrs. Hicklebee would say if this poor, smelly thing sat anywhere near her?"

The irony is, although this illustration has stood on the pages of Scripture for quite a number of centuries, the church is still engulfed in this same shallow attitude. I remember a story, which I presume takes place before the turn of the twentieth century, and it illustrates our point. There was a certain man who went regularly to a local church to hear the vicar preach. Although he went every Sunday and was not in very good health, he frequently had to stand because the church was usually full. He observed that the best-dressed people were always ushered to a good seat. So one Sunday he resorted to a little subterfuge. He happened to own a very large and beautiful ring—he was not rich, but he did own this. He put the ring on and put his glove on over it (they wore gloves in those days). He went to church and hung around in the foyer while all sorts of people passed by. Then he took off his glove and with a studied effort at being indifferent about it, he just sort of raised his hand to the level of his ear so that the ring was displayed. Immediately, he was ushered to a comfortable seat— precisely the thing James wrote about so long ago. It is amazing how easy and how common it is to perpetuate this attitude.

Before we are quick to condemn, we need to ask ourselves a question. If Bill Gates or Warren Buffet came to our church for a visit to inspect the claims of Christ, are we sure they would receive no special deference over anyone else, that we would not go out of our way to make them feel at home? Would we treat a very poor person with an equal measure of respect? I think we can all admit how elated we might be should Warren Buffet come to Christ and get interested in our work for the Lord. The temptation is very real, very real, and James is saying that this is an attitude from the world. Visually, it is a stunning blemish in a splendid setting, a setting which draws its brilliance from the Lord of glory. I cannot help but think that when James wrote this he must have been thinking how our Lord left His glory in heaven to enter the poverty of a carpenter's home—voluntarily. For a person who puts his faith in such a Savior, it is inappropriate to be a respecter of persons.

After finishing his illustration, James concludes in verse 4 that those who show partiality and favoritism cause divisions and cliques and become judges with evil thoughts of other Christians. Some translations stick "motives" here instead of "thoughts," probably thinking of the usher's motive of getting money from the rich man.

However, this really is not the word for motives. I tend to think James is talking about the evil thoughts the judge has about the person he judges. The word for judge here is "critic." One who criticizes another is a judge. He lifts himself over the other person and even verbalizes his evil thoughts about that person. James says this type of reasoning, *dialogion*, is very dangerous because it is based on face value, on externals. Someone may do something to us, which at face value seems cruel and unkind. Or he may do something to another, which at face value appears harsh and merciless. But James says it is dangerous to evaluate people based on externals alone. We do not know all of the facts, perhaps, or we may have misinterpreted the facts we have. Judging the appearance of an event is the same as judging the appearance of a person.

The son of the pastor I served under while going to seminary in Dallas passed along an interesting story that illustrates my point. There was a young attorney at a law firm in Dallas, about twenty-eight or twenty-nine, who lived alone in an apartment. It was customary every Thanksgiving for this law firm to distribute turkeys among its employees. But the young bachelor could never figure out what to do with his. Being single, he didn't want to cook the thing and even if he did, he couldn't eat it all. Every Thanksgiving he was faced with the problem of what to do with his turkey. He couldn't refuse it since the president of the company was always the one to distribute the turkeys. The turkey giving was done with great pomp and ceremony.

Well, one Thanksgiving some of the young attorney's friends decided to play a little practical joke. They stole his turkey and replaced it with a bogus one made of papier-mâché. It was wrapped in brown paper with the neck and tail of a real turkey showing. It looked just like all the rest. When the president of the law firm handed out the turkeys, our unsuspecting lawyer took it home with him on the streetcar. He was sitting there with this thing in his lap when a man came down the aisle and sat next to him. He was obviously down on his luck, a little shabby and run down. They struck up a conversation, and the man said he had been hunting for a job all day without luck. He only had a dollar or two left in his pocket with which to buy a Thanksgiving meal for his family. He was anxious not to let his children down.

So the light bulb flashed in our young attorney's mind. He said to himself, "Here's where I can do my new friend a service and get rid of this turkey at the same time." His first thought was to give him the turkey but then he thought, "No, to give him the turkey might offend him. I'll sell him the turkey." So he asked the man how much money he had with him. "Two dollars," the man said. The lawyer replied, "Tell you what, I'll sell you this turkey for two dollars." The transaction was made and both men were very happy. The poor man got off the streetcar with his turkey, and the lawyer went home with his money.

Well, you can imagine the scene when the man got home. The children were all excited; they gathered around the table and unwrapped the phony bird. And you can imagine what the man must have thought about the lawyer. "What a rotten, dirty slob. Of all the dirty, low-down blankety-blanks, this guy takes the cake." Of course, we can also imagine the horror of the lawyer when he went to work after Thanksgiving and all his sly friends slapped him on the back and told him what they did. And they, in turn, felt terrible when they learned how their practical joke had backfired. In fact, they all rode the streetcar for days and even advertized in the paper to try to straighten things out with the unfortunate family.

This story sticks in my mind because it shows how impossible it is to judge someone at face value. The bachelor lawyer's heart was right when he sold that turkey, but judging from the exterior of the situation, it would take a full moon before you could convince our jobless friend of that. We never seem to have all the facts, but even when we do, our interpretation can often be faulty. It is simply best to avoid evaluating from the appearance of things.

James wants to drive his point home, so he backs up his principle with three reasons why favoritism and partiality should disappear from the Christian scene. These reasons all revolve around the inconsistency of favoritism.

Inconsistencies Associated with this Problem (2:5-13)

Inconsistent with Future Reality (5)

> **Listen, my beloved brethren: Has God not chosen the poor of this world *to be* rich in faith and heirs of the kingdom which He promised to those who love Him?**

Notice that verse five begins with "hearken," listen. The same word, *akouo*, was translated in verse 19 as "hear." James is still trying to tell us what it means to be quick to hear. He is saying that our eyes, which make value judgments so quickly, can deceive our ears. Listen, he says, don't make that kind of judgment. Did not God choose the poor of this world to be rich in faith and heirs of the kingdom He promised to those who love Him?

Usually, this verse is used to support the idea that God chooses the poor to become Christians because it is easier for a camel to go through the eye of a needle than for a rich man to get into heaven. But I don't think the verses suggest that at all. The contrast is not between the poor man who has faith and the rich man who does not. It is not a contrast between a believer and an unbeliever. The contrast is between the poor man who has a lot of faith and the rich man who has only a little faith (see 1 Cor 1:5; Eph 2:4; and 1 Tim 6:18 for analogous expressions). The poor man is rich in faith. He has a lot of faith. And because he does, he is an heir of the kingdom. This does not merely mean the poor automatically get into the kingdom. It means they have heirship there, which is another question.

We need to remember that more often than not inheritance is viewed as a reward in the NT. Paul says in Colossians 3:23-24, "And whatever you do, do it heartily, as to the Lord and not to men, knowing that from the Lord you will receive **the reward of the inheritance**; for you serve the Lord Christ." Getting into the kingdom is one thing; inheriting it is another. Let's return to the illustration of Warren Buffet. Suppose he becomes a believer and decides to give a large sum of money to our seminary and wants to build an extraordinary physical complex where he lives in Omaha, Nebraska. He also builds a home for my family and invites us to live there as long as we wish. Finally, he dies and in his will has allowed us to inherit the home we are living in. Now we are owners. Before we were the guests. See a similar use of the word "inherit" in Revelation 21:7. With a little bit of faith we can enter the kingdom of God (the house). As our faith grows, so does our inheritance in that kingdom (we become owners of the house). The greater our faith, the greater our inheritance in the kingdom of God (God's house).

At Mt. Nebo Moses told the new generation to do two things regarding the land of Israel: enter the land and then possess the land. Although they never fully possessed the land, the Israelites became the first self-governing country until the United States. What do I mean by that? They had a king for hundreds of years. They had something else, too. An inheritance. The first thing they did after taking possession of the land was to divide it into states, so to speak. Each tribe got its piece of the nation.

Then what happened? Individual families got a piece of the land as well. They called this piece of land their inheritance. Figuratively, they could mortgage their inheritance, but it could not be foreclosed on. Every seven years any debts accrued on their land were forgiven. Why? Because private property gave them a sense of ownership and initiative. It is one reason why after they were scattered outside the land that they have become entrepreneurial leaders, creative artists, financiers, and professionals in so many fields. Uniquely intelligent? Probably. But they also had a taste of inheritance. As western civilization developed, the common people in other countries were serfs. They earned a subsistence living while most of their labor made landowners wealthy. That is why some believe the average American fighting in the war for independence from England was two inches taller and lived fifteen years longer. Why? Because they came to America with hope. Hope for what? To own a little piece of land, to have an inheritance they could pass down to their children. It gave them initiative and drive. The opportunity for an inheritance can be transformative.

This reminds us of our Lord's words, "Lay not up for yourselves treasure on earth, but lay up treasures in heaven." When you think about that, two conclusions are inescapable: 1) The way to be rich in the kingdom is to lay up treasures in heaven; and 2) The way to be poor is by not laying them up. Simply then, a Christian who does not lay up treasures in heaven will not have any there waiting for him. This all goes back to our Lord's words in Luke 6:20, "Blessed are the poor, for yours is the kingdom of heaven." Who owns the kingdom? Jesus says the poor do. The Sermon on the Mount begins in a similar way: "Blessed are the poor in spirit, for theirs is the kingdom of God." It seems clear that poverty either in spirit or financially is a predication for possessing the kingdom. He says the kingdom is yours. He is not talking about getting into the kingdom, but about owning it, possessing it, inheriting it—heirship.

Let this sink in. In times of testing, who is more likely to depend on God, the rich man or the poor man? The poor man has nothing else and no one else to trust. He has no other resources. The temptation of the rich man, however, is to trust in his own resources and his own abilities. This is why the poor man has an abundance of faith. It is easy for him to trust God because he has nowhere else to turn. It would seem that a man's faith is in an inverse ratio to the accumulation of his wealth.

John Wesley is supposed to have said at one point in his life that he knew of only four men who had become wealthy without suffering deteriorating consequences spiritually. Later in his life, he said he did not know any. That is interesting, and I think it illustrates a principle frequently in operation. As our material wealth increases, our ability to trust God often diminishes. It is difficult for a rich man to be right-minded; conversely, it is difficult for a right-minded man to become rich. The right-minded man is busy laying up treasures in heaven. Ironic, isn't it? In a world in which everyone seems to be running around wildly, trying to possess more and more, James seems to say it would be wiser if we looked for ways to have less on earth, and more in heaven. His point is that showing partiality to the rich and dishonoring the poor is shortsighted, for one day the rich man (more often than not) will be poor and the poor man will be rich.

Of course, these are generalities. Some of the finest believers I know are extremely wealthy. In fact, I am writing these words in a mega-million dollar home in Snowmass Village, CO. It belongs to some wealthy Christians, and they have basically dedicated all they have to God's glory. They are donating its use to me while I write. A couple of days ago while walking, I took a path called Ditch Trail. As I was walking along, some people I met pointed out the home of Michael Eisner, the CEO of Disney, in the valley below. There are wealthy people all over the place up here. Some of them are very humble Christians with far more balanced lives than some of us poor folk. So there is nothing wrong with wanting to be rich. The only question is where do you want to be rich? The fact remains that if you get rich here, you will be poor there, if you don't send the majority of those riches ahead of you to welcome you home when you stand before Him.

Yes, favoritism is inconsistent with Future Reality; but it is also inconsistent with Present Reality (2:6-7).

Inconsistent with Present Reality (2:6-7)

But you have dishonored the poor man. Do not the rich oppress you and drag you into the courts? Do they not blaspheme that noble name by which you are called?

James says it does not make sense to show favoritism to rich people who blaspheme the name of Jesus Christ and stab you in the back. I saw this contrast the summer after my first year in college. I am from Nashville, TN, the home of the Southwestern Company, an organization that during the summer employs only college students. They send them out selling Bibles and other educational books for the family. Well, my mother wanted to get me away from a girlfriend I had back in Tennessee. So she called me at Rice to let me know she had found this great job for me. "What's that, mom?" It was selling Bibles door-to-door. I thought, who wants to sell anything door-to-door? But I was a new Christian who had fallen in love with the Bible, so I figured, why not? I thought the Bible might be one thing I would be willing to sell. What mom neglected to tell me when I went home to Nashville for sales training was that the company always sends its employees away from home so that they will not be distracted. They sent me to Shawnee, Oklahoma. I rode a bicycle around town, just like the Mormons.

Well, one thing I learned real fast. If I wanted to get the door slammed in my face, all I had to do was go to the rich neighborhoods, but if I wanted to sell some books, just go to the country folks. They lived off the land and seemed to have a greater sense of dependence on the Lord, since the weather had a lot to do with the kind of harvest they got.

Again, this is only an example of a generality. But, in this particular experience and in James' argument, it was the rich people who were rude and had ugly things to say about Christians and Christianity. James is saying that it is not only inconsistent to show favoritism to the rich because they will be poor in heaven, but also because of how they often mistreat people of faith in the present life. Favoritism is inconsistent with Future Reality and Present Reality. It is also inconsistent with True Legality (2:8-13).

Inconsistent with True Legality (2:8-13)

> If you really fulfill *the* royal law according to the Scripture, *"You shall love your neighbor as yourself,"* you do well; but if you show partiality, you commit sin, and are convicted by the law as transgressors. For whoever shall keep the whole law, and yet stumble in one *point,* he is guilty of all. For He who said, *"Do not commit adultery,"* also said, *"Do not murder."* Now if you do not commit adultery, but you do murder, you have become a transgressor of the law. So speak and so do as those who will be judged by the law of liberty. For judgment is without mercy to the one who has shown no mercy. Mercy triumphs over judgment.

Here James turns to the law, both of Christ and of Moses. His point is simple. In effect, when you set the rich man ahead of the poor man, you are not loving that poor man. You are not treating him as you treat yourself. You would not like to be treated that way. Therefore you violate the royal law of love, and in so doing, all of the other morality you may claim is set aside. The law is a unit, a seamless garment. Break one link and you have broken the whole chain. Break part of a window and the whole window is shattered. If I go out and rob my neighbor, it matters very little that I pay my taxes. I have constituted myself a criminal, a lawbreaker.

There is a rather amusing story that illustrates this point. This is supposed to have happened before a rather well known jurist by the name of Judge Kent. A man had been apprehended for robbery. In this particular robbery it seems the man had cut a hole in a tent where some people were camping. He stuck his right arm and head through the hole and extracted certain valuable objects. He was caught and brought to trial. His lawyer, as lawyers often do, put up a perfectly ridiculous defense.

The lawyer said, "You cannot call this man guilty because his whole body was not involved in the crime—just his arm and his head." So in his final plea, after the case had been argued, Judge Kent said to the jury, "Now if you feel there is validity to this argument and only part of this man's body is guilty of the crime, then you are instructed to find a verdict of guilty against all the parts of the body you find culpable here." So the jury went out and soon came back with a verdict. They found guilty the head, the right shoulder, and the right arm of the man in question. He was called before the bar of the judge, and Judge Kent sentenced the head, the right shoulder, and the right arm of the man to two years hard labor at the state prison. Then he added, "You can do anything you please with the rest of your body."

Obviously, the body is a unity, and so is the law. When you break the law of love, you are guilty of breaking the whole law. Judgment will come, and here I think he means the Judgment Seat of Christ. At that time we may go before the Judgment Seat expecting great reward for our faithfulness in attending church, in teaching Sunday School, in serving on the board. But James says if you come to church and do these things with favoritism in your heart, your religion is in vain. There will be no mercy for the merciless. Jesus said, "I will have mercy and not sacrifice." Again, "Blessed are the merciful, for they shall obtain mercy." And John wrote that love will have boldness in the Day of Judgment. The world is full of favoritism, partiality, and prejudice. James says, "OK. But not in God's house. There is no room for these attitudes here. That is not in accordance with the royal law of love."

James talks about the materially rich and poor in his example of our shallow, worldly attitude. We can also show partiality to people who are rich and poor in other ways. When I was a youth pastor we had a very dedicated young person in the core group of about thirty kids who suffered from cystic fibrosis. His name was Craig Powell. Most kids with his malady die by the time they become teenagers, but Craig was still with us. Unfortunately, he was an ugly duckling. Craig had to start the morning in a lung machine to clear the phlegm from his breathing so he could go to school. He only weighed about ninety pounds and walked with a decided limp due to a deformation in his right leg, almost like a clubfoot. Furthermore, he had a severe case of acne and had trouble with drooling. It goes without saying the other kids were uncomfortable around Craig. He was their Ugly Duckling, sort of pushed to the side.

In this particular youth group I had taught them how to share their faith with strangers by going out to Love Field, a local airport, once a month. We did this for three years. We were never obnoxious—just asked people sitting by themselves if they would like to take a religious survey. If they did, when the survey was over, we would ask them if they would like a more personal relationship with God. If they said yes, then we would offer to share how they could have one. If they invited us, we would continue to share how they could do that. We were never pushy. Craig never missed. He would just limp up to people and go through the routine.

Those were the days of Sunday evening services, and the pastor was always aware of Love Field Sunday for our youth group. He would give part of the evening service over to the youth who had gone to Love Field if they wanted to share. Craig was always the first one down the aisle, limping along, sharing his story that day in his gravelly, little voice.

I graduated from seminary and moved away to help start a church. But Craig and I kept in touch. He graduated from high school and went on to college. One day he called me and said, "Dave, I just can't get a girl to go out with me. I know no one is going to marry me, but I just would like to have a friend to talk to." I didn't know what to tell Craig. Sometimes tears would roll down my cheeks as I listened to him talk. I reached into space for words to comfort and encourage him, but felt so inadequate. Here was the Ugly Duckling incarnate, but to me he seemed like an angel in disguise.

One day his mother called to tell me Craig had died. He had lived several years longer than the typical person suffering from cystic fibrosis. He lived long enough and deeply enough to learn how to share his faith with more boldness and faithfulness than most of the healthy kids his age. I firmly believe when I see Craig again on the other side, I won't be looking at an Ugly Duckling at all, but one of the most beautiful swans in heaven. Some of us who think of ourselves as swans will turn out to be ugly ducklings. For man looks at the outside, while God looks at the heart. **To be a good listener, don't let your eyes get in the way of your ears.** And the good news is that God, through the Spirit, can take any ugly duckling in this life and turn him into a beautiful swan in the next.

"THREE LITTLE PIGS"

James 2:14-17

One afternoon a friend called me up for lunch. While we ate he discussed some of the proceedings on the home he was building. After lunch we went over to take a look at the progress. I really wasn't prepared for what I would see as we rounded the corner. I have seen a number of houses go up from ground level, but never one quite like this. What appeared before my eyes was the beginning of a slab of concrete which, when combined with fill dirt, would be four and a half feet thick. I couldn't believe my eyes. Why would anyone want such a colossal piece of concrete? Sensing my amazement, my friend began to explain the necessity of the slab. First of all, he said that the ground in that area had shifted over a period of time. So special precautions were necessary to make sure the shifting ground would not crack the slab. Secondly, the house was going to be extremely large with two and a half stories. Hence, such a house would need a very firm foundation. Therefore, all sorts of extra precautions were taken in making the slab especially durable. My friend explained the obvious—the slab was probably the most important part of the building process. No matter how fine the interior and exterior of the rest of the house, it would all come tumbling down if there was not a foundation or if the foundation were not sufficiently durable. Once that slab was properly laid, the workers could build with confidence, knowing that what they erected would be there awhile, since it rested on a very firm foundation.

How firm a foundation does your life rest upon? I often wonder if we are as particular about the foundations on which we build our lives, as we are about the ones on which we build our houses. We should be. Otherwise, when the ground of our being begins to shift and the storms come, our lives may come tumbling down because the slab has cracked and crumbled, leaving only sinking sand.

This illustration of our life as a house and the necessity of a firm foundation is certainly not my own creation. It was made famous centuries ago by Jesus Christ as He concluded the most famous sermon ever given, the Sermon on the Mount. At the end of Matthew 7 we find His closing illustration about building a house on sand or on rock. What Jesus teaches is fundamental to understanding this controversial passage in James 2:14-26. Keep in mind that the closing remarks of a sermon are often considered paramount in the mind of the preacher. Apparently, Jesus thought the truth of this parable extremely important.

Now, quite often the rock in this parable is identified with Jesus Christ. I think this is probably due to the fact that Jesus said to Peter, "Upon this rock I will build my church," and Jesus is usually identified as the cornerstone or rock upon which the church is built. However, that is not the case in this parable. Here Jesus contrasts a wise man and a foolish man. Both of them build houses. Obviously, Jesus is not actually talking about house building. He is using house building as an illustration. The house represents life. And that is a good illustration because we live in houses. What Jesus wants us to pay attention to here is the difference in foundations. One is rock; the other is sand. One is firm, while the other is soft.

What could these foundations represent? Jesus tells us. The rock foundation is the concrete slab of **hearing plus doing** the Word of Jesus. The soft slab is hearing only. Slab building, even today, involves pouring a large amount of sand down as a cushion, but the sand is capped with concrete to make it firm. Hearing only (without doing) is just sand. Hearing plus doing is concrete poured over the sand, a firm foundation. So Jesus is saying if you base your life on hearing and doing His teaching, when the storm winds blow, your life will weather the storm; your house will not crumble. But nothing can save the house of the fool in the storm. For he has built and based his life merely on hearing the Words of Jesus but without doing anything he heard. The very same storm blows against the life of the foolish man as blows against the life of the wise man, but the house of the fool comes tumbling down, and great is the fall of it. Nothing could save him in the hour of that storm because he had a soft foundation for his house.

This is the long way around to James 2:14-17, but if you have followed me, we have a head start on understanding this problematic yet pivotal portion of James. For you see, I am convinced James was thinking of this very parable from the lips of our Lord when he wrote this section on hearing. Be quick to hear, says James, in time of trial. This is one of the first qualities needed to weather the storm. He goes on to explain that hearing without doing is empty, vain, and worthless. **Hearing plus doing** is exactly what Jesus spoke of on the mountain. James writes in 1:21 that we need to listen carefully to God's Word when a storm hits. For God's Word is able to save us from destruction in the midst of that storm if we do something about what we hear. So True Hearing involves Good Listening; it also involves Good Attitudes; and finally, expanding on the theme already set forth at the end of chapter one, it involves Good Actions. Hearing plus doing is the foundation we need for our lives to be saved when the wind blows. With that background, I think James 2:14-17 will start to make sense.

In James 2:14-17 James sets forth a proposition, a premise, a thesis, a big idea. He says, "Faith without works is dead." Then in verses 18-19, opposition arises. Someone says faith without works is not dead. The demons have no good works at all, but at least they tremble. Then in verses 20-26 James refutes the objection raised and proves that faith without works is dead. In this lesson we will only focus on James 2:14-17. This is his big idea: faith without works is dead. He sets forth the Principle of Profit in 2:14; then an Illustration of this principle in 2:15-16; and finally, his Conclusion in 2:17.

The Principle of Profit (2:14)

What *does it* profit, my brethren, if someone says he has faith but does not have works? Can faith save him?

James leads up to his big point that faith without works is dead with a question. The question is, "Where is the profit?" Other translations (ESV, NIV) will, "What **good** is it . . .?" The NAS says, "What **use** is it . . .?" They are translating the word *opheilos*, which certainly can mean "use, benefit, good." But it can also mean, "profit." I prefer this translation because of the context. We have to be very careful of context here. What are the verses just preceding 2:14-26 about? The Judgment Seat of Christ where believers are rewarded for what they have done since they became believers. What is the context immediately following 2:14-26? "My brethren, let not many of you become teachers, knowing that we shall receive a stricter judgment" (3:1). When will teachers get that stricter judgment? Again, the Judgment Seat of Christ is in view. We are responsible for the light we have received, and since teachers of the Word spend more time, on average, than those who do not teach, they are exposed to more light. Thus, they have a greater responsibility and will receive a stricter judgment. But, again, when? At the Judgment Seat of Christ (JSC). If the verses leading into 2:14-26 are about the JSC, and the immediate verse coming out of this section is about the JSC, it is not a big leap to ask ourselves if the intervening material is also about the JSC. I believe it is very logical.

In the Parable of the Talents (Matt 25:14-30) the Lord returns after giving talents (sums of money symbolic of spiritual gifts and opportunities) to three different servants. Two of these servants have doubled their money. One buried his. The Lord is upset with the "unprofitable" (v. 30) servant. He tells him he should have at least put the money into a bank where it could earn interest. What's the point? The Lord is looking for profit. He made an investment in us. He wants us to use what He has given us. But if we sit on it or bury it, when he returns, there will be no profit. This does not make Him happy. At the JSC the Lord is looking for profit.

Understanding that this entire passage (2:14-26) may be about the JSC, I would suggest that "profit" is the preferred translation here. And if it is, then the whole passage makes sense from the get-go. We will see why as we move along, but first let's get a feel for the controversy surrounding this verse. For that we go back to Martin Luther, who because of this passage never accepted James as part of the Bible, even though the canon of the NT was established before 400 AD by the church fathers. Luther called James "a right strawy epistle."[5] He said it belongs in the trashcan, not in the Bible. Why?

Luther had been an Augustinian monk for years. Prior to the Reformation he spent his entire life serving God in the church of his day. From youth he had been indoctrinated with the teachings of selling indulgences to buy the sinful dead out of Purgatory, doing penance to earn forgiveness for sin, and doing good deeds to stay in God's grace. Then there was a move to get back to the Scriptures as a basis for faith and practice. They wanted to read them in the original Hebrew and Greek. When Luther learned Greek, he was forced to slow down in order to translate. While translating Romans and Galatians, it became clear to him that eternal life comes by faith alone. Works were not required by God for salvation. Galatians 2:16 says, "Knowing that a man is not justified by works of the law, but by the faith of Jesus Christ . . ." Such verses became the keys to unlock the chains of legalism holding Luther down, the fetters which bound him in a prison of ritual and dogma. In Luther's own words, "When, by the Spirit of God, I understood these words, 'The just shall live by faith,' I felt born again like a new man; I entered through the open door into the very presence of God."[6]

It was a Damascus road experience for Luther. He immediately

---

[5]   Martin Luther, http://www.sbts.edu/media/publications/sbjt/sbjt_2000fall3.pdf.

[6]   James Montgomery Boice, *The Minor Prophets: An Expositional Commentary*, vol. 2, Micah-Malachi (Grand Rapids, Michigan: Zondervan Publishing House, 1986), pp. 91-92, quoting F.W. Boreham in *A Bunch of Everlastings or Texts that Made History* (Philadelphia: Judson Press, 1920), pp. 20, 27.

identified with Paul and his writings. He saw how Paul, too, had been trying to earn a position of favor with God by all of his zeal for keeping the Law of Moses as he was trained in the Jewish system growing up. Eternal life is God's free gift. No one could ever be good enough to earn it. So Martin Luther broke with the Church of Rome over this very point. The Church taught eternal life was a "reward" God gave those who earned it by living a good life and supporting the Church and taking communion. Martin Luther said emphatically, "No. Eternal life is the gift of God through Christ." So from that day forward the Church of Rome began to frown on Paul's writings while Luther championed them.

We can imagine, then, Luther's consternation when he read a passage like James 2:14-26. He said, "This teaching conflicts with Paul who said, 'Yes, faith alone is all that is necessary for eternal life." Luther could not harmonize James with Paul, so he threw James out. The Church of Rome couldn't harmonize James with Paul either so they threw Paul out (figuratively). But here they are, both in our Bible. So obviously the two fit together somehow, or the Holy Spirit was not the Divine Author behind one of them. So let me give you three explanations for James 2:14. The first is a Roman Catholic approach; the second a Reformed approach; and the third a Dispensational approach.[7]

1. The Church of Rome today (along with many Protestant church denominations) explains it this way: "Yes, we believe eternal life is the gift of God, but we also believe we must do something to keep that gift after we have received it."[8] So there is Paul's doctrine—eternal life is a free gift—and there is James' doctrine, which says: we must have good works to keep our gift. Of course, we would not accept this explanation for the simple reason that it conflicts with the definition of a gift, as well as

---

[7] I realize there are many dispensationalists who have adopted the Reformed approach, I think, without realizing how it conflicts with their dispensationalism.

[8] This is a direct quote from a conversation with a Roman Catholic priest.

other portions of Scripture. A gift is not a gift if I must do something to keep it after I received it. That is a bribe. Here then, is a second explanation. It is the most popular one in evangelical circles, and it is the one found in the notes of many study Bibles.

2. They would translate the end of verse 14 like this: "Can **that kind of** faith save him." Their argument is that this isn't genuine saving faith at all. It is false faith, spurious faith, and insufficient faith. An illustration is usually given of a wax museum. We enter the museum and look at all the figures. They seem very real, but when we get next to them, we realize that they are just fake. They are lifeless statues. So faith without works is dead, meaning not real, not valid, not genuine.

But there are real problems with this approach. The wax museum illustration doesn't fit this passage. At the end of this chapter James likens faith without works to the body without the spirit. That is the biblical definition of physical death. Now if I went into a wax museum and said, "This place is full of dead people," you would think I was really weird because the wax figures are not dead people. They have never been alive. But a dead person was once a live person. And so the faith James talks about here is a faith that was once very vibrant and alive. Then trials, persecution, and storms set in. What happened? Their faith slowly lost its life, its vitality. It was numbed by the storms like so many shots of Novacaine. It became inactive. It lost its liveliness.

May I suggest that we never use the word "dead" for something that is fake, false, or spurious? We don't do that in the English language, and they didn't do it in the Greek language. We do, though, use the word "dead" for something that is inactive, not moving or lifeless. "That is a *dead* football team," for example.

If then this passage has nothing to do with keeping the gift of eternal life by good works after receiving it, and if it doesn't mean good works are proof that faith is genuine, what else could it mean?

3. Simply this: the word "save" means the same thing it did in James 1:21, in which James is interested in saving our lives in the midst of our trials. The controversy around this passage is based on an assumption as to the meaning of the word "save." We are conditioned to think that means "go to heaven when you die." But I wish to make a radical suggestion. James uses the word "save" five times in this letter, and I think we can prove that none of the five has anything to do with going to heaven. As we get into this, it may help to remember that this is not a book about the Way; it is a book about the Walk. It would be a little strange to find a major portion of the book talking about the Way. It would be out of sync with the overall theme of the book: Triumph through Trials. This section (2:14-26), like all of the sections in this letter, is about the Walk. It is how to have a dynamic, vital walk of faith.

Let's examine how James uses this word "saved." We will start at the end of the letter first, since the two uses in James 5 are relatively easy. We must be conscious of two assumptions we are bringing to the text: 1) We cannot earn our salvation through good works; and 2) We cannot lose our salvation. With these in mind, let's look at James' uses of "save" one by one.

a. James 5:20—"Let him know that he who turns a sinner from the error of his way will save a soul from death and cover a multitude of sins." If a brother is a brother (which we established earlier in 1:16-18), then this passage cannot be talking about how to get to heaven since James is addressing brothers who already have heaven secured and cannot lose it, which was one of

92

our presuppositions. Since the word for "save," *sōzō*, has the basic meaning of "deliver or rescue," it could mean that the sinning brother is rescued from an early grave if he were to persist in his sins. Or it could mean he is rescued from a life of misery, depression, and defeat—Paul's frequent use of death in his writings. See 1 Tim 5:6 for the widow who is dead even though she lives.

b. James 5:15a—"And the prayer of faith will save the sick, and the Lord will raise him up." We know from verse 14 that this is a sick Christian who is calling for the elders to pray for him in his sickness. Their prayer of faith may save the sick brother. Save him from what? From his sickness. This one is so obvious most other translations translate the word *sōzō* as "restore" (NAS) or "make well" (NIV). At any rate, it is not talking about getting him to heaven. It is a sick brother who already has heaven.

c. James 4:12—"There is one Lawgiver, who is able to save and to destroy." At first blush this might look like a typical "go to heaven" usage. But closer examination of the context reveals that once again James is addressing brothers (4:11) who are bent on judging each other. He wants to motivate them to stop doing this. He argues that when they do this, they have usurped God's role as lawgiver and judge. He does not motivate them to stop judging each other by reminding them that God could send them to hell. Since they are brothers and cannot lose their salvation, it would be a tautology, a line of reasoning that does not advance the argument. They might say, "Why bring that up?" But if the JSC is in view, which I think it is throughout this book, then it is there that the Divine Judge will save or destroy our works as a

93

Christian (1 Cor 3:11-15). That's His job, not ours. So stop judging each other. At any rate, whatever meaning you want to assign to "save" here, he is talking to brothers, and it would be out of context to introduce the heaven or hell issue to them.

d. James 1:21—"Therefore lay aside all filthiness and overflow of wickedness, and receive with meekness the implanted word, which is able to save your souls." We have covered this ground previously, but by way of review, do you remember that this instruction is to the "beloved brethren" of verse 19? Heaven is not an issue for them. And if it were, this verse would teach salvation by works. No, we saw that "soul," *psuche*, here should be translated "life," as in our time on earth. James is trying to teach them how to have victory over trials by seeking God's wisdom during them through meekly receiving God's Word, which is able to make their lives count for eternity. Wow. What a concept. Out of a trial can come something that will be saved for eternity. Puts a new twist on trials, doesn't it?

e. James 2:14—"What *does it* profit, my brethren, if someone says he has faith but does not have works? Can faith save him?" Okay. We are back at our verse in question. So far, of the four other uses of "save" in James, none refers to going to heaven when we die. So what are the chances that the fifth and last use means that? I'd say, slim to none. Since this verse occurs in the midst of a context dealing with the JSC (2:12-13 and 3:1), the likelihood of the intervening verse dealing with the JSC is very high. When we stand before Him, He will be looking for profit. Destiny is not the issue. We don't even stand before the JSC unless we are believers destined to spend eternity with God. The issue is profit. He gave us so many years (time on earth = your **life**) and so many gifts and so many opportunities with which to serve and glorify Him. What did we do with those years, gifts, and opportunities? He is examining our lives for profit. If we show up with just our faith but no works, there will be no profit and our time on earth will not be saved. Faith alone, in this sense, cannot save our lives.[9]

So, it is this option for "save" which best fits the context immediately and remotely. To repeat and make the point as clear as possible, James asks the question, "What profit (reward) will you have at the JSC just mentioned in verse 13 if you only have faith?" God will not judge you for your faith in that day. He judges you in that day for your works. If you have no works, there is no reward, no profit. Your faith gives you eternal life just as Paul says. But your works will determine whether the value and worth of your life will be saved, preserved, kept for eternity or not. Faith and faith alone gets you a ticket to heaven, but works are your redemption stamps for extra benefits when you get there. They save your life's worth and significance forever. Faith alone cannot save you in the sense of saving your life at the JSC. Remember, not once does he use the word "save" in reference to going to heaven. What will save us in that day at the JSC? Our faith plus our works. The sacrificial, self-denying life is filled with works worthy of reward.

So, in verse 14 we have seen what I am calling the Principle

---

[9] Some of my friends want to point out that the translation of "that kind of faith" is sticking something into the text that is not there. Not really. This is known to Greek grammarians as an anaphoric article, which means the article preceding the word faith is pointing back to the faith just mentioned, that is, a faith that is unattended by works. Well, since the issue here is the JSC, the translation is a perfectly good one. The faith that shows up at the JSC without works will not save him, that is, save his life to glorify Christ for eternity. As Jesus says, he will have lost his own life—its true meaning and significance.

of Profit. Now, like a good preacher, James gives an illustration in 2:15-16.

The Illustration (2:15-16)

If a brother or sister is naked and destitute of daily food, and one of you says to them, "Depart in peace, be warmed and filled," but you do not give them the things which are needed for the body, what *does it* profit?

Here is a concrete example of a good work that could be profitable both here and in eternity. If we share of our material goods to help this hungry brother or sister, it certainly profits them, and there is profit for the giver, both here and in eternity. Here and now, it leads to happiness (1:25). And hereafter, it leads to a reward at the JSC. These rewards are not selfish things. There is no concept of selfishness in the world to come because we do not have a sinful nature, the essence of which is selfishness. Our rewards will glorify our Savior forever, but that is a different topic for another book.

Obviously, if we pass up opportunities to help the helpless, we still have faith, but we have lost a chance for profit—for the destitute, for us, and for the Lord. Here is the opportunity to save someone else's life physically and to save mine spiritually at the JSC. If I do this act out of love and concern for the needy, it is a sacrificial act acceptable unto the Lord. It may become a ruby or diamond in one of the crowns I'll cast at his feet (Rev 4:10). There will be profit. But if I selfishly refuse to help my brother or sister, I have no sacrificial works of love to give eternal value and significance to my life before the JSC.

After giving us this principle of profit and an illustration, James brings the idea to a conclusion in 2:17.

The Conclusion (2:17)

Thus also faith by itself, if it does not have works, is dead.

My faith, concludes James, without any works, is dead. This does not say my faith was never alive. It is dead. Paul talked about the root.

James talks about the fruit. Paul looks at the tree and talks about the root where it began. James looks at the tree and talks about the fruit. He does not say it is a fake tree, but that the tree, which was once very much alive and productive, now has no fruit. It has lost its life. It needs rejuvenating, revitalizing—something we will cover in 2:18-26.

Now before we finish this section, there is a question begging to be answered. Why didn't Martin Luther think of this solution to the text that appeared to contradict the teachings of Paul? After all, we don't think we are smarter or more spiritual than Martin Luther, do we? Of course, not. Here is the answer: the solution we have presented would never have occurred to Luther. Why? Because he was an amillennialist. Oh, now don't go throwing big words around. This just means he did not believe that Jesus was coming back to reign on the earth for 1,000 years as Revelation 20 promises. Martin Luther was a victim of the teachings of Augustine. Remember, he was an Augustinian monk. And Augustine taught that Revelation 6-19 (what we call the Tribulation Period) was fulfilled in the first century A.D. As for the millennium, he taught that it began in heaven when Christ ascended to sit at the right hand of His Father, and that it is just a spiritual kingdom in heaven for a thousand years, not something to be fulfilled on earth.

With this approach to the future, Martin Luther did not believe in a Judgment Seat of Christ (JSC) for just believers after the Rapture of the church. For him there was just one final judgment which would separate the sheep from the goats. The concept of "saving your life" for eternity as revealed at the JSC was not on his radar. Thus, as Augustine taught, everything was about destiny—heaven or hell.

James says there is so much more to life than heaven and hell. To James, our life is like a house we are building. Capturing our Lord's parable from the Sermon on the Mount, he says if we build on the firm foundation of hearing and doing, i.e. faith plus works, our house (meaning our life), will endure, and be preserved in the storm. It will be saved both literally and figuratively. The life lived in accordance with God's Word will be a healthier and happier life on earth, and its value and worth will be saved and preserved for eternity at the JSC.

But the Christian who builds his life, his house, on just hearing God's Word without aligning his life with it is a fool, says Christ. He builds his house on sand with no concrete. The first big storm will send it crumbling. He will be miserable in this life, and his life will have no profit to show at the JSC.

That is why we stress God's Word. According to James 1:21, it has the potential to save our lives, both on earth and in heaven. God's Word touches every area of our lives. When we hear and do as it instructs, we are like wise men who build their lives on a solid foundation. We will find success in this life and significance in the next. Every area of our lives that we submit to the wisdom of His Word can have eternal value and worth—family, business, recreation, friendships, health, worship, parenting, you name it. God is interested in preserving far more than our spirits for eternity. Our spirits are preserved by faith alone. He also wants to preserve every area of our life on earth, so it can weather the storms and yield fruit for eternity. This requires more than faith. It requires hearing and doing. That dynamic combination of faith and works has the potential of giving us a healthy, happy life today, the value of which is being preserved in the world to come. With a life built on God's Word, no storm can blow our house down.

How firm is your foundation? I have mentioned two houses, but I want to add a third. Three different kinds of houses are being built today. It reminds me of the three little pigs. One house is built of straw; one of sticks; and one of bricks and cement. An unbeliever builds the house of straw. This little pig has no hope for the future and no foundation for today. He's not afraid of the big, bad wolf because he doesn't believe he exists. Consequently, the smallest puff of air from the big, bad wolf blows the straw house down.

The second little pig is a bit smarter. He received Christ as his Savior. He has a hope for the future, a very bright hope indeed, but that is all that concerns him. He just wants to come to church Sunday after Sunday, sit in the same pew and oink now and then when the preacher says something he agrees with. He just wants to make sure his place in heaven is secure; he has no concept of orienting his life to God's Word. This little pig does not get serious about what God's

Word says, because he already knows he is going to heaven. And so with a huff and a puff, the big, bad wolf is able to blow his house down.

This is not the way the story goes for the third fellow. He was a wise little pig. He built a solid house with a firm foundation. He based his hope for heaven on the free gift of Jesus Christ, *and* he built his happiness today using the concrete instructions in God's Word. It took much more work, but it paid off, because it was in peace and comfort that he sat in his rocking chair, knowing that the big, bad wolf could huff and puff all he wanted and his house would never be brought down.

Which little pig are you?

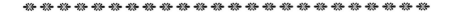

Ken Wilson was entering his senior year in high school when I met him. He had grown up in a Christian home and had assurance of his salvation, but his spirit and sharp mind told him there was more. He wanted to find it. He began coming to my office after school to hang out. As we opened the Scriptures together, his eyes got wider and wider. He fell in love with the Bible and theology and seriously considered becoming a theologian. His dad wanted something more solid for him as far as earning a living, so instead of theology, Ken aimed for medicine. He was valedictorian of a class of nine hundred and was able to skip the first year of college. Bypassing a year helped, since his medical training would take twelve years: four in med school, then residencies in general surgery, plastic surgery, orthopedic surgery, and a fellowship in hand surgery.

After finishing his training, Dr. Wilson moved to Portland, Oregon, where he taught on the full-time faculty at OHSU medical school for years. Eventually, with four children depending on him to be a father, he decided to go into private practice to spend more time with his family and in ministry. He did very well and has a number of inventions in his field, but by age forty-eight he was getting bored with medicine and his dreams of studying theology had not diminished. He had been an avid Bible student all these years and an elder and substitute preacher in his church. His spiritual hunger finally overtook him and drove him to seminary.

While continuing his medical practice, Ken was able to finish his MDiv and ThM degrees. By then we had begun our seminary, Grace School of Theology, and Ken wanted to help. At first he helped monetarily. He gave the seed money that allowed us to launch the seminary and hire a couple of professors while I continued to pastor. That wasn't enough for Ken, though. He still wanted to teach theology and asked the advice of multiple Christian leaders about the need for a top-flight theologian within Free Grace theology. He applied for acceptance at the oldest existing educational institution in the world, Oxford University in England. They must have wondered what a hand surgeon in his fifties intended to do with a doctorate in theology. I am happy to say that Ken now has his Doctorate of Philosophy from Oxford. He is teaching full time for our school and practices medicine on the side.

What is the greatest driving force in Ken's life? Undoubtedly, it is for him to be found well pleasing to Jesus when He comes. For Ken, the return of the Lord is motivating in two ways: 1) The positive rewards that he can use to glorify Christ forever; and 2) The punitive damages at the Judgment Seat of Christ. He is convinced that a greater emphasis on the negative repercussions at the JSC would keep more believers from taking advantage of God's grace. One thing is for sure: Dr. Ken Wilson will have plenty of profit to show for the investment of grace Christ has made in his life. After all, like the third little pig, Ken has built his life on a firm foundation.

"THE GREAT DIVORCE"

James 2:18-26

Our subject in this lesson is divorce. Not the kind of divorce that takes place in a courtroom when husband and wife put asunder what God has joined together because of incompatibility, but the divorce that takes place in a Christian between what he hears and what he does because of inconsistency. As a general rule, people do not like change. But in the Christian life a refusal to change puts the big kibosh on the Holy Spirit's work in our lives, which is supposed to be utterly transformative (2 Cor 3:18).

Lack of inner change within correlates to lack of change without. I have often wondered if church doors are actually magic erasers that wipe away everything we have heard as we walk out. When we leave church, how much of the truth we heard sits down behind the wheel of our car? How much of it walks into our living room when we get home? How much of it really touches the student in his classroom or the businessman in his decisions or the way we raise our children or the way we relate to a roommate or speak to strangers. This is truly the Great Divorce.

The ridiculous masquerade of Christians going to church proclaiming one thing and then going home living out another message is not hidden from the world. They see us and ask, "Why bother getting married? Why bother going to church? Why bother becoming a Christian? Their sermons are divorced from their lifestyles. I don't see how Christianity has any effect on their lives except to help them form another social club!" The reaction of the world to our inconsistencies betrays us. What we hear and what we do are contradictory, making us an ineffective, repulsive bunch. James deals with this at the end of chapter two. All of chapter two and part of chapter one have revolved around the relationship between hearing and doing. James says when trials bombard our lives like hand grenades, merely hearing God's advice will not help. We must both hear and do. We can only be saved from the destructive elements of trials by listening carefully to God *and* following His instructions. The exciting thing James reveals in 2:14-17 is that God is interested in more than just saving our spirits for eternity. He has a plan of salvation for every area of our lives. He wants to feed us solid truth that will yield a healthy, happy life on earth. By rewarding the faithful, selfless works of His children, He preserves the value of our lives for eternity. Without works what we do with this life will not be saved. Our spirit is saved by faith, but our life is preserved by works. Therefore, the divorce between faith and works is profitless, pointless, and purposeless. Even to the world it is repulsive. Truth severed from works is dead. Like a body is dead without the spirit, a faith divorced from works decays.

Based on James 2:14-17, I said that the word "dead" does not mean non-existent or false. A wax museum is not full of dead people. It is full of wax figures, which never were alive. James isn't talking about false believers, imposters. He is talking about people whose faith was once alive but is now dead. He is talking about a faith that was once vibrant, but after too many storm seasons has become cold, numb and sluggish. Again, by "dead" he means "inactive, unproductive, fruitless." This is exactly the use of "dead" in Romans 6:11 and 7:8. James is saying there is a vital connection between faith and works. Works, he says, bring faith to life. Works inject vitality and energy. When works are not wedded to faith, faith loses the Gillette edge; it becomes dull and lifeless, unproductive and inert. Dead.

This is precisely how we use the word "dead." Some people may be critical of a church by saying, "My, what a dead church." They aren't saying there are no Christians in the church. They mean these Christians do not seem to be alive for the Lord, which is what James is indicating.

He isn't saying that genuine faith is not present, just that without any works genuine faith cannot save you in the midst of a storm. It is of little value to you in the midst of a trial. It is as good as dead.

That was the Proposition: Faith without Works is Dead (2:14-17). James realizes that not everyone will agree with him. He knows those who have no works but do have genuine faith will object. They will want to defend themselves. They will want to show proof of their faith's vitality. This leads us to an imaginary Objector who voices a dissuading argument.

The Opposition: Faith without Works is not Dead (2:18-19)

But someone will say, "You have faith, and I have works. Show me your faith without your works, and I will show you my faith by my works. You believe that there is one God. You do well. Even the demons believe—and tremble!" (Adapted)

The objector is the one speaking through verse nineteen.[10] He claims there is no connection between faith and works since the same belief can produce markedly different works. Though both Christians and demons believe in the same God, believers do good works based on their faith,[11] while the demons tremble. Same belief—two different responses, says the objector. Like any complacent believer, the objector builds this argument to prove that faith without works will suffice when God judges our Christian lives at the JSC. That is a summary; here are the details.

The objector says in verses 18-19, "You have faith. I have works. I will prove that there is no necessary connection between faith and works. State what you believe and then back it up with the works of your life. If you can do that, I will do something more difficult. I will show you the works of my life and you can guess what I believe based upon them. Obviously, this guessing game is absurd because there doesn't have to be a connection between what I do and what

---

[10] See 1 Cor 15:35-36 and Rom 9:19-20.

[11] See the same Greek expression in Matt 5:44, *kalos poieō*

I believe. Look at the demons! You both believe the same thing: there is one God. But you say your faith produces your good works, so why does it only produce trembling in them and not the same good works? The same belief causes at least two different reactions. Therefore, there is no correlation between belief and behavior. So just because I don't do all the good works you are pushing, that doesn't mean my faith is dead or that I never had faith. I don't need works to prove I believe."

I firmly believe, however, that the objector is wrong. What a man believes has a vital connection to what he does. If I believe Christ might return today, it will impact how I spend the next twenty-four hours. If, hypothetically, I didn't believe in life after death, that would emphatically affect how I live. As Paul wrote, if there is no resurrection from the dead, then we are of all men most miserable (1 Cor 15:17-19). We have no hope. This life is all we get. For millions of people whose existence is one of perpetual struggle, despair becomes their only reality without the hope of life after death. There are many lifestyles that stem from disbelief in life after death. Hedonism—what feels good? Apathy—who cares? Despair—what's the point?

What we believe dramatically affects how we live. There is a vital connection between faith and works. As James set forth in verse 17, **Faith without works is dead**. He sets out to prove this in 2:20-26, by contrasting two Old Testament characters of very different backgrounds to show the vital link between faith and works: Abraham and Rahab. He begins with Abraham.

The Refutation: Faith without Works is Dead (2:20-26)

Example of Abraham (20-24)

> But do you want to know, O foolish man, that faith without works is dead? Was not Abraham our father justified by works when he offered Isaac his son on the altar? Do you see that faith was working together with his works, and by works faith was made perfect? And the Scripture was fulfilled which says, *"Abraham believed God, and it was*

accounted to him for righteousness." And he was called the friend of God. You see then that a man is justified by works, and not by faith only.

These verses appear at first to be another front-on collision with what Paul taught. In verse 21 and 24, it seems like James says that we are justified by works. Conversely, Paul says just the opposite, that we are justified by faith, in Galatians 2:16 and Romans 5:1. How can the two ideas be harmonized?

First, let us establish that the word "justify" means "to declare righteous." It is equivalent to our use of "to become a Christian." Second, the key to understanding Paul and James is to see that Paul speaks of justification before God, while James speaks of justification before men. Third, we must realize that both writers recognized the type of justification referred to by the other. Romans 4:2 shows us that Paul recognized justification by works, but he goes on to say such justification is not before God. It is before men.

Let's look deeply at what he said in Romans 4. Abraham was justified before God long before Isaac was born. In 4:17-22, Paul makes it clear that Abraham's faith was in a God who could bring life from death. He was referencing how God enabled Abraham and his wife to conceive when he was one hundred years of age. When Abraham believed, it was before God. It was an act of faith only. No work had been performed and God counted it as righteousness. Abraham's faith justified him before God. Paul argues the same point again in Galatians 3:11 when he says, "No man is justified by the law in the sight of God, it is evident; for the just shall live by faith." Paul talks about justification in the sight of God and says it is by faith only, although he also recognizes justification by works before men (Rom 4:2).

In James, we read about this justification in the sight of men. That is why verses 22 and 24 begin with seeing. In 22, James emphasizes that men see and he recognizes justification by faith. But then in verse 24, he says that is not the only way man is justified. Man is justified by faith before God, and justified by works before men. God can see into a man's heart and see his faith, but men cannot do that. The only basis men have for declaring us righteous is what they see. What do men see? Our works.

At 100 years old, when Abraham believed God would give him a child, only God saw the faith in Abraham's heart. At that moment, Abraham was justified by faith in the sight of God. This event is found in Genesis 15, long before the birth of Isaac. In Genesis 22, some twenty-five years after Abraham was justified by faith, God tested Abraham's faith in God's resurrection power by asking him to sacrifice his son. Hebrews 11:17-19 says Abraham had faith that God would raise Isaac from the dead. Sacrificing Isaac was an outward, visible work, which justified Abraham before men. They called him a friend of God.

It is interesting that even today, Abraham is known in the Muslim world, the Jewish world, and the Christian world as a friend of God. No one knew or could see when by faith Abraham first trusted in the God who resurrects. Only God saw that. But all men could see Abraham's love for God by his willingness to sacrifice his only son. Abraham was justified by faith in the sight of God when he believed God's promise of progeny as numerous as the stars in Genesis 15. He was justified by works in the sight of men when he walked to the altar to offer up his son Isaac. God said, "Abraham, you are righteous," when he saw Abrahams faith in his heart. Men said, "Abraham, you are righteous, a friend of God" when they saw the works in his life. It's possible that 25 years elapsed between the events of Genesis 15 and Genesis 22. Perhaps this chart will help:

ABRAHAM BELIEVES	ABRAHAM SACRIFICES
Genesis 15	Genesis 22
Faith before God	Works before Men
Romans 4 and Galatians 3	James 2 and Rom 4:2
Faith is Born	Faith is Perfected
Justified before God	Justified before Men
Judicial	Experiential
A Believer	A Friend

Look at James 2:24 again. James never says a man is justified by faith plus works. That is heresy. James never combines faith and works into one system for justification. He says, "There are two systems. One seen by God; one seen by men. One is justification by faith; the other is justification by works. One is before God; the other is before men." Verse 24 concludes: "A man is justified by works also; he is not justified only by faith." To emphasize his point, James selects Rahab the harlot as another example.

Example of Rahab (25)

Likewise, was not Rahab the harlot also justified by works when she received the messengers and sent *them* out another way?

Abraham was a moral, male Jew. So next James picks an immoral, female Gentile to demonstrate that this principle works for all people. Rahab was justified by works, says James. If the two-fold system of justification is consistent, then Rahab must have been justified before God by faith before she could be justified before men by works.

Let us look at Hebrews 11:31 to see if Scripture supports this idea. There it says Rahab had faith the moment she received the spies into her house with peace. However, Joshua 2:14 and 20 make it clear that only God could see Rahab's faith when she received them. The spies did not know whether Rahab would betray them or not. They shook as they waited upon the roof because they did not know her heart. Only God knew. He could see the root; they could only see the fruit. It was not until she sent them out the other way that she proved her good faith to them. Therefore, Rahab was justified by faith before God when she received the spies with peace. She was justified by works before men when she sent the spies out the other way.

In Rahab's case there was also a lapse of time between her faith and her works:

RAHAB RECEIVES	RAHAB SENDS OUT
Heb 11:31	Jas 2:25
Faith before God	Works before Men
Declared Righteous by God	Declared Righteous by Men

It is clear both in Abraham's case and Rahab's that there are two different systems of justification. One is before God; the other before men. One is by faith; the other by works. Paul recognized justification before men (Rom 4:2), but emphasizes justification before God. James recognizes justification before God (Jas 2:24), but emphasizes justification before men. They both acknowledge the two-fold system of justification.

Now, having waded through all this complicated theology, one might be tempted to say, "Who cares about being justified before men? It is God's opinion that counts, not man's." So here is where the connection James makes between faith and works becomes important: **faith without works is dead**. Justification before God gets its vitality from justification before men. In verse 26 he compares the human body to faith and the spirit to works, illustrating this principle.

Example of Death (26)

For as the body without the spirit is dead, so faith without works is dead also.

Logically speaking, we might expect James to illustrate this principle of "faith without works is dead" in a completely opposite way than the one he uses. If I wanted to illustrate visible things, I would pair the body with works. If wanted to illustrate invisible things, I would pair the spirit with faith. However, James does just the opposite. He is making a case for the connection between faith and works. James is arguing that works do for faith what the spirit does for the body. They animate! The spirit gives life to the body. Likewise, works animate our faith! They bring faith to life. Works give our faith vim and vigor.

That is why verse 23 says that faith and works go hand in hand.

They work together. How? Faith is made perfect, complete, and mature (*teleioō*) by works. When Abraham first believed God could bring life from his loins, he really believed. It was genuine faith or else God would not have imputed it to Abraham for righteousness. When Abraham was asked to sacrifice Isaac, his faith in a God who could resurrect was tested. Through this test his faith became strong and mature.

As verse 23 says, the Scripture that said God counted it for righteousness was *fulfilled*. That verse of Scripture, Genesis 15:6, was not a prophecy. Verse 23 does not refer to a fulfilled prophecy. "Fulfilled" means that the original seed of faith in the heart of Abraham found its fullest significance and meaning when it grew to the point that he was willing to sacrifice his son. Abraham's works fed his faith, made it stronger, and gave it meaning and significance. It "filled out" his faith to completion, maturity.

It's like James is saying, "What good does it do to have a driver's license if you never drive a car? What sense is there in having that piece of plastic in your billfold?" Faith is your license to drive—so drive! Some time ago, a coral snake was killed a couple houses down the street from us. Suppose that snake had bitten me and I knew the hospital had antivenin that could save my life. All I have to do is jump in the car and get to the hospital. I'm licensed to drive. The antivenin could be pumping in my veins within moments, restoring my vitality. If I don't take advantage of my license to drive, I will lose my life.

Or, let's suppose I am a senior lifeguard. There is a badge on my swim trunks to prove it. What significance does the badge have if I see someone drowning in the pool and don't jump in to save him? None. The driver's license itself cannot save me if I am wounded. The badge cannot save someone who is drowning. If anyone's life is to be saved, I must *do something*. There must be action.

James must mean, "Though I have the badge of faith sewn to my heart, until I act by adding works to my faith, that badge can do nothing to help in the midst of trials, both my own trials and those of others." Abraham and Rahab had badges of faith and they acted on them. Rahab saved her life literally by her works, meaning she was not killed when Joshua's army took Jericho. Abraham saved his life figuratively by his works, meaning he gave it eternal significance, which will be revealed when the OT saints are judged for what they did on earth to glorify God (Dan 12:2-3). But both Abraham and Rahab were justified before men by their works.

To conclude, I want to make three points. The first is based on the theological distinction we made between Paul and James concerning justification before God and justification before men. Simply put:

1. **God sees the root, while men see the fruit**. We have a large tree in our front yard that seems to be dead during the winter. No one driving by would be able to tell if it is alive or dead because there are no leaves on the tree. Some of the branches have fallen, which might indicate that it is dead. Without digging, only God can see the roots of the tree. Only He knows if the tree is alive or dead. In the spring, if leaves spring forth from the tree, then everyone can see that it is alive. During the winter, because our knowledge is limited, we cannot make a judgment. The lack of leaves may look bleak, but it is not definitive evidence. The tree could be dead or alive. Only God knows.

   Have you ever judged a person as not being a Christian because of the lack of fruit in his life? We should not make such judgments. Men see the fruit, but God sees the root. There may well be a root of faith hidden from the view of man that only God can see. Faith is enough to justify that man before God. We mere men must be cautious about judging a man's eternal destiny based solely on his life. To be sure, his life is an indication of his degree of judgment after death, but it is not a conclusion regarding his eternal destiny. We may question, but we do not have the right to determine. Men see the fruit; only God sees the root.

2. **Faith without works is dead**. James was written long before Paul's letters. Most scholars think James was the first

NT book written, based on the need for encouragement from Jerusalem after the Jewish Christians were dispersed around the Mediterranean world. In this early stage of Christianity, James was not trying to split theological hairs in this letter. He had a point to make—**faith without works is dead**. Like a dead body, inactive faith reeks with decay. A corpse is repulsive. When people near such bodies, they are turned away. Howard Hendricks called this the "Sit, Soak, and Sour Syndrome." He was talking about the believers who **sit** in our churches for twenty years, **soak** in the truth, and then **sour** because they aren't doing anything about the truth they have heard. Tim Hawks, Senior Pastor of Hill Country Bible Church in Austin, Texas, guesstimates that 50% of his 5,000-person congregation fits into the sit-soak-sour category. He says about 20% of his people are very dedicated and active. Another 30% are new and excited. Sitting in the middle are the folks who have been around awhile without getting involved. They start to sour and when they sour, they smell. Christian cadavers.

3. **Works can light up our life; works bring fire to our faith.** James doesn't mock his readers. He knows they are suffering. That kind of suffering leads to depression and spiritual lethargy. James wants them to rally. He says, "Let's pump up. Let's lift some iron." Adding works to our faith can get us off the couch. It brings fire back to our faith. I haven't commented on this yet, but I am particularly impressed by the kind of works James mentions. He does not bring up preaching, teaching Sunday School, serving on the church board, or singing in the worship team. All those are fine. The problem with them is that they can be self-serving. James says to go find someone in worse shape than you are, perhaps a widow or an orphan. Do an act of mercy. Help the hungry. Feed and clothe them. These acts of mercy are less likely to be self-serving, and

the opportunity is always there. Jesus said, "The poor you will have with you always" (Matt 26:11).

Dr. Steve Tucker says he lived most of his Christian life defeated and just going through the motions for his family. He could see no practical use for Christianity other than a ticket to heaven after death. The son of a pastor and extremely intelligent, his family had great expectations for him, especially after he left the West Coast where he grew up to go to a conservative Bible college in the East. He would probably follow in his father's footsteps. To the contrary, Steve found the college so legalistic he couldn't make himself stay. He moved back to the West Coast, finished college, and went to medical school. He became a dermatologist, married his sweetheart, and began having children.

Professionally, all went well. He had a thriving private practice, taught once a week at a local medical school, and had some inventions in curing skin cancer. His children were also off the charts. Two of the three were valedictorians of a large 5A high school. One was an all-city basketball player who even made a run at professional golf after earning a master's degree in electrical engineering. Anyone looking in from the outside would say that Steve had it all.

Very few people in this life have it all. Though he was rich on the outside, he was poor on the inside. He had been a believer for around forty years, but had no fire. Steve wrestled with anger. His temper would explode on the freeway, in his home, and even on the golf course. He had been a deacon in our church, but resigned when he realized his Christian walk was a sham. Why compound his problems with hypocrisy? He continued to faithfully attend church and he was generous with his giving, but he shut down spiritually.

Then Steve had an experience with the living God through the Holy Spirit. All of a sudden, he encountered the third member of the Trinity. Nothing ecstatic happened and he did not roll on the floor, but he began to realize there were "rivers of living water" (Jesus' reference to the Holy Spirit in John 7:37-39) inside him. His walk burst into life. At the time, he had enough money to retire, but he suddenly saw his office as a launching pad for ministry. From then on, many, if not all, of his patients left his office with inspirational books.

Steve's church participation was reinvigorated. He began attending the Saturday morning men's breakfast at seven. He and his wife began coming to a prayer meeting for our seminary (Grace School of Theology) right after the men's breakfast. He started being invited to speak to groups about his story, a story about a man who really began his journey for Jesus at age fifty-five. Steve's experience was no flash in the pan. He is sixty-six today. He lives each day to make a deposit into the lives of others and into his account in heaven. He has discovered the true riches of walking by the Spirit day by day. His life is a testament to the vital connection between faith and works.

"A MEASURE OF MATURITY"

James 3:1-12

Have you ever seen a ninety-eight year old man play golf? Golf was a new game for me when I was fifteen. I grew up like a lot of kids playing baseball, and in baseball you swing hard. So one day, I was on the third tee at Richland Country Club in Nashville, getting ready to tee off. I heard a whirring noise behind me and turned around to see what it was. It was the first golf cart I had ever seen. In 1960, if you wanted your clubs carried, you hired a caddy.

The two old men in the golf cart pulled up alongside me and asked if they could play. Why not? Since I was already teed up, I thought I'd show these old geezers how to do it. I swung hard. The ball flew far. Unfortunately, it was in the wrong fairway. The old men teed off, hitting right down the middle. Old Ben, aged ninety-eight, got out of the cart and trudged down the fairway to his ball. Uncle Jim, aged ninety-two, offered to give me a lift to retrieve my ball. On the way, Uncle Jim told me the story of Old Ben, how he took up golf at age sixty-two and became club champion three times. Well, when we caught up with Old Ben, it was with some respect that I watched as he unleashed all ninety pounds on that little white ball and sent it straight at the green. Seeing the admiration on my face, Uncle Jim looked at me with a twinkle in his eye and said, "When Old Ben matures, he's gonna be good."

I chuckled as I walked down the fairway, pondering physical maturity. How do you know when you've matured? There are a number of ways to know when we have matured physically, are there not? It takes some longer than others, but there are signs. What about spiritually? I was not a believer at the time, but I never forgot Uncle Jim's comment. Years later after becoming a Christian, I wondered how we could know when we had "grown up" spiritually. Are there indicators, measurements? The answer is affirmative. Yes, there are indicators, one of which is found in James 3:1-12. This is a section called "A Measure of Maturity."

As we move into James 3, we should reorient ourselves with the book as a whole. Here is our outline, once again:

JAMES

"TRIUMPH THROUGH TRIALS"

Salutation (1:1)

Introduction (1:2-18)—The Value of Trials

Theme (1:19-20)—Qualities Needed

Body (1:21-5:6)—Qualities Developed

    I. In Regard to Hearing (1:21-2:26)

    II. In Regard to Speaking (3:1-18)

        A. The Lips are a Dangerous Display of Wisdom (3:1-12)

        B. The Life is a Discrete Display of Wisdom (3:13-18)

From the outline you can see that we are moving into the second quality James thinks we need if we intend to be victors over our trials. The first quality was to be quick to hear, as stated in 1:19. It is difficult to hear God speak when we are not listening. The second quality is to be slow to speak. Again, it is hard to hear God speak when we are speaking ourselves. So in the first part of chapter three James will tell us to be slow to speak. Why? Because *our lips* are **a dangerous display**

of wisdom. In contrast, he will tell us that *our life* is **a discrete display of wisdom** at the end of the chapter. Let's start with the lips.

In 3:1 we are warned: **"My brethren, let not many of you become teachers, knowing that we shall receive a stricter judgment."** To understand this verse we need to imagine the NT assembly for worship (church), which probably looked quite a bit different from ours today. These Christians were being persecuted. They probably met in homes. Many NT scholars believe we have no evidence for a church with greater than fifty people after the dispersion from Jerusalem. That isn't necessarily true, but judging from the end of Romans and other factors, it could be.

1 Corinthians 14 gives us a picture of what one of these church meetings might have been like. One huge difference between their meetings and ours is that one person did not get up and filibuster their services. Many different people would speak. One would bring a psalm, another an exhortation, another a biblical message, and so on. They were submissive to one another (Eph 5:21). It sounds like a beautiful setting, but the possibility of many teachers also opened up the door to doctrinal competition and one-upmanship, the old I-Know-More-Than-You syndrome.

Into this kind of setting James speaks a warning: "Let not many of you become teachers." For the next eleven verses he defends this admonishment. It may surprise you that he wouldn't want everyone to become a teacher. His first reason is that the teacher will receive a stricter judgment. Why? I mentioned this before, but it does not hurt to repeat: the teacher (of the Bible) receives more light because of his prolonged exposure to the Word, and we are responsible for the light we have received. Each of us will be judged according to the light we have received.

My very first message as a new pastor of my first church was "The Danger of Starting a Bible Church," which was exactly what we were doing. What is the danger? Exposure to the light. The greater the light, the greater the responsibility, and guess what—the greater the judgment. This then must be especially true for teachers, who are conduits of light. James says let's not rush into this teaching thing.

The judgment he refers to will be at the JSC (Christian family only). That does not mean that people don't hold preachers to a higher standard, as well. Ultimately though, we answer to God. Our ministry of teaching isn't evaluated until we see him at the JSC. The fact that this verse immediately follows James 2:13 (and its warning of 2:14-26) is further evidence that those verses involve the Judgment Seat of Christ (JSC).

James has more to say about this. He wants to develop his warning. He launches into an exposé of the tongue. Verse two is the basis for this lesson: A Measure of Maturity.

> **For we all stumble in many things. If anyone does not stumble in word, he *is* a perfect man, able also to bridle the whole body.**

The word "for" tells us James is giving reasons to support his warning. He has already mentioned stricter judgment. The following verses most likely give support for the stricter judgment. He doesn't mention greater light and greater responsibility, but he does discuss difficulties with the tongue. He starts on a positive note. His thesis, his big idea, is that anyone who does not stumble in the use of his tongue is a mature Christian. The word "stumble" is somewhat rare in the NT. *Ptaiō* means to "make a mistake, go astray, or sin," according to our best Greek-English dictionary (BDAG). In other words, **the degree to which we can control our tongues is roughly equivalent to the degree of our spiritual maturity**. How 'bout that? Want an indicator of spiritual maturity? Want a sign? A measurement? God put a spiritual thermometer in our mouths to measure our maturity—our tongues.

The word for perfect does not mean sinless perfection. We were introduced to this word in the third verse of James: "But let patience have *its* **perfect** work, that you may be **perfect** and complete, lacking nothing." It's the adjective *teleios* in both 1:3 and 3:2. We also saw the verb form of this word used to describe Abraham's sacrifice of Isaac. The sacrifice helped bring Abraham's faith to maturity, completion. After Genesis 22 we do not hear much of Abraham, perhaps because his faith had reached completion by that sacrifice. His life after meeting the Lord is a lesson on spiritual maturity. As a new believer he made a lot of mistakes (Pharoah, Lot, Hagar, Abimilech), but he kept growing. The Lord kept stretching his faith . . . until he passed the ultimate test; he was willing to sacrifice the son in whom his hope for the future rested. Abraham had gone as far as he could go. He became a mature believer.

God wants to do that with each one of us. James 1:3-4 tells us that it is through testing that we mature. Do you remember how Genesis 22 begins? "Now it came to pass after these things that God tested Abraham." The sacrificing of Isaac follows. The first time I translated this in Hebrew I cried. When you are new to a foreign language, translation is slow work. But it forces you to have a more intense experience with the text. The magnitude of what Abraham was doing overwhelmed me. That was almost forty years ago. I am typing these words high in the mountains of Colorado, much higher than the hills of Judea, but not nearly as high as Abraham was when he stood beside his son on Mt. Moriah.

We have grappled with the word *teleios* before. It does not refer to sinless perfection; it speaks of maturity. It is not without exceptions. Some people are just quiet, and their tongue might not be the best indicator of their spiritual maturity. But as a general rule, **the degree to which we can control our tongues is roughly equivalent to the degree of our spiritual maturity.** James supports his thesis in two sections: The Control Ability of the Tongue (2b-5a) and the Uncontrollability of the Tongue (5b-12).

The Control Ability of the Tongue (2b-5a)

James starts on a positive note, the ability of our tongues to control our drives and our destinies. The tongue has Control Ability.

The tongue can control our drives (2b-3).

. . . able also to bridle the whole body. Indeed, we put bits in horses' mouths that they may obey us, and we turn their whole body.

James makes a bold statement. He claims that if a man can control his tongue, he can control his whole body in both restraint and direction. To illustrate this point, James uses two examples. The example of the horse and bridle primarily emphasizes restraint. As you who ride know, the bit that goes in the horse's mouth is the instrument used to keep the horse from running away from you. It is the reins that control the direction of the horse.

I learned this lesson early, in my years of playing Roy Rogers. Our family owned a couple of horses when I was a kid. One of these horses always had an impulse to head for the stables where he was fed. He always moved very slowly when riding away from his oats, but point his head in the direction of those stables and he was gone. Well, one day King Calico pulled a dirty trick on me. As we rounded a training track and his head was temporarily pointed toward the stables, he got the bit in his teeth and took off for home. This means he chomped down on the bit and I lost control. He was going full steam ahead right toward an orchard near the stables. I knew he was going to try to wipe me off on some branches. The only recourse, I injudiciously decided at the time, was something I had seen Roy Rogers do on TV—jump off Trigger. So that's what I did.

Unfortunately, at age of eleven I had not yet studied Newton's laws of motion. One of those laws says that a body in motion tends to stay in motion unless hindered by an opposing force. Well, this body was in motion to the tune of over thirty miles an hour when I jumped off. And this body met an opposing force—the gravel road. I felt like a pogo stick bouncing down the road on my head. It really hurt. But I learned a valuable lesson. I never watched Roy Rogers again. No, just kidding. I learned never to let that horse get the bit in its teeth again.

The point is that if the tongue can be controlled, then the other powerful impulses of the body can be restrained as well. What would you list as the top drive of the human body? Hunger? Thirst? Sex? None of the above, says James. The strongest drive in the human body is the urge to talk. If we can control that drive, we can control the other drives of the body as well. Talk about a diet plan! Want to lose weight? Just learn to control your tongue. After all, it's hard to eat with your mouth shut! It's true. The strongest drive, urge, or impulse in the human body is the urge to talk, and all too often that impulse comes at a most inopportune time. If we can learn to control it, we can control our other drives, as well. This is positive and encouraging.

But now James moves into somewhat neutral territory. He is headed toward negative ground, but before he gets there, he uses another example of the Control Ability of the Tongue. The tongue can control not only our Drives; it can also control our Destinies.

The tongue can control our destinies (4-5a).

Look also at ships: although they are so large and are driven by fierce winds, they are turned by a very small rudder wherever the pilot desires. Even so the tongue is a little member and boasts great things.

James goes nautical, using the example of a ship and rudder. The emphasis is on direction. A rudder does not restrain a ship as a bit restrains a horse, but it harnesses wind power to guide the ship. In biblical times, the winds symbolized fate and men at sea were thought to be at the mercy of the winds. Or as Bob Dylan sang years ago, "The answer is blowing in the wind." Your destiny lies with the wind. The ship and rudder illustration show that the rudder, not the wind, is in control. Hence, the rudder controls our destiny. Properly used, the ship will reach its destination. Improperly used, your life will be shipwrecked on the shoals of destruction. This hints at the tongue's capacity for destruction. The word "desires" carries with it the idea of impulse. If the impulse is wrong, the ship wrecks and its destination is never reached. An impulsive tongue can destroy God's desired destiny for a Christian life.

"Even so" (*houtō*), the tongue, concludes James, though small, can control our drives and our destinies. The first is a positive virtue; the second is somewhat neutral with the possibility of destruction. The third metaphor used by James is negative and begins the section on the Uncontrollability of the Tongue.

The Uncontrollability of the Tongue (5b-12)

See how great a forest a little fire kindles! And the tongue
***is* a fire, a world of iniquity. The tongue is so set among our**
members that it defiles the whole body, and sets on fire the
course of nature; and it is set on fire by hell.

James shifts to the destructive nature of the tongue. In the first
section, the tongue did the controlling. Now we read that the tongue
itself cannot be controlled. Have you ever tried to control a forest fire?
Unlike a hurricane, which dissipates as it moves on shore, a forest fire
continues to gain strength as it plows along. So the tongue, which is
a microcosm of evil, can start a fire with destructive potential that
increases as words are passed from one to another. It consumes words
and lives like a fire consumes trees and forests. Rumors, lies, put
downs, destructive criticism, character defamation, false witness, and
so on. It is sobering to realize that three of the seven things on God's
hate list (Prov 6:16-19) are sins of the tongue.

The tongue is situated in our members as a small fire, defiling the
whole body, and like a forest fire it inflames the cycle of life. Our life
is a succession of events. And the tongue, being a fire, can cause a
conflagration of events with consequences that affect the whole cycle
of life.

It has been said that a little boy in a Hungarian village was playing
with matches and started a fire that destroyed two hundred and
thirty houses and sent the village into bankruptcy. Huh . . . just a little
match. That is exactly the point James makes here. An ill-timed word
may light a fire that will burn through successive consequences in our
lives as it rolls inexorably forward. Oh, how I wish I could take it back.
Oh, if only I had never said it. But it has been said, and the calamitous
consequences roll on. And it is particularly solemn to realize that this
conflagration can be traced to hell.

Destructive words are lit by the fires of hell. Remember when
Peter said, "Be it far from you, Lord," in reference to Jesus going to the
cross. Christ replied, "Get behind me, Satan." Our Lord recognized
that Peter's words were kindled by hell. And so often a word that is

unkind or critical has its direct source in satanic inspiration and does tremendous damage as a result. Some of the most demonic things you will ever hear will come out of the mouths of Christian brothers and sisters. It is one of Satan's favorite tactics to divide and conquer. The tongue is like a fire, which is almost impossible to control. To further emphasize its uncontrollability, James attributes two characteristics to the tongue.

It is Insubordinate (3:7-8).

> For every kind of beast and bird, of reptile and creature of the sea, is tamed and has been tamed by mankind. But no man can tame the tongue. *It is* an unruly evil, full of deadly poison.

It is impossible to tame the tongue. Anyone who has visited Sea World or a similar show for sea creatures has been amazed at how the trainers can control such enormous animals with their whistles and signals. I am pretty sure this verse was written before James had witnessed anything like this. It is another witness to the supernatural character of the Scriptures. We have seen all different types of creatures—cobras, lions, parrots, killer whales—tamed by man, but no one can completely tame that little instrument in the mouth. It has been said that the most ferocious monster in the world lives in a cave behind the pearly guardrails of the orifice known as the mouth!

The tongue is also "full of deadly poison." An interesting account tells of a West Indian church in which someone noticed a deadly cobra moving through the meeting—an unwelcome visitor in any church. Someone went out, grabbed a hoe, and cut its head off. After the meeting, the people who had been attending the church gathered around this dead cobra, looking at it. One of the young men stomped on the head of the dead cobra and immediately let out a shriek. Within an hour he was dead. The fangs of the cobra still had deadly poison within them capable of killing a person. Long after life had gone out of the snake, there was still enough residual poison to kill.

That is typical of the tongue. Even after we are gone from the scene, the poison that has spewed out of our lips continues to bring forth deadly consequences. People can be injured and hurt by the things we have said long after we are removed from the surroundings. "Full of deadly poison"—its potential to kill is important. Today, texting and emails often assist the tongue in spreading its poison. Behind the cover of the computer people will say things they would never voice face to face.

The tongue is not just Insubordinate; it is also Inconsistent.

It is Inconsistent (9-12).

> With it we bless our God and Father, and with it we curse men, who have been made in the similitude of God. Out of the same mouth proceed blessing and cursing. My brethren, these things ought not to be so. Does a spring send forth fresh *water* and bitter from the same opening? Can a fig tree, my brethren, bear olives, or a grapevine bear figs? Thus no spring yields both salt water and fresh.

We have images here of a well and a tree. James views the mouth as a well. Drawing water out of a well is like drawing words out of the mouth of a man. Problems arise when the water rushes out too fast. A rapidly flowing river soon collects mud. Or like the fountain pen whose directions say, "When this pen runs too freely, it is a sign that it is nearly empty." When we exercise the tongue too much we are like a well spouting both salt water and fresh, or a tree producing both ripe fruit and rotten. For the tongue is a strangely inconsistent tree, a strangely inconsistent well.

Xanthus, a Greek philosopher, was planning a dinner for his friends. "Go buy the best thing in the market," he told his most trusted servant. So the guests came in to dinner and the servant set before them tongue. All forms of tongue: boiled tongue, fried tongue, baked tongue, sautéed tongue, TV dinner tongue—whatever technique they used in those days.

But after the fourth course of tongue, Xanthus got a little annoyed at this, and he said to his servant, "I thought I told you to go into the market and buy the best thing available."

"Well," replied his servant, "what is better than the tongue? The tongue is the organ of friendliness, the organ of worship, the organ of eloquence, and the organ of encouragement."

"All right, all right," sneered Xanthus. "Tomorrow I want you to go out and get the worst thing you can find."

So the guests came in for dinner the next night and the servant set before them tongue. All forms of tongue: boiled tongue, fried tongue, baked tongue, sautéed tongue, TV dinner tongue—whatever technique they used in those days.

But after the fourth course of tongue, Xanthus got a little annoyed at this, and he said to his servant, "I thought I told you to go into the market and buy the worst thing available."

"Well," replied his servant, "what is worse than the tongue? The tongue is the organ of blasphemy, the organ of lying, the organ or slander, the organ of deception."

This is exactly what James is saying. Strange is the inconsistency of the tongue. With it we bless God and we curse men. We sit in church and sing the praises of God and then we walk out and have the preacher for dinner, if you know what I mean. That is the tongue—strange, perverse, inconsistent creature that it is.

Now James 3:1-12 doesn't tell us how to control the tongue. Therefore, we must be extremely cautious in using it. Dr. John Gill, a preacher in London years ago, wore long clerical robes as well as a white neckband that hung down in front of his robe. One day during the week a lady who attended his church waited on him and indicated to him in no uncertain terms that she considered a long white neckband to be a symbol of ministerial pride. She lectured him for quite some time on the sin of flaunting one's clerical status by wearing long, white neckbands. Then she held out a pair of scissors and suggested that Dr. Gill hand over his long, white neckband and she would trim it down to a size she thought was in keeping with ministerial humility.

So Dr. Gill, who had listened with great patience, handed over the long, white neckband, and the woman quickly trimmed it down to the appropriate size.

Then he said to her, "Now I have let you trim my neckband and I have noticed that you have something a little long. I would appreciate it if you would let me trim that down."

"Oh, by all means," said the woman, "feel free to go right ahead."

"All right, then," said Dr. Gill, "dear sister, stick out your tongue!"

Wouldn't it be nice if we could shorten our tongues a bit (or sometimes the tongues of others)? But we can't. There seems to be a built-in problem in this passage. On one hand we are told that anyone who can control his tongue is a mature believer. On the other hand, we are told that no one can control his tongue. There doesn't seem to be much encouragement in this passage. Ah, but that is the way it is with most of commands to holiness in the NT, is it not? We really can't do it. That is precisely where the Holy Spirit steps in. One of the fruits of the Spirit is called **self-control**. It really isn't self-control though, is it? It is **Spirit-Control**. That is why we say control of the tongue is a mark of spiritual maturity. The more I walk by the Spirit, the more I enjoy His fruit. And the fruit of self-control can harness our tongue. **The degree to which we are able to control our tongues (by the Spirit) is roughly equivalent to the degree of our spiritual maturity.**

We would be wise to remember the destructive potential of the tongue and be judicious in its use. We are trying to have triumph over our trials. To triumph we need to get God's wisdom. We can't hear Him if we are talking. Remember Proverbs 17:28: "Even a fool, when he holds his peace, is counted wise, and he who shuts his lips is esteemed a man of understanding."

It was Abraham Lincoln, possessed of wisdom to an uncommon degree, who said, "It is better to remain silent and be thought a fool, than to speak out and remove all doubt."[12] It has also been said, "All speech is a hazard. Oftener than not, the most dangerous kind of

---

[12] Abraham Lincoln, http://www.brainyquote.com/quotes/quotes/a/abraham lin109276.html.

deed." And Dionysius the Elder said, "Let your speech be better than silence, or be silent."[13]

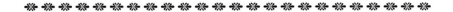

This passage has played a big part in my life. I grew up in a family where there was a lot of verbal sparring. We honed our verbal skills through arguing, put downs, and sarcasm. If my home did not offer enough opportunity to display my wares, there was always school. My friends and I prided ourselves in who could "out-cut" the other. Though I became an accomplished verbal fencer, it always seemed to leave a bad taste in my mouth. There really wasn't any pleasure in being able to "out-argue" another person, but once the match began, I had a compulsion to win. Even my teachers would say, "If you don't become a lawyer, you will have missed your calling."

But I was miserable. My first taste of lasting happiness was when I received Christ in the back seat of a Greyhound bus going up Lookout Mountain just outside of Chattanooga on the way home to Nashville. Through faith alone in Christ alone I found forgiveness for my sins and a hope for the future. It was also my first taste of inner peace.

Unfortunately some old habits die hard. Some don't. Cussing disappeared from my vocabulary almost instantly. Every cuss word in my mouth tasted like dirt. Be that as it may, the verbal sparing did not stop. When I went to Rice many of us prided ourselves in being able to out-argue the other. But as I was to learn the hard way, Dale Carnegie is right: you never win an argument. Oh, you might win the argument, but you will often lose a friend. Nevertheless, my compulsion to win continued right into seminary. And seminaries are fertile soil for those who like to argue. There are all sorts of theological debates to explore. But each encounter still left an after-taste, even if I "won."

By this time I was a Youth Pastor at a local church, while still studying at the seminary. The Senior Pastor asked me to preach one

---

[13] Dionysius the Elder, http://quotationsbook.com/quote/37148/.

Sunday evening. I was scared to death, never having given a sermon before. I worked a month on that sermon. I checked with my favorite NT professor to go over my interpretation of the passage. Then I gave the sermon. In order to grab their attention, I used a song by Simon and Garfunkel, "The Sounds of Silence," and a reference to the new movie, *The Graduate* starring Dustin Hoffman. The head of the homiletics (preaching) department of the seminary was listening and called me into his office.

This particular professor was called "Big Red" by the students because of his reddish shock of hair. He was not respected as a professor because he never taught us much. We even used to make fun of some of his assignments and say the only reason he was teaching at the seminary was because the president of the school was his brother-in-law. So with some trepidation I sat down in his office. Then he began. He accused me of stooping to the muck of the world in order to be relevant. At the time, *The Graduate* was a shocker from a morality standpoint. As Big Red droned on I could actually see his point. I got people's attention with my intro, but not with the right content. I sat silently taking all this in. He was angry and offended that I should import this kind of salacious material into the hallowed sanctuary of his church. And he was right. I was convicted.

But then Big Red crossed the line. He began to tear apart my exegesis or interpretation of the passage. Say what you want about my preaching (whoever wanted to be a preacher, anyway?), but don't criticize my exegesis, especially when I had it developed and verified by the best NT scholar in the school. I felt my old weakness setting in. My counter-arguments were multiplying in my mind. I could hardly wait to tear into this igmo and give him a lesson in biblical interpretation he couldn't afford to lose.

Ironically, just before this encounter, I had been memorizing James 3. I realized I had issues in this area, so I thought hiding God's Word in my heart might help. Just as I was ready to pounce, James 3 popped into my mind. I swallowed hard and kept my mouth shut. I listened patiently as Big Red finished his tirade. I swallowed hard again and thanked him for caring enough about his church, the seminary, and even me to call me on the carpet. I admitted I had made a mistake and hoped I would learn from this. I didn't mention the exegesis. Then I walked out—a changed man.

The Holy Spirit used James 3 to change my life. Oh yes, I still make my share of mistakes. As a preacher I have offended many through the years. But if you only knew how bad it used to be. On a daily basis as I interact with people I have the same old temptations to jump into the fray and "help them with their thinking." But by God's grace and His power, I usually refrain. It has actually caused some people to think of me as a quiet person. Not. What's true is I studiously try to avoid the verbal sparring I reveled in as a teenager.

Funny thing about Big Red's assignments. I had him not only for preaching, but also for Pastoral Ministries. Most of us in the class never thought we would become pastors, so again, we used to laugh at some of his assignments. One of them was to read *How to Win Friends and Influence People* by Dale Carnegie. We all thought, what a waste. But after forty years of pastoral ministry, I can say with conviction that Carnegie's book should sit on the desk of every pastor. For one thing, it helps us learn how to be slow to speak.

"A WORD TO THE WISE"

James 3:13-18

We have seen that the Measure of Maturity is the degree to which one can control his tongue. Of course, James says no man can really tame his tongue. Fortunately, the Holy Spirit can because one fruit of the Spirit is self-control (Gal 5:23). But if one does have his tongue under control by the power of the Holy Spirit, what evidence will there be? What would that sound like? Can we learn about light from darkness, about cold from heat, about the wise man from the fool, the spiritual from the carnal?

James gives us the Marks of Maturity, the evidence of one whose tongue is under control. In James 3:1-12 we received the Measure of Maturity and learned that our lips are a Dangerous Display of Wisdom. Now we receive the Marks of Maturity and learn that our life is a Discrete Display of Wisdom:

JAMES

"TRIUMPH THROUGH TRIALS"

Salutation (1:1)

Introduction (1:2-18)—The Value of Trials

Theme (1:19-20)—Qualities Needed

Body (1:21-5:6)—Qualities Developed

   I.   In Regard to Hearing (1:21-2:26)

   II. In Regard to Speaking (3:1-18)

       A. The Lips are a Dangerous Display of
Wisdom (3:1-12)

       B. The Life is a Discrete Display of
Wisdom (3:13-18)

We will look at the heart of the wise man and then the heart of the foolish man. The heart is inside. Then we will look outside, to the fruit of a foolish man's heart, and then the fruit of a wise man's heart. Before we go there, let's look into the OT at the wisest man who had ever lived at that time: Solomon.

It has been noted that a tree is best measured when it is down. It usually refers to looking back over a man's life to see what he has accomplished. Before he was bewitched by his wives and concubines, Solomon was an author, diplomat, poet, writer of songs, king, philosopher, philanthropist, financier, architect, and engineer. He was a man of royal blood with intense creative ability, a builder of one of the Seven Wonders of the World. His name meant peace. How did Solomon accomplish so much? Wisdom. God gave him the ability to work with people (2 Chron 1:11). Biblical wisdom has more to do with the relational than the technical. We all know technical geniuses that don't seem to have much wisdom. In the business world, it is often the man who achieves horizontal harmony who rises to the top. In God's economy, a mark of a wise man is knowing how to get along with other people.

Whether it is in the church, the mission field, a parachurch ministry (Young Life, Navigators, Campus Crusade), or elsewhere, knowing how to deal with people requires wisdom. I have seen seminary graduates with a library of theological knowledge between their ears march into churches and split them wide open due to their lack of wisdom. So let's get on with it. We will start with the Heart of a Wise Man (13) and then the Heart of a Foolish Man (14-15). That's on the inside. Then we will look outside at the Fruit of a Foolish Man (16) and the Fruit of a Wise Man (17-18). This is a chiastic construction: A-B: B-A, or Wise-Foolish: Foolish-Wise.

The Heart of a Wise Man (13)

Let's remember from James 3:1-12 that the context for James 3 is the early church meeting, in which there were a few too many teachers a bit too eager to share their spiritual knowledge with the group. It was the cause of much contention and strife within the church. We concluded that a dangerous way to display our doctrine is with our lips. We learn in 3:12-18 that a discreet way to display our doctrine is with our lives. Not our lips, but our lives—that is the message of James 3 in a nutshell. That is wisdom. Let's allow the verses to speak for themselves. Let's look into the heart of a wise man.

> **Who *is* wise and understanding among you? Let him show by good conduct *that* his works *are done* in the meekness of wisdom.**

It sounds like the second chapter, where James says, "Let's see what you believe from your works. Let your works do the talking." In other words, "Put your morals where your mouth is." He adds a couple descriptive phrases in verse 13 that tell us two basic qualities of the heart of a spiritually wise man. One is "good conduct," and the other is "meekness." These descriptors indicate the inward condition of the wise man's heart. Let's look closer.

A Willingness to Change

The Greek word *anastophē* means "change, conversion, turning inside out or upside down." Behind the word is the concept of "life style." It refers to the internal willingness to change one's life style to conform to God's Word. Do we change the Truth to match our lives, or change our lives to match the Truth? The first mark of a wise person is not how high his IQ is, how sparkling his sense of humor, how impressive his delivery, or how many people he speaks to on Sunday morning. It is how much change has taken place (or is taking place regularly) in his life so that his life patterns itself after the truth.

We are so enamored with degrees of higher learning. I remember when I was about to get my Ph.D., my church members started calling me Dr. I really did not want that, so I said, "You know, I come from Tennessee. You can just call me Bubba." So they started calling me Dr. Bubba. I got up in the pulpit and said, "Look, I really don't want to be called Dr., so if you don't think Bubba shows enough respect, you can call me Abba Bubba. After all, my wife calls me Hubba Bubba." When I graduated, they made a nameplate for my desk. It read, "Dr. Abba Bubba."

Interestingly, the man who most influenced my Christian life during my seminary years was a professor who did not have Dr. in front of his name. He could have easily had that. In fact, a well-known seminary in Germany offered him a Ph.D. if he would turn his work on textual criticism over to them for publication. He turned them down. He told me, "If I have to have letters in front of or behind my name for credibility, there is already a problem." No doctorate. His credentials for the ministry were not degrees of higher learning, but a life that was patterned after the Truth.

Under Control

The term "meekness" often makes us think of a person who is rather spineless and shrinks back from the challenges of life, a Mr. Milk Toast who hides in the closet when his Mac Truck Wife comes home from work. Not so. Our Greek dictionary uses other synonyms to define the word *prautēs*: gentleness, humility, courtesy, and considerateness. Can you see how this virtue would help someone get along with people?

The word is also used in taming or breaking a wild horse. What does that mean? Has the horse lost any of its spirit or power? No. Its power has been brought under control. In Plato's day this word was used of a teacher who could dialogue with his students without getting angry. It was used to describe Jesus: he was meek and lowly. Power? He was omnipotent, but under control.

Meekness is the mark of the heart of a wise man. By contrast, what is in the heart of a fool?

The Heart of a Foolish Man (14a)

But if you have bitter envy and self-seeking in your hearts, . . .

What is in the heart of a foolish man? Bitter jealousy and selfish ambition. Notice now that these are in the heart. They are not tattooed on his chest nor monogrammed on his t-shirt. No one wears a sign his head saying, "I am a jealous, ambitious person." These qualities are hidden in his heart.

Bitter Jealousy/Envy

What is the difference between jealousy and envy? Our Greek dictionary defines the word used here (*zēlos*) as both jealousy and envy and more specifically as "intense negative feelings over another's achievement or success." Envy is mourning with empty hands because you do not have what someone else has. Jealousy is mourning with full hands because you are afraid of losing what you have. Envy begins with nothing and wants something. Jealousy begins with much and fears losing it. A jealous spouse fears losing his or her mate. A jealous worker fears losing his job to someone better qualified. A jealous preacher fears losing his congregation to another preacher. Do not think jealousy is absent in Christian circles. Singers and musicians can be jealous of each other, just as preachers and professors can be. There is competition and rivalry to see who can win the greatest following. After all, if the disciples of Jesus were still arguing over which of them was the greatest during the Last Supper (Luke 22:24), what about us? The flesh, being in all of us, travels into churches, seminaries, and onto the mission field.

One of my associate pastors went to Kenya as a rookie missionary. He started more churches in Nairobi in one year than the other missionaries in his denomination had during the previous twenty years. He was making the veterans look bad, so they sent him to an outpost on the northern border of Kenya. It was a year of huge drought in that area. A whole tribe of Sudanese people crossed the border to find food. John led them all to Christ. When his denomination heard about it they sent out a reporter and a cameraman to cover the story. John's picture showed up all over the missionary quarterly report. More jealousy ensued. They sent him to Tanzania next. Same thing. So they sent him to the Sudan. And on it went. He was just gifted and had a lot of energy. But jealousy in other Christians stalked him everywhere he went.

Selfish Ambition

In the heart of a fool is selfish ambition, the desire to push oneself to the top. In churches a fool wants to be seen and be the one with authority. Shakespeare captured the heart of this man in one of his plays: "I am Sir Oracle—when I op' my lips, let no dog bark."[14] When I speak, you had better listen. Oh, my! It is by the grace of God that anyone listens. It is His grace that gives any of us an audience. If God wants to promote you to a specific role like being a teacher or deacon or elder, let Him do it. If God wants to move you ahead in business, let Him do it. If you feel this is God's path for you, let Him open the doors. Let Him push you through and slam the door and lock it behind you. He can do that. And believe me—He will.

In the heart of the wise man is the willingness to change and the willingness to be under control. The heart of the foolish man also contains two qualities: jealousy and selfish ambition. God has let us in on what is in the heart of every wise man and every foolish man. Yet only He can see clearly into each person's heart. How can we as men perceive the condition of a heart? God does not leave us

---

[14] William Shakespeare, *The Merchant of Venice*, Act i, Scene 1, Gratanio.

in the dark. He gives us a list of symptoms that indicate the heart condition of any man.

Here is the list of symptoms which point to "heart trouble" in a foolish man.

Fruit of a Foolish Man (14b-16)

> . . . do not boast and lie against the truth. This wisdom does not descend from above, but *is* earthly, sensual, demonic. For where envy and self-seeking *exist,* confusion and every evil thing *are* there.

As we move into these verses, I need to jump start the discussion with the word "demonic." Mark it down. If you are observing divisiveness and strife in a Christian setting, the wolf got through the door, the demons are swinging on the chandeliers and dancing on the crucifix. Who let them in? The funny thing is, you might even be right and the other side wrong, but you can be so right sometimes that you are wrong. Know what I mean? I have seen church boards and church staff get into a dither over whatever. As soon as division sets in among believers, the devil is at work. It can set in through the voices of those who are ostensibly the wisest men and women in the church. The Bible says they are fools. The correct point of view can be the very wedge the devil uses to pry believers apart. Every Christian group should be on guard for division in its ranks. It is the one of the clues, if not the first clue, that the devil is sitting in the pew. Or as one of my professors, S. Lewis Johnson, used to say, "If you want to find the devil, don't look in the pews; look in the pulpit."

Moving on, let us see what kind of fruit tells us we are listening to a foolish man.

Arrogance

The word for "boast" here is *katakauxaomai*, which means to be full of pride because of one's authority or position of importance. This man likes to strut and pound his chest. When his tongue begins to move, he will find a way to let you know how great he is. The tongue, once again, betrays his heart.

This man is usually moved by jealousy and ambition to make it to the top. But when he gets there, he begins to exult and boast in his triumphs. Of course, he does not want to be too obvious about his braggadocio, so he couches his triumphs on the cushion of God's grace. What a flippant way to use grace, to bolster our own ego. It has been said that grace humbles a man without degrading him and exalts a man without inflating him. After all, what do we have that doesn't come from the grace of God? The arrogant man is always searching for little ways to impress us with his own magnanimous character.

Lying

Lying is how we become arrogant. We change the truth to fit our lives. It is like building a house. We get one wall up and then discover it is mismeasured, so we change the scale of the rest of the house to accommodate the mismeasured wall. Because of the first mistake, the whole house is out of whack. We have changed the ruler to fit the mistake, rather than fixing the mistake to meet the standard of the ruler. It is like being in business and robbing the till and then changing the books to make them read right. Lying against the truth. The New English Bible calls it, "defiance against the truth." A liar is a person who lives in sin and alters the truth to make it okay.

Very important: if you catch the foolish man in "little" lies, beware. He has mastered the art of rationalization. The truth may convict him, but he will find a way to adapt the lie into truth in his situation.

Earthly

The scope of this wisdom is strictly horizontal. The measures of success are earthly, meaning worldly: worldly standards, counsel, methods, and advice. Your spirit will sense when the wisdom you are hearing is from the world. It leaves you dry, empty, wanting. In churches it usually comes from board members or preachers who want to run things the way they do in the business world.

Another thing about earthly wisdom I have observed over the

years is it often puts programs over people. The NT teaches that the church is a family. It is not the world. It is a business, but not a worldly business. It is a family business. In a worldly business people are expendable. The bottom line is all-important. Well, not in God's business. People come first in a family. If we can't reach our intended bottom line without running roughshod over people, then we need to change the bottom line, not the people.

There is no doubt that sometimes a Christian organization needs to have changes in personnel. But there is a godly way to do it and an earthly, worldly way to do it. Wisdom from below is earthly. If you witness a number of key people being hurt in a church, you can bank on the fact that the wisdom behind it is earthly.

Natural/Unspiritual

The word here is *psychikos*, from which we get our word psyche. The human being is made of body, psyche, and spirit. Our psyche is our unique combination of mind, emotions, and will. This word speaks of human wisdom from our own mind, emotions, and will—not the spiritual wisdom from the Holy Spirit speaking through our human spirit. When we hear wisdom from our own mind, emotions and will, it does not resonate with our spirits as being from God.

I was blessed to serve in a church for about twenty years in which I never had to plead for money. We always exceeded our budget, and once a year I just got up and said, "Thank you." However, I do remember a financial challenge early in my tenure. Giving was behind schedule. I listened as various elders offered advice—anything from pleas to pledges. Then one elder said, "We need to give more to missions." Say what? We are facing a crisis and you want us to give more money away? "Yep. We are getting too wrapped up in ourselves and our own success." Wow. Voice of the Spirit. That's what we did, and within a couple of months we were back on target.

Demonic

What a final blow. There is a wisdom that comes from us which can resemble the advice of a demon. It may be astute, and even brilliant, but it does not produce peace and harmony. We remember earlier in this chapter on being slow to speak that James said the tongue is aflame with the fires of hell. Pretty strong stuff and so sobering. The words you are hearing may be a demon speaking through a Christian, just like Peter. If the devil could speak through someone as close to the Lord as Peter, what about the rest of us?

How can you discern when you are listening to wisdom that is from below? Just look around. The unwise man cannot get along with people. There is confusion and every evil thing. Confusion, *akatastasia*, means disharmony and antagonism. According to our Greek dictionary, it means "disturbances, division, disorder, opposition to and undermining of established authority." When this foolish man or woman walks into the room, you can feel the tension and electricity. "Every evil thing" means that much of the undermining of authority will be accomplished by false accusations, especially by accusations of various forms of immorality. This is how the foolish discredit those in authority.

I have been privileged to work with many great people. I will never forget one of them with whom I still work. He co-owned a successful law practice, made piles of money, flew the company plane, all that. But he really wanted to spend his life in ministry. So when I decided to go full time with Grace School of Theology, I offered him a job as our Executive VP of Operations and General Counsel. Understand that when anyone hires a trial lawyer, he is hiring someone who can probably out-argue him. So there was some risk here.

To the contrary, Tom never tried to out-argue me. We have had our differences of opinion on various decisions regarding the school, as would be expected from two different people, but after making sure his opinion was clear, he would always say, "OK, what do you want to do, boss?" What do you want to do, boss? I had not seen such great respect in all of Israel. So, I asked Tom, "Where did you learn to respect authority like that?" He said, "West Point. Chain of command is one of the first things they teach you. They want you to be able to think on your own, but in the final analysis, the decision belongs to the person above you, your boss." Wow. That is wisdom from above. Without it, you are on your way to *akatastasia*. It is not a matter of the boss getting his way all the time. It is a matter of leadership. Without proper respect for those in authority, confusion is sure to follow.

So much for the symptoms that indicate a heart full of bitter jealousy and selfish ambition in an unwise man. Now what is the fruit of the heart of a wise man who willing to change and be under control?

The Fruit of a Wise Man (17-18)

> **But the wisdom that is from above is first pure, then peaceable, gentle, willing to yield, full of mercy and good fruits, without partiality and without hypocrisy. Now the fruit of righteousness is sown in peace by those who make peace.**

As we delve into the life of a wise man, will you notice a characteristic of his that is repeated three times: peace. We might also say harmony. We're back to horizontal relationships, back to Solomon (peace). Let's inspect them one by one.

Purity

The morals and motives of this man will be pure. Why? Because he is continually willing to change his life to fit the truth and he is under the control of the Holy Spirit. That's what a mature Christian is, a person who walks by the Spirit and does not fulfill the lusts of the flesh (Gal 5:16). Ludwig Richter, the painter, told of his mother's formula for overcoming temptation. She said, "Repeat the beatitudes and repeat one of them seven times." Which one? "Blessed are the pure in heart, for they shall see God." Why will the pure in heart see God? They make it a practice to confess their known sins. By doing so they walk in the light. Their hearts and lives are pure. They see God working in their lives and the lives of others. Blessed are the pure in heart.

Peaceable

Would you like to write a best selling book? Write one on how to find peace. Scarcely a book has been written with "peace" in the title what has not sold well. People are searching for peace, but only the Prince of Peace can give it to them. A mark of the wise man is that he is peaceable because the Prince of Peace reigns in his heart. He will not be abrasive, but soothing. He will not want to stir up strife. Rather he will avoid quarrels and want to patch things up. Some will say, "Well, I am not by nature a peaceable person." That's the whole point. You are not by nature pure either. I know we are not by nature peaceable. Apart for the Prince of Peace we can neither find peace nor dispense it.

Gentle

This word is a little different from the word "meek" in verse 13. That word, *prautēs*, was inward. This is outward. Remember in verse 13 we were looking at the root; now we are looking at the fruit. The word is *epieikēs*, and it refers to the person who does not press the last tittle of his legal rights. It is used of God in the OT who was legally right in wiping Israel off the map when she broke the law, but He chose not to press His rights. We live in a day when everyone seems bent on declaring his rights. However, there are times when the wise man will forfeit their rights to keep the peace. Philippians 4 is a perfect example. Two leading women in the church, Euodia and Syntyche, were having a feud which threatened the unity of the whole church. So Paul gave them a prescription for peace. One of the pills they were to swallow was labeled "gentleness," or "yieldedness." If proving he is right runs the risk of destroying the unity of a group or a relationship, the wise man will opt to be peaceable. He is more interested in relational harmony than being right. He understands that we can be so right we are wrong.

Easily Persuaded

This person is the opposite of one who is obstinate and stubborn. The word is *eupeitheis,* which can mean, "willing to yield, submissive, reasonable, compliant, easily persuaded." This person does not say, "My way or the highway." You can reason with her. She is not impervious to change. She is open and teachable.

I always think my way is right; my way is the best way and why can't you see that? In contrast, the mark of a wise man and wisdom from above is being conciliatory, amenable, and reasonable. You can work with him. When the Holy Spirit transforms the heart of the fool into the heart of a wise man, he is molding a heart that is open and teachable—willing to learn a new way or to improve the present one. Are you easily persuaded or hard to budge? When we have the Holy Spirit, we develop a tolerance and a teachability that says, "Hey, I'll think about that. That is a good suggestion. I will really consider it." It is the opposite of being so strongly opinionated we cannot be persuaded by the facts. "My mind is made up so don't bother me with the facts"—you know, that kind of thing.

Full of Mercy and Good Fruits

Here is a twin blessing. Neither of these fruits is natural to us. By nature we are cynical, hard, and harsh. The word mercy (*eleos*) is used in the NT in regard to our attitude toward someone who has been wronged deservedly or undeservedly. Our heart goes out because we remember God's mercy toward us. Mercy is the attitude; good fruits are the actions. We cannot say we have truly felt mercy toward someone until we have tried to help him (Luke 10:37, *eleos*).

There was a cartoon in *Newsweek* some time ago. It was a picture of a starving man leaning on his haunches and staring at an empty pan. Clearly, the pan was for food. On the other side is a very fat man with a big bag, a hat on and a long cigar. And this opulent, corpulent character is dumping something out of the bag and into the pan— words. The caption reads, "Too many words; not enough deeds." Remind you of James 2:15-16: "Be warmed; be filled"? The Christian ranks are filled with people with big bags of words, dumping them into the empty pans of the needy. When the Holy Spirit takes over our hearts, He fills them with mercy (an attitude) and good fruits (actions).

Not Argumentative

This word translated "without partiality" is *adiakritos*, and opinions differ on how to understand it. Some say, "unwavering, unshakeable." But if you remove the "a" from the front it becomes *diakritos*, which our dictionary (BDAG) says is a "quarrel." So put the "a" back on the front and it is like going from "moral" to "amoral." No morals. Here it would mean "no quarrels." I think this fits the context best, so I would suggest "not argumentative." As Dale Carnegie says, "You can't win an argument."[15] If you win the argument, you lose a friend. Wisdom is all about horizontal harmony.

Without Hypocrisy

True wisdom never claims to be something it is not. The Greek word refers to an actor who plays two parts. In the Greek theater the same actor would play several parts, using the appropriate mask suitable for the part. Aesop's fables get the point across in a satire in which two men run into each other on the road. They have never seen each other before and it is a cold, wintry day. As they start talking and working up a friendship, the first man starts to blow on his hands. The second fellow says, "Ah, what are you doing?" "I'm warming my fingers because the day is cold: haa, haa." A little later they have lunch together and are served two bowls of soup. The first fellow lifts his spoon with a spoonful of soup up to his mouth and says, "Woo, woo." The second man says, "What are you doing?" "Well, I'm blowing on my soup. It is so hot, I'm blowing to cool it off." The other guy stands to his feet and says, "In no way will I be your friend. I renounce your friendship." "But why?" asked the first man, stunned. "I will have nothing to do with one who blows hot and cold with the same mouth." Sure, it is a silly, childish illustration, but it is precisely what hypocrisy is all about.

Some of the biggest problems I ever had in church work stemmed from people who blew hot and cold out of the same mouth. They would flatter me to my face, and defame me behind my back. One case was so bad and caused so much turmoil in the church that,

---

[15] Dale Carnegie, http://www.quoteland.com/author/Dale-Carnegie-Quotes/352/.

to this day, I find myself shutting down whenever I hear flattery. I practically go into anaphylactic shock, which basically means I am highly allergic to flattery. I just don't trust people who are high on the flatter-o-meter.

We have witnessed the heart and fruit of a fool, and the heart and fruit of a wise man, who in this context is a mature Christian (3:2). What is the result of true wisdom? The man who is willing to change and is under control, as demonstrated by these characteristics, will be a peacemaker. He will have horizontal harmony. He will be rightly related with other people. He will get along well with others. That is the overall mark of a man with spiritual wisdom. Not great intellect, not technical skill, not biblical doctrine stored in his mental attic. It is horizontal harmony with his fellow men, especially those of the household of faith. Since he is a peacemaker, he will reap what he sows. He will sow the seeds of peace and the seeds of all the other fruits of righteousness and reap their harvest. Would you like that kind of life? Here is a word to the wise. Pray the prayer of St. Francis of Assisi. Ask God to make it true in your life.

> Lord, make me an instrument of your peace.
> Where there is hatred, let me sow love;
> where there is injury, pardon;
> where there is doubt, faith;
> where there is despair, hope;
> where there is darkness, light;
> and where there is sadness, joy.
> O Divine Master, grant that I may not so much seek
> to be consoled as to console;
> to be understood as to understand;
> to be loved as to love.
> For it is in giving that we receive;
> it is in pardoning that we are pardoned;
> and it is in dying that we are born to eternal life. Amen[16]

---

[16]   St. Francis of Assisi, http://en.wikipedia.org/wiki/Prayer_of_Saint_Francis.

❊ ❊

Sam is a natural leader. Even when he was not a Christian, he was the leader of the pack, mainly in sports. He was confident and assertive. When he became a believer, he turned his thoughts to Christian leadership. Just like in his football days, he wanted to call the plays—to be the quarterback. He attended a well-known Christian university and headed off to seminary. Leadership options were many after seminary, but Sam was drawn to the church. After an associate's position for a couple of years, he started a church. It grew fast. Sam was a gifted spiritual leader.

Everything turned to gold for Sam in his church for about twenty years. Then trouble came knocking. Sam's worship leader had been off at a Spiritual Life seminar and bought into a new twist on how to get close to God. He started bringing his new approach to the Christian life into the worship service and the staff meetings. When Sam didn't buy into what his worship leader was selling, the devil had his beachhead. Each staff member had one of the elders assigned to get close to him and support his ministry. The worship leader began sharing his grievances concerning Sam with "his" elder. The elder began looking at Sam in a different light.

Suspicion of motives and distrust set in. Once trust leaves a relationship, everything the other person does or says can be seen through jaundiced eyes. Rumors began about Sam's overbearing leadership style. The elder board was divided, some siding with the worship leader and some with the pastor. Then people began looking for character flaws in Sam's life. Criticism of his wife and children began. Before long it was more than Sam could stand and he resigned from his church—his life's work.

That's not the end. The worship leader rounded up those people sympathetic to his new "light." He split Sam's original church and started his own. It lasted a couple of years and folded. Then, believe it or not, this same worship leader was hired by a church in another city in the same state and did the same thing all over again. The pastor he ran off this time left the country to find a new job.

Unfortunately, I know another ten stories not dissimilar to this one. Where does the devil find a beachhead? Look for sources of distrust, undermining authority, character assassination, slander, jealousy, and internal strife. Whoever that source is does not speak for God, but for the devil. His wisdom is not from above, but is earthly, sensual, and demonic.

"A MAN'S BEST FRIEND"

James 4:1-6a

It was Ralph Waldo Emerson who said, "The only way to have a friend is to be one." Proverbs 18:24 echoes, "A man who has friends must show himself friendly." Everyone wants to have friends. If you find a man who does not want friends, it is because he previously tried to make a friend and failed; therefore, as an ego defense, he has built a shield of aloofness to keep from getting hurt again. But as a general rule, everyone wants friends. We especially like to have best friends, really close friends. Best friends know all about you and love you just the same. A best friend magnifies not the dross in you, but polishes the gold. How can we distinguish between a best friend, a close friend, a casual friend, and an acquaintance?

Bill Gothard gives us a four-fold breakdown of friendships and tells us how we can identify each level. Here is his chart:[17]

---

[17]   Bill Gothard, *Institute in Basic Youth Conflicts*, "Friends," 1975.

LEVELS OF FRIENDSHIP

ACQUAINTANCE	Spasmodic contact; freedom to ask general questions; personal questions are taboo
CASUAL FRIEND	Based on common interests and hobbies; freedom to ask more specific questions about life goals, etc.
CLOSE FRIEND	Based on common life goals; projects done together to help reach these life goals
INTIMATE FRIEND	All the above in addition to the freedom to correct each other's faults; a mutual love and trust allows character building. Prov 27:6—"Faithful are the wounds of a friend."

What does this have to do with James? It is our friends who help pull us through times of trouble. Our troubles often reveal who our friends really are. James has a lot to say about friendship, especially our close, intimate friends. Only his primary concern is not friendship on a human level, but rather on a cosmic level. Who is your best friend, he asks: God or the world? Abraham was a "friend of God" (Jas 2:23). James 4:4 says we can either be a friend of God like Abraham or a friend of the world. Unfortunately, he says we cannot be best friends with both. I can't even have the world as a casual friend and God as an intimate friend. James says if the world is my friend, then God is my enemy. Our best friends can drag us down or pull us up. The amount of peace and satisfaction we find in this world depends on our friends, so I hope to use chapter four of James' letter and Gothard's levels of friendship to help us decide who really is our best friend on a cosmic level. Knowing that, perhaps we can understand why life is so frustrating or satisfying for us, as the case may be. Let's re-establish the context. Here is our outline of James so far:

JAMES

"TRIUMPH THROUGH TRIALS"

Salutation (1:1)

Introduction (1:2-18)—The Value of Trials

Theme (1:19-20)—Qualities Needed

Body (1:21-5:6)—Qualities Developed

    I.   *In Regard to Hearing (1:21-2:26)*

    II. *In Regard to Speaking (3:1-18)*

    III. *In Regard to Anger (4:1-5:6)*

        A. Cause of Conflict—Pride (4:1-5)

           1. A Proposal (1)

           2. A Proof (2-3)

           3. A Problem (4-5)

        B. Cure for Conflict—Humility (4:6-5:6)

You can see we are entering the third major section of the body of the letter. The three qualities we need in order to triumph through trials are: quick to hear, slow to speak, slow to wrath (1:19). We have dealt with hearing and speaking. Now we must learn a little anger management (4:1-5:6). In this section we will look at the Cause for Conflict (4:1-5) in our lives. We will make a Proposal regarding Worldliness (1), a Proof of our Proposal (2-3), and then explain the Problem of Worldliness in more detail (4-5).

Worldliness: the Proposal (4:1)

Where do wars and fights *come* from among you? Do *they* not *come* from your *desires for* pleasure that war in your members?

The Conflicts

What is the Cause for Conflict in our lives? Let us first determine what kind of conflict James is talking about. It might seem as though James is looking at the world and asking, "What's the cause of all these wars going on in the world today? Why so much fighting and bloodshed?" But I remain unconvinced of that. The context of the letter so far has been the local church and interpersonal relationships. In the previous section, great verbal displays of spiritual knowledge have caused competition between teachers, jealousy, rivalry, and verbal battles. So when we come to James 4, I believe James still has the church scene on his mind.

There is a distinction between wars (*polemoi*) and fighting (*machai*). The first refers to the "continual state of agitation which bubbles below the surface of one person's attitude towards another." It speaks of the long-standing grudge hidden in the heart of one brother or sister against another because of a previous injury or injustice. Complete forgiveness has not occurred. There is a hidden war going on. The second word refers to open clashes that result because of a grudge.

If you picture the believer as a volcano, you'll get it. The continual bubbling and agitation going on deep inside a live volcano is the war. And then from time to time the volcano rumbles, stirs and spouts flaming hot lava. That is the fighting. We all demonstrate caution with an active volcano by keeping a safe distance from it, for we know the volcano could explode at any time and destroy our lives. This is the picture in James' mind, and how true it is of so many local churches: one group pitted against another in continual antagonism beneath the surface. From time to time these fleshly attitudes surface in open skirmishes. How pitiful, yet how typical.

The Cause

James says, "So you want to know what causes these wars and fighting?" Answer: worldliness. The agitation comes from our lusts. Lust, *hēdonōn*, is not a neutral word. It always refers to evil pleasure in the NT. And so James is saying, "It is your own worldly lusts which smolder within your members; it is these which erupt from time to time and burn you and those around you."

By this time we can compile a fairly complete picture of the group to which James is writing. Their chief characteristic is worldliness, which is the love of pleasure and material gain. They honor the rich (2:1-6; 5:1-5); they neglect the poor (1:26-27; 2:1-5, 15,16); they envy each other on a material level (4:1-2); they rival each other in spiritual things, especially in their displays of wisdom (3:1, 13-15); and they use their tongues to claim great things in both the material (4:13-17) and spiritual spheres (1:26; 2:14-19; 3:1-18). This is a group of worldly, self-seeking people. But I wonder, really, if they are much different from us. Doesn't James sound like Paul does in Romans 7 when he says, "The problem is inside us"? As Pogo claimed, "We have met the enemy, and he is us."[18] Even on a grand scale God is not responsible for our wars. We cannot look outside ourselves for someone to blame. We must look inside ourselves. Man is the great enemy of mankind. Our sinful nature drools like a monster starving for trinkets and fruits of this world to satisfy its appetite, and its appetite is insatiable.

James seems to echo his thoughts from chapter one when he says every man is tempted when he is drawn away by his own lusts and enticed. He speaks of deserved suffering. He says many, many of our problems, trials, conflicts, and turmoil we bring upon ourselves because of our own worldliness. Job is a prime example of this, yet again. Now in chapter one Job endures a number of *undeserved* calamites. His response to them does not offend God but then the rest of the Book of Job yields quite a different picture of him.

By the end, Job doesn't even like himself very much. He sees himself for what he really is and repents in dust and ashes. There is a paradox here of true life. Basically, Job was a righteous man—outstanding, undoubtedly head and shoulders above his contemporaries. Yet within him was an element of spiritual pride, which dies hard, and comes out over and over again in his debate with his friends.

---

[18] Pogo, http://wiki.answers.com/Q/What_is_the_origin_of_the_phrase_'I_have_found_the_enemy_and_it_is_us.'

It takes God confronting him face to face to make Job realize there is something undesirable deep within his heart. I think that is often our experience. We go through experiences that are real trials for us. Yet these experiences are necessary because of things within us that are unacceptable to God. These things are brought out and exposed by the trials we endure. And in some cases we bring the trials upon ourselves.

Another good illustration of the cause of conflict is David. After his great sin with Bathsheba, Nathan announced to him that the sword would never depart from his house and that his neighbor (a general word) would lie with his wives in the sight of the sun. Later we discover that some of this is fulfilled through Absalom, David's son. If you read the third Psalm, you realize it was written when David was fleeing from Absalom. It is a lovely Psalm of trust and repose in a time of testing. In it, David doesn't seem conscious that what he is going through at the hands of Absalom is a result of his own sin. He speaks of lying down and sleeping and God guarding him and avenging him on his enemies and all the rest of it. However, it is obvious that the suffering, which his own sin brought upon him, became an occasion for David to learn to trust God more deeply. In the midst of a trial that he brought upon himself, David experiences a time of deep blessedness with the Lord.

This encourages me. If the only kind of trouble in which I could find joy and benefit were undeserved trials, then the number of trials I could have joy in would be greatly reduced. One of the things I have discovered about ministry is that in trying to help people, we often make mistakes that are deeply trying, which create large problems; we must live with them and trust the Lord in. Often, we have caused the whole problem. To know that this is a trial from the Lord designed for our good can bring out new stores of faith that were not there before and can also bring out the impurities of our faith. That is tremendously encouraging. When we read the Book of James, let us not think of these trials as just undeserved tests from the Lord, but let's realize that his readers brought many trials upon themselves. They were worldly, talked too much, were arrogant and full of spiritual pride, and they fought among themselves—no wonder they were assailed on all sides by trials. Yet they could count it all joy, knowing that these trials were for their benefit.

All right. The proposal has been made: conflicts are caused by the lusts within us (worldliness). But can James prove it?

Worldliness: the Proof (4:2-3)

Lust without Possessing (2a-c)

You lust and do not have. You murder and covet and cannot obtain. You fight and war.

Here James says we lust after something and do not get what we want. We murder. I believe James means mental murder here because the word is followed by envy. If I literally murder someone, I no longer envy him, obviously. He is out of my way. James has been heavily dependent on the Sermon on the Mount, and it was there, you'll remember, that Jesus said anger against one's brother without a cause is judgment worth. But even taken literally, we need to realize how terrible is our potential for violence. One justice of the United States Supreme Court made the statement that the only difference between the man on death row and the man on the street is a difference in what they do, not what they are. Everyone one of us is a potential killer. If driven hard enough and frustrated over a long enough period of time, we just may destroy in order to reach our desired goals.

Lust without Praying (2d-3)

Yet you do not have because you do not ask. You ask and do not receive, because you ask amiss, that you may spend *it* on your pleasures.

James says the reason we are not satisfied and fulfilled is that we are living independently from God. We have swallowed the world's philosophy that we either can reach or have reached all our goals on our own, which is the epitome of pride. We are alive today by God's grace. He could have taken our lives in the night. Though we depend on His grace for life every day, we don't even bother to ask Him to fulfill our soul's thirst for satisfaction. Or if we do ask, it is consumed by our lusts. We hold off praying as long as we can, but then if we cannot make it on our own, we humbly turn to God for help. Then when He doesn't come through, we think He let us down. Of course, it has not occurred to us that our prayer was for God to help us fulfill our selfish lusts. "Oh Lord, help my stock go from ten to twenty. I will give you ten percent, Lord, and I will keep ninety." "Oh Lord, give me a Christian wife so we can serve you better together. Now here are the vital statistics I was thinking of, Lord. What do you think?"

We can learn three simple principles about prayer here. **First** of all, God simply wants us to ask for what we want. That shows our dependence on Him. We do not have to snow Him with our prayer. Simply ask sincerely. This reminds me of the man who stood up in prayer meeting to pray one of those long, windy, theological prayers. He began with, "Oh, thou great God who sitteth upon the circle of the earth, before whom the inhabitants are like grasshoppers . . ." A lady seated behind him began to tug on the back of his jacket and said, "Just call Him 'Father' and ask him for something." That's all He wants. You have not because you ask not.

Second, ask according to his will. Sometimes we presume to use the Father to accomplish our own ends. We attempt to misuse His power to accomplish our program. We want our desires met our way according to our schedule but that may not be God's way. Patience in prayer is difficult, but God wants us to pray with the attitude, "Lord, in your own time and in your own way." This leads to the **third** principle: Wait.

A friend of mine used to tell the story of a man who was on his rooftop fixing something. He lost his footing and as he slid off the roof, he managed to grab hold of the gutter. He found himself hanging about twenty feet off the ground and he began yelling for help. There was no one around to help, so looking up to heaven, he said, "Is there anyone up there who can help me?" A voice came out of the sky saying, "I can help." "What should I do?" the man asked. The voice from above said, "Let go." The man thought a moment and cried out, "Is there anybody else up there who can help me?"

All too often that is the way we pray. We say, "Lord, help me." And God says, "I will—in my own way, and in my own time." So we start casting about for another solution instead of trusting, waiting, depending on the Lord. "Lord, if you are not going to help, then I'll have to do it my way. I've tried the spiritual route and it did not work, so now I will take my own path." Well, my way is more often than not the world's way, simply because God's thoughts are not my thoughts and God's ways are not my ways.

Worldliness: the Problem (4:4-5)

James has proved his proposal—our conflicts come from our worldliness. We might ask, "So what? I get tired of praying without seeing the answers I want. What's the problem if I do it my way?" James then declares two major problems with doing it our way. The first is becoming an enemy of God (4:4); the other is provoking His envy (5-6a).

Enemy of God

> **Adulterers and adulteresses! Do you not know that friendship with the world is enmity with God? Whoever therefore wants to be a friend of the world makes himself an enemy of God.**

We have chosen the world as our friend and made God our enemy. That is why James makes the shocking, startling address of verse four, "Adulterers and adulteresses!" All that is in the world—the lust of the flesh, the lust of the eye, and the pride of life (1 Jn 2:16)—all of this is at odds with God. Therefore, if we make friends with the world, we become God's enemy, His opponent. Self-assertiveness is the essence of worldliness. It is the world's creed. If you want to get ahead, then do it for yourself. No one else will do it for you. You have to claw and kick your way to the top of the heap. You only go around once, so you have to grab the brass ring. You have to get what you want out of life, so squeeze it like an orange.

When we adopt this philosophy we are unfaithful to God. We have become adulterers and adulteresses. A shocking statement, yet vivid imagery. This has never happened in my home, of course, but I have heard it said by some husbands that they wake up in the morning, let their eyes adjust to the light, peer around the room, and what do they see but their wife sitting in front of her dressing room table mirror. She is still in her faded flannel nightgown and her hair is up in curlers. She doesn't have a smidgeon of makeup on. Her eyes are droopy with sleep and the first thought that crosses his mind is, "Could this be the charming, romantic woman I married?"

Trying not to answer the question our dutiful husband shuts his eyes and attempts to go back to sleep. With this vision of his wife still in his mind, you understand, he goes off to work. And that evening, perhaps as he is going home from work, maybe a little bit late, under one of the streetlights on the corner he meets an overly friendly woman. She is exactly the opposite picture of the vision he last had of his wife. She has false eyelashes glued on and her eyelids are tinted with eye shadow. Her cheeks are smeared with rouge and she wears bright, red lipstick. Her hair is dyed platinum blond. Long earrings hang from her ears and around her neck is a string of pearls. Many bracelets circle her wrists. She wears a dress that barely qualifies. He recognizes her perfume as "Heaven Scent," his favorite. She presents a striking contrast to his wife, and he probably does not pause to think that in the cold, grey light of dawn this woman of the streets is probably just as unappealing or even less appealing than his wife. So he says to himself, "Perhaps I should strike up a conversation with this woman. I could tell my wife I needed to work late at the office. We could go out to dinner, perhaps a little dancing. I don't want to break up my marriage; all I want is a little friendship. After all, what's wrong with friendship?"

We can all recognize how foolish and hazardous this is. What begins as friendship leads to adultery. There are early morning, unromantic times in our Christian experience. These are times when our relationship with God seems drab and routine, depressing and uninspiring. It is at just such a time that we may meet the world on some street corner of our life. All of a sudden, dressed up in all its allurements, the world seems so attractive. Intellectually, physically—whatever appeals the world has to offer. Because of what seems to be the drabness of our Christian experience, we are attracted to it. We say to ourselves, "I don't want to break off my marriage with God, but why can't I have a little friendship? A little fun? Why can't I go along with the world to a limited?"

That is precisely what James warns us of. It is adultery. "You adulterers and adulteresses. Don't you know that friendship with the world is enmity toward God?" Then in verse five he adds another warning—the envy of the Spirit.

Envy of God (5)

> Or do you think that the Scripture says in vain, "The Spirit who dwells in us yearns jealously"?

The word *pneuma* is a reference to the Holy Spirit who has come to dwell within us and is jealous for our affection for God. When my heart flutters off in the direction of the world in any area, when I want to have a little affair with the world, the Spirit within me is jealous. I think James chose the word "friend" carefully. The root meaning is "affection." *Philē*, the Greek word for emotional love, comes from the same root. When I develop affection for something in this world to a high degree, I become a friend of the world and an enemy of God. God is jealous. He wants our affections.

How can I tell who ranks higher on my list of friends: God or the world? That is where Gothard's chart comes in. Let's take the world first. Acquaintance? Each of us is acquainted with the world. We are in it—can't avoid that. But an acquaintance is not a friend. Where are your interests? Look at the chart. If your interests are primarily wrapped up in the world, then the world is at least your casual friend. Close friend? Perhaps. What are your life goals? Are they temporal or eternal? Are they seeking for pleasure or seeking for people? Are they found in the world or in the Word? Intimate friendship? Is the world squeezing you into its mold? Is your character and conduct being conformed to this world? If so, you and the world have an intimate relationship. In fact, any of the last three relationships mean the world is your friend and God is your enemy.

Wouldn't you rather be God's friend? Perhaps you are. Let's see. Have you met Christ? Do you see him spasmodically either privately or even publicly at church? Then, at least you could say He is an acquaintance. Do you have a number of common interests with God, such as His children? Perhaps you are casual friends. Or perhaps your life goals are the same as His. You are committed to reaching the world around you for Christ and you want to build up your brothers in Christ. That is close friendship with God. But intimacy—oh, how sweet. Have you given God free reign to mold and shape your character into that of His Son? That is intimate friendship.

Who ranks higher on your scale of friendship? God or the world? James is a book about trials and troubles. In such times we may need the help or advice of a friend. Woe to the man whose only friend in hard times is the world. It will chew you up and spit you out. For the wisdom of this world is foolishness with God. It is completely backward. For example, take this bit of wisdom from the world. The world says a man's best friend is his dog. That's typical. Give the pundits credit for getting the letters right, but they have it spelled backwards. A man's best friend is not his d-o-g, but his G-o-d. He wants to be your friend and mine. If we would only call on Him and depend on Him, at all times but especially in times of trouble. How close can you get to God? It is up to you. Emerson said, "The only way to have a friend is to be one." The Proverb says. "A man who has friends must show himself friendly." And James 4:8 says, "Draw near to God, and he will draw near to you."

❋ ❋

Mike was just one of those guys who had it all going for him—top of his class, all-city athlete, Hollywood looks. If he wasn't Most Likely to

Succeed in his high school yearbook, he should have been. He went on to medical school and residency after college. With a gift in the fine motor skills arena he became one of the best neurosurgeons in the state and earned all the money that went with it. He had a beautiful wife, a gorgeous home, two cute kids, and a Corvette.

I met him when his wife kicked him out of the house for infidelity.

Distraught, Mike found refuge in his younger brother, who was a Christian. He sought forgiveness in Jesus through the witness of his little brother. Because he lived in another city, the younger brother was calling conservative pastors at random who lived near his brother to find someone to follow-up on his decision. I agreed, and the surgeon was open to being helped. Slowly, he began to grow and even became part of a growth group within our church. Outrageously funny, Mike kept the group in stitches. He easily could have made a living as a stand-up comedian.

But Mike had one albatross around his neck that limited his growth. He could not give up his old friends. These were his carousing buddies, none of whom took Mike's new faith seriously. Before long he was back to some of his old ways, and his wife divorced him. He went through cycles of sin, repentance, growth, and back to sin. Though he seemed to have a genuine experience with Christ, his friends kept dragging him down, especially his best friend: the world. Mike loved the good life his money could buy: a condo in Deer Park, Utah, bigger houses, nicer cars, and always pretty girls. After he had been through three marriages and was getting ready for a fourth, I asked him what he had learned about marriage in all of this. I'll never forget his answer. He said, "Well, they all turn out about the same: business as usual. A marriage is a small business. Someone has to pay the bills; someone has to take out the trash; someone has to get the kids to the doctor. And the business side seems to take away the fizzle. If I had known that a long time ago, I would have stayed with my first wife."

Then Mike got involved in cocaine. All his friends were doing it, so why not? As a physician it was easy for him to get it legally at first. But then it evolved into something else. He began snorting before surgery. He never hurt anyone, but he did get caught and lose his license to practice medicine. In time he lost his last wife, lost all his money, and filed for bankruptcy. He began coming to church again to try to get his life right with the Lord. He joined a small group that was truly supportive. After eight years of staying clean, he asked me to appear before the State Medical Board of Examiners as a character witness so he could get his license back.

Mike worked in a pain clinic for a couple of years before he slipped up by giving some pain meds to friends who were not patients. He lost his number to prescribe drugs and with it, his job. Then his health began to go: two hip replacements and prostate cancer. This past Christmas Eve he called me to see if I would give him $100 to buy some gifts for his two kids by his fourth wife.

Is Mike really a believer? Only God knows. Mike was a good friend to my family and me on many occasions, and I tried to be a friend to him, but I was never his best friend. His best friend took him down. Friendship with the world is enmity with God.

"THE MOST DANGEROUS GAME"

James 4:6-10

Years ago a book was released which was destined for success in America because it scratched where we itch, *Games People Play*.[19] If you have read this book by Eric Berne, you know how penetrating and deep the scratching goes. It concerns the way we use psychological gimmicks to get people to do what we want them to do, hopefully without letting them know it. Three years after it was published and had been on the best sellers' list for many months, a couple of Christians published a companion volume called *Games Christians Play*.[20] An artist was employed to depict each of these games. The games we play in church reveal how we do a lot of things in Christian circles, wishing to conceal our true motives. Let's look at some of the games Christians play.

The first game is called, "I don't know why they don't do something about her." This is usually played by people who are gullible and spineless. It is usually riddled with the ubiquitous word "they," as in, "I don't know why **they** don't do something about the rowdies in the balcony." Or, "I don't know why **they** don't do something about the man who always puts his arm around his wife in church." Or, "I don't

---

[19]   Eric Berne, *Games People Play*, (New York: Ballantine Books, 1964).

[20]   Judi Culbertson and Patti Bard, *Games Christians Play*, 1967.

know why **they** don't do something about all the young people who take up our seats on Sunday morning." "I don't know why **they** don't do something about those people who smoke in front of the church." The "I Don't Know Why They Don't Do Something About It" game is a very popular game in churches.

An even more popular game is this one. It is called, "Opposing New Fangled Gimmicks." The artist depicts a very straight-laced, erect man in his fifties. He is teaching junior high boys. He has been teaching them for thirty years, always following the lesson manual, and gives out pencils at Christmas. The last creative thought he had was in 1986. His common response when spoken to by the superintendent about changing his approach is, "I'm doing the best I can," or, "Nobody is more faithful than I am." You want to say, "Unfortunately," but then he comes back with, "This is the way we've always done it." And so he has received a little award, a little banner he can wear across his chest. He is the guy who feels discussion is the first wayward move toward sensitivity training. He feels that any approach that involves the class talking is the first step toward liberalism. He believes you really teach when you say, "Sit there and listen and don't respond. Just listen."

The third game is "When You Have Been a Christian as Long as I Have." The guy depicting this game is wearing a halo. He apparently was born in the choir loft and learned to swim in the baptistery. He has never known a time when he didn't know the Lord, and he is tired of Him. When a new Christian comes in, Bible in hand, excited about a new discovery, saying "I didn't even know there was a book called Habakkuk in the Bible," our game player puts his arm around the new believer and says, "Well, when you come across the main theme—the Chaldean taunt in chapter two—you will find the real truth." His listener says, "The Chaldean taunt?" He thinks it's a disease or something. He doesn't know what it is. The new Christian says, "You know, I am getting interested in South America." Our game player responds, "Yes, well, new Christians always go to extremes. I went through that when I was eleven, but now as an adult, I don't worry about those people. It's childish."

The fourth game: Prima Donna. If you are going to play Prima

Donna it helps to have an Austrian accent or to have been brought up in the Eastern schools. It also helps to have $100,000 for the new sanctuary. You want everyone to know what you are doing, so you ask to have your name inscribed on a plaque someplace prominent so it can be seen by anyone walking in. The Prima Donna can usually sing "Amazing Grace" in Latin, you know, that kind of individual. She is the classic namedropper. "When I was talking to Billy the other day, I mean, Dr. Billy Graham as you might know him...." "Adrian and I were so very close," meaning the late Adrian Rogers. This kind of person tends toward playing Prima Donna.

I have saved my favorite for last. This game is called, "Welcoming the New Convert." The depiction is a lady marine getting out of a Mac truck in the church parking lot. She spies one of the new members and rushes over. She says, "Oh, honey, I am so glad you are coming; we've signed you up for the nursery for the next five months. You will serve, won't you?" Or she takes it upon herself to instruct the new member on how to dress, what to say, what is wrong with the youth of today.

You may think playing games in church is 21st century stuff, but it isn't. It is as old as the NT church. As a matter of fact, if I read my Bible correctly, there were games being played as early as the first book of the NT written, the Book of James, written perhaps as early as AD 35. James characteristically points out games. Only, when James points out a game, the people don't laugh. When James points his finger, it hurts. This section is no exception. James points his finger at the most dangerous game ever played. It is called PG. See if you can figure out what the letters stand for before this lesson is finished. PG—the most dangerous game.

We are now in the final main section of James. It deals with controlling our anger. In particular, James says our own worldly lusts hatch most of our conflicts with others. The cause of conflict is worldliness. I asked you for the cure for conflict. We find that it is humility. This is the theme woven into the fabric of James 4:6-5:6. Humility: before God, before men, and before the world. Let's start with humility before God.

We realized as we finished 4:5 that blaming God for our troubles is ridiculous, at least if many of our troubles come directly from the lusts of our hearts. We can't blame God for our own foolishness and sin. It is discouraging to realize that even after I become a believer, I still drag these lusts around with me and suffer from their influence in my life. I am defective. How can a defective creature correct his own internal foul up? Can a defective computer correct itself? Obviously no, so despair could easily triumph. That is the moment James steps in with encouragement. He says that God's grace is sufficient for all our need. His grace is greater than our sin. Although the first installment of grace came when we received Christ, even more grace is available for the believers who would like to cure their conflicts.

In Paul's language, by grace are we saved through faith (Eph 2:8). We are saved from the penalty of sin by the substitutionary *death* of Christ. But now we need to be saved from the power of sin. This is done through the substitutionary *life* of Christ (Rom 5:9-10; Gal 2:20). The first is what most people call our **salvation**; the second is what many call our **sanctification**. The first deals with the penalty of sin; the second deals with the power of sin. But note well: we are completely dependent on God's grace for salvation, and we are completely dependent on God's grace for sanctification. We cannot be saved by our own power, and we cannot be sanctified by our own power. In other words, we need more grace. That is exactly what James is saying and promising. **"He gives more grace" (Jas 4:6a).** But how do we get more grace? Can we earn grace? Of course not. James gives us the answer in 4:6:

> **But He gives more grace. Therefore He says:**
> ***"God resists the proud,***
> ***But gives grace to the humble."***

Humility is the key to God's storeroom of grace. We need more grace to overcome the problems we've had **since** becoming believers. This is true not only of our battle with our lusts, but in ministry, too. We make mistakes, large mistakes that cause problems with which we have to live. Discouragement says, "Quit!" But God's grace says, "Go on. My grace is greater than your sin. It will cushion the blows and enable you to reap fruit from the wreckage of your mistakes. No one yet has out-sinned my grace." "Grace, grace, God's grace. Grace that will pardon and cleanse within. Grace, grace, God's grace. Grace that is greater than all our sin." With God's grace burning before me as the only source of light in the darkness of my trial, I reach out to Him and say, "How do I get more grace?"

God resists the proud, but gives grace to the humble. The answer is obvious. Humble myself before the Lord. Bury my spiritual pride. Worldliness is the cause of my conflicts; humility is the cure. OK, if I am going to bury my pride, I better know what that is. Pride is a compound word meaning "to appear above." *Hyper* (above) + *phaneroō* (to appear). The latter is the one from which we get phantom in English. What is a phantom? Just an appearance. Nothing real. Pride is just an appearance of being above others. It is not reality. We are all equal—just ants crawling around in the dust. That is reality. We are all equal before the Lord, but we like to dress ourselves up in the fine clothes of our material or spiritual accomplishments and we like to let our fine intellectual hair hang down. These are all efforts to lift ourselves above the common dregs of mankind. We want to appear above. The proud convince themselves that their material and spiritual attainments have been reached through their own cleverness, diligence, determination, prowess, and charisma. Oh my—it is only by God's grace that we were even born in a country which encourages and allows us to go freely where we choose in life. Even Warren Buffet acknowledges that the greatest factor in his attainment of wealth was being born in America. He calls that "winning the ovarian lottery."[21] We call it grace.

To suppose we are humanly responsible for these blessings is pride. A false appearance. A façade of superiority. Such self-deceiving pride must be destroyed if we wish for a further measure of God's grace. Humility must be cultivated. But how do we get humility, and what is it?

Humility is the opposite of pride. Humility means getting the real

---

[21] Warren Buffet, http://www.youtube.com/watch?v=LiTkU9eIFPs.

picture of who I am. If pride gives a false appearance, humility gives the true picture. Humility is the lowliness of mind that acknowledges my total dependence on God's grace for both the privilege and the power to live this life. Satan, the author of pride, deceived himself into thinking more highly of himself than he should have, and gave evidence of this pride by acting independently from God. True humility would reverse Satan's act. I must see myself as I am—a recipient of God's grace—and give evidence of lowliness of mind by making a declaration of dependence upon God. That is where 4:7-9 leads us, to verse ten, which speaks of humility. Verse six ended with humility; verse ten begins with humility. Verses 7-9 tell us how to get there. Humility is the goal of this subsection. It is God's winding staircase from the attic of pride down to the basement of humility. Here are the steps.

Step#1: Submit to God (7a)

Therefore submit to God.

We have seen this word "submission" before. It is another compound word in Greek, which means "to put yourself under." We have used the illustration of God's protective umbrella. When I submit to God, I place myself under the protective umbrella of His will. I acknowledge my need for His protection. To step out from under the umbrella is to expose myself to the full force of the storm. To put it another way, to step out from under God's protection is to put myself within the radar range of Satan's submarines, which are constantly trying to torpedo my ship.

In particular, these words are dedicated to those who would rather fight than surrender. To submit to God means to stop the fighting, give up, surrender. Do you remember what it was like when we were growing up? From age six to twelve, the big game was to see who could wrestle the best. We would go at it until someone shouted, "I give." That was the goal, to hear the opponent say, "I give." We would wrestle and miss a meal if we had to waiting for one or the other to say, "I give." We long to hear those words from the other guy, not from ourselves. They are the very last words we want to say. We will let him beat us to a pulp before we'll say, "I give." Why do we wait so long? Pride.

"I give." That is what it means to submit. Lord, I give up. I am beaten. But how much better to say it before the fight begins. Don't make God send an angel to wrestle with you as He did Jacob. Stop scheming and start submitting. Say, "Lord, I am not going to assert myself any longer. I will not force my will on the world any more. I give up. I lean on you."

Step #2: Resist the Devil (7b)

Resist the devil and he will flee from you.

What a great promise. This is God's Word. If I actively choose to stand against the devil, then he will flee. Awesome. However, we usually don't see this verse in its context. We are to resist the devil's sin, pride, which is an attitude of superiority that compels us to act independently. Obviously this would be the first temptation we face after Step #1. We have just humbled ourselves before God—we have declared our **dependence** on Him. So the first temptation would be to step back out on our own, to get out from under the protective umbrella of God's will for our lives. We need to resist the devil and say to God, "Your will, not mine, be done."

Bob was a good-looking guy with a lot of pretty girls interested in him. He grew up in a Christian home with strong family values. His parents and church instilled in Bob the desire to save himself for marriage. They sent him to a Christian college. Toward the end of school he found the right woman for him. They married in a wonderful ceremony, a true witness to Christ and the Church.

Two weeks later it was over. They didn't even have time to open the wedding gifts. She announced to Bob that she was gay and had no desire for a man. She walked out and never came back.

Bob had been under God's umbrella. He was trying to do it God's way. "And this is what I get?" he reasoned. The temptation was very strong to step out from under the umbrella and do it the world's way, the devil's way. Why look for a Christian wife in church? Why not just head for the bars? The good news is that Bob's strength from his upbringing in Christianity and family values helped him to resist the devil and draw close to God. Today he has a wonderful Christian home.

Step #3: Draw Near to God (8a)

Draw near to God and He will draw near to you.

After putting myself under God's authority, Satan tempts me to step away, to reject God's authority. I resist him, though, and he flees. I haven't arrived at humility, yet. I need to step closer to God still. It's important to note that I can be under God's authority without putting my heart into it. The next step from the attic to the basement is to draw close to Him. **It is very hard to be proud when you are standing next to Jesus.** When Isaiah caught a glimpse of God, he saw himself in all of his sinfulness. He thought he would die (Isaiah 6).

Getting closer to God makes us more aware of just how riddled with sin we really are. Oh yes, I know we are forgiven saints who sin from time to time, but we can become much more deeply aware of our sin so that it is more than just a fact of life—it is an utter grievance. As Paul went along in his life, he became more acutely aware of his own depravity. Early in his walk he called himself the "least of the apostles" (1 Cor 15:9, around 56 AD). Later on he went so far as to say he was the "least of all saints" (Eph 3:8, around 62 AD). Finally, at the end of his life he called himself the chief among sinners (1 Tim 1:15). I don't think he was more sinful in his actions at the end of his life than when he first became a Christian. As Paul grew closer to the Lord he grew more aware of his sinfulness and how completely dependent he was on God's grace to continue on. By drawing near to God we learn true humility.

Step #4: Deal with Sin (8b-9)

Cleanse *your* hands, *you* sinners; and purify *your* hearts, *you* double-minded. Lament and mourn and weep! Let your laughter be turned to mourning and *your* joy to gloom.

Again, what happens when we draw close to God? We see more of our own sinfulness. So now we need to deal with our sin. In 1 John 1:6-2:2 the apostle explains three errors we can make regarding our sinfulness once we see it. Each one is a form of denial. Denial of sin is a symptom of spiritual pride.

There are many ways to deny some aspect of our sinfulness, one of which is to say we are no longer sinners; we are now saints. To refer to believers as sinners misidentifies the children of God, or so they say. But right here in our text, James is addressing the brethren (who are born again—remember 1:16-18) and calls the double-minded among them "sinners." Some people in the Exchanged Life movement tell us that we no longer have a Sin Nature. They say our Sin Nature was **exchanged** for a New Nature. Our current battle with sin, they claim, comes from the residual patterns of sin left over in our fleshly bodies after being born again. Though I resonate with much that is taught in the Exchanged Life ministry, I do not agree with this aspect. Just look at the words *hē harmartia* (sin) in Romans 6:7-23 and on into Romans 7 for evidence that the Sin Nature lives on after being deposed in 6:6. Deposed; not destroyed.

It is a crucial error to deny the extent of our sinful condition after we become believers. Perfectly sanctified in our position in the heavenly places in Christ (Eph 1:3-13), yes, but still very much sinners in our condition on earth. That is what Luther was trying to say in his famous statement *simul iustus et peccator*: at the same time justified and a sinner. Justified in our Position; sinful in our Condition.

As I see it, the problem with denying our sinfulness is that it cuts us off on our way down the stairway to humility. If I can get close to Jesus without being made more aware of my sinfulness, I have a serious case of denial and very little chance of finding any degree of humility. God gives grace to the humble, not the proud.

I must deal with my sinfulness. One aspect of sin James lands on is having a dirty heart because of our double-mindedness. This double-mindedness is a result of trying to have God and the world be our intimate friends at the same time. Can't happen. So James wants us to repent of this sin. He talks about mourning, weeping, and gloom.

Very heavy. We get the idea that his readers have had blinders on and suddenly realize how wrong they have been in their worldliness. They need to radically change their approach to life. It may involve mourning and weeping over their current lifestyle.

Dealing with our sinfulness actually has more to do with honesty than tears. There are times when tears are called for. This seems to be one of those times for James' readers. But as a general rule, I think we are reading some insight on the nature of true confession. It is more than just naming a sin as sin. When we agree (*homologeō* means to agree or confess in 1 Jn 1:9) that something is sinful, we are agreeing with someone. That someone is God. That means we should have the same attitude toward our sin that He has. Our sin grieves Him (Eph 4:30) and He hates it (Zech 8:17). True confession involves some degree of remorse for my sins and some degree of repugnance. I want to turn away from it; I yearn to stop; I crave deliverance.

Step #5: Declare my Dependency (4:10)

Humble yourselves in the sight of the Lord, and He will lift you up.

The final step into the basement of humility is declaring complete dependency. That is what it means to humble oneself in the sight of the Lord. Having seen God in all His holiness and myself in all my sin, what else can I do but cry out and cling to Him? I declare my dependence on His grace! When we do this, He will shower us with His grace, for He resists the proud but gives grace to the humble. When we do this, He exalts us. I do not necessarily think the exaltation referred to here means a place of prominence before men; I lean more to the idea that, though I was down and dejected and in despair over my sin, He lifts me up. He gives me more grace. He restores the joy of my salvation.

I think we can safely say that God will only put a man or woman in a place of prominence before men when he or she has come to the bottom of the stair steps to humility. We all think of John the Baptizer in this regard. If any man could have been tempted to take the glory, it would have been John the Baptizer. They flocked after him in the most incredible of circumstances. They came out into the wilderness where he preached. He did not have a church with plush pews in the center of town or on a freeway. He did not wear expensive suits; he was not attractive; he didn't even have an appealing, positive message. Yet they came to him by the droves.

They finally asked, "Are you the Messiah?" He said, "I am not even worthy to bend down to loosen His sandals." "Who are you? Are you the Light?" they asked. "No, I'm just the lamp." "Are you the Word?" "No, I am just the voice, the voice of one crying in the wilderness." The voice stops, but the Word goes on. The lamp goes out, but the light lingers. The secret of his life? "He must increase; I must decrease" (Jn 3:30). I wonder, whom did the Lord exalt? Like few others, He exalted John the Baptizer.

Games Christians Play. Have you figured out the most dangerous game a Christian can play? It is called PG. PG—Playing God. That is what pride is all about. Pride says, "God, I don't need you. I can handle things quite nicely by myself, thank you very much." At the very least, it is to claim credit for what God has done for us. Self-exaltation—that's pride. Do you remember what that word "resist" means? It means God stands against the proud man or woman in battle array. Woe to the man, woman, or child who goes to battle against God. If God be for us, who then can be against us? But if God be against us, who then can be for us? How would you like to see everything you do in life be bomb-shelled—your family, your business, your church life—everything? There is a sure-fire way— Play God.

On the other hand, the cure for conflict is humility. Submit to God; resist the devil; draw near to God; deal with sin in your life; declare your dependence. I have wondered through the years which of these steps is the most important. Perhaps we cannot single one out. However, if forced to choose, I would say the most important step is to draw near to God. I think I began to understand this verse years ago when my first child was about five. We were living in a four-bedroom house. The master bedroom was set apart from the other three. My son was in one of those other bedrooms and my daughter, who was about three, was in another. We used the fourth for reading and TV.

On Saturday nights I always liked to save a couple of hours before bed to mediate on the ministry of the next day and to pray. It was something of a ritual for me. So, the kids were asleep and I had my back to the wall, leaning back on a Hollywood couch. While meditating with my eyes open, I noticed the door handle slowing turning. The door inched open a bit, and a little hand started crawling around the edge of the door as it was pushed slightly wider.

Now you have to understand that I did not like being disturbed during my ritual. Finally, the door was open, and Jimmy stepped in. He was a cute kid with big blue eyes, and they were wide open. He wrestled some with nightmares, and I could tell he was scared, but I didn't want to be disturbed. I was being spiritual, you understand. So I asked, "Jimmy, what do you want? You are supposed to be in bed." He looked at me with those big eyes and said, "Daddy, I don't want anything; I just want to be close to you."

Ah, man, what're you gonna do? "Jimmy, what do you want—a pony, a Cadillac? Come over here." I held out my arms to him and he ran over and jumped up against my chest. I drew him close with my arms around him. That's when I began to understand this verse. "Yes, Lord, I know you are busy. But things are tough in my life right now, and I am scared. I'm not even asking for anything. I just want to be close to you." That is nearly irresistible. He will wrap his loving arms around you and pull you close. When I am that close, safe in His arms and close to His heart, I cannot help but to see more of His infinite holiness and my pathetic sinfulness.

There are three things that I think will amaze me when I get to heaven: 1) All the people who are there who I did not think would be there; 2) All the people who are not there I thought would be there; 3) The fact that I am there—that is God's grace.

A college girl from years ago sent me a letter from school. It included a poem that really hits the nail on the head concerning this attitude of humility.

To have been the cup His lips touched and blessed;
To have been the bread that He broke;
To have been the cloth that He held as He served;
Or the water He poured as He spoke.
To have been the road He walked on His way;
To have been His print in the sand;
To have been the door that opened His tomb;
. . . but I was the nail in His hand.

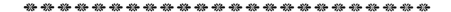

One of the people I have been graced to know was a veterinarian from England named Paul Barrett. I met him when he was well established in his practice and about forty. He had been a Christian for a couple of years and was already drifting toward a subtle form of legalism. We did some Bible study together and Paul did an about-face. When he began to unfold the petals of God's grace, he could not get enough. He taught himself Greek and began absorbing huge chunks of Scripture like a sponge in water.

Paul was an endearing man with his somewhat shy, retiring ways and his English lilt. He was not the type of man you would notice in a crowd—balding, slight of build, scholarly-looking. Very humble. He had almost single-handedly developed the largest veterinary practice in our county. He had a mind like the proverbial steel trap. Yet I never heard a boastful word from his lips. After about three years of growing faster than a yearling on a Kentucky horse farm, I suggested he teach a Sunday school class.

"Me?" he asked with a hint of fear and trepidation in his voice.

"Sure, Paul. You have all this knowledge. And you are a gifted man. Why not share what you have learned?"

After a little more encouragement, he dove in. We announced the class and a modest group of six showed up.

Within a year there were sixty people coming to Paul's class, which was one of our larger classes, if not the largest.

"How did you do that?" I asked him.

"Well," he began in his usual diffident manner, "I did the same thing I did to build my vet clinic. I wrote a note of appreciation to everyone who visited my class and continued to write to them periodically if they came back."

Wow, I thought to myself. I don't remember ever getting a note from a Sunday school teacher.

With Paul's keen mind, solid exposition, and clever wit he soon became the most popular and beloved man in our church, the pastor (me) not excepted. It was a beautiful thing to watch, and it brought tears to my eyes when I remembered from whence he came. His animal practice became almost a sideline for him as he pursued a transcendent purpose for his life.

One day I was having lunch with my staff at The Black-Eyed Pea and noticed Paul across the way eating with his staff. I was going to lead a tour of Israel in a month and had not found a preacher to substitute for me. I enjoy teaching gifted laymen to preach, so I thought, why not? Paul was such a shy type I was pretty sure he had never given a speech in public, but with his teachable attitude, he could learn. I sauntered over to his table, plopped myself down and popped the question. Again, "Me?" as he practically choked on his food. Yes, Paul, you; you're ready.

I thought he would turn me down, but to my surprise Paul called me in a few days and accepted. Great, I said, let's get together for lunch and I'll give you some tips. Since it usually takes me several months to train someone and we only had three weeks, there wasn't much I could do. I handed him a book on preaching and asked him to read it and just pick up a couple of main points. I wasn't worried about the exegesis of his passage because the two of us had been over it in a previous study together. But exegesis is a long way from the pulpit. As I was about to leave we met one more time. I said, "Paul, whatever you do, don't get up there and apologize. You are a gifted man, so just share your gift."

When I got back, I couldn't wait to listen to the tape of his sermon. I was told by others that it went well, but he was so nervous and his knees were shaking so badly he had to sit on a bar stool to get through the sermon. As I began to listen, he started off by saying, "Well, Pastor Dave asked me to just share my gift, so I am going to spay a cat." That brought down the house. Then he told a couple of jokes about the Queen of England to help people get used to his accent. Just before launching into the text he said, "Now in the Old Country if we hear something we like, we don't say 'Amen.' We say, 'Hear, hear.' So, if you hear anything at all you like in this message, it would be much appreciated if you would say, 'Hear, hear.'"

I could pick up an occasional "Hear, hear" on the tape as the message went on, but when it was over, the entire congregation rose and cheered him with a rousing, "Hear, hear!" in unison. It was marvelous. I could not have been happier for both him and our church to have such a wonderful example of one who was willing to put his life in God's hands for His use. While others his age were going through mid-life crises and buying gold chains and fancy sports cars, Paul was in a mid-life concert with Jesus as the maestro. Did his popularity and burgeoning knowledge puff him up? Never. If possible, he became even more self-effacing and humble.

At some point, Paul noticed his speech beginning to slur a bit. One of the doctors in our church checked him out in my church office one Sunday. More tests were run, and it was confirmed—Paul had ALS, Lou Gehrig's disease and what some call the "cruelest disease." The muscles slowly degenerate, usually over about a five-year period. Eighty percent of its victims die of suffocation when their lungs no longer operate. The rest choose to go on a lung machine. In the final months those on a lung machine must have a nurse available 24/7 to put drops in their eyes because they can no longer blink and their eyes dry out. All this time, the mind never looses its capacity to think, which is why it is thought by many to be the cruelest disease. It was agonizing for us to believe our beloved Paul was afflicted with this dark disease. I used to write a small devotional for our church newsletter. But Paul was actually a more gifted writer than I, so out of love and respect for him during the last couple of years of his life we turned the task over to him. Each article he wrote was so special, it not only became the highlight of the letter, but the electronic subscriptions, even from people who were not part of our church, soared. Paul never indulged in self-pity. He was his old self—witty, insightful, and relevant. For about the last year of his articles, he was reduced to using a computer that could recognize a code from the blinking of his eyes to communicate which letter to type. Letter by letter, word by word, he blinked away his heart, his mind, and his tears.

Though he had been to Israel with me once before, and I can still see him jogging down the steps of Masada, Paul wanted to make one more visit before he died so he could focus without distraction on his Savior and his future home. Of course by then he could not walk, so men from the church carried him everywhere we couldn't push him in a wheelchair. God used this to impact the owner of the tour company, a Jewish Zionist from South Africa, to receive Jesus as his Messiah.

When the Zionist shared his new faith with me, this sixty-year old man said, "It was when I saw you all carrying the man with ALS around Israel that I knew you had something I wanted. You have a way of dealing with suffering I had never witnessed before. As a tour operator, I deal with lots and lots of pastors from the States, many of them who seem to me to be very hypocritical. But I knew this was real. I've been processing this decision for years. I could wait no longer."

Yes, Paul Barrett was a humble man who found more grace to enjoy intimacy with his Savior than most of us will never know. That same grace enabled him to endure with unparalleled dignity and faith a disease that could drive any person crazy. Although his lifetime was truncated by that merciless and macabre disease, I am confident when he stands before his Savior for a pass in review of his time on earth, Paul Barrett will see the Lord open His mouth to say affirmably, "Hear, hear."

"THE BADGE OF HUMILITY"

James 4:11-12

God has stamped everything with a mark of identity. Amazingly, the first coral snake I saw in the wild was in my own neighborhood. We lived near some woods and a multicolored snake about two and half feet long was killed. I went over a little jingle in my mind slowly as I held the dead snake in my hands: "Red on black, friend of Jack; red on yellow, kill a fellow." I went home and, since this was before the days of internet, I looked in the encyclopedia to be sure. There it was. So I held up the dead snake and thought, "So this is a coral snake." It felt weird to be holding death in my hand. You see, there was no antivenin for coral snakes in America. To make the antivenin you had to milk the snake. Even today there just aren't enough incidents in our country to warrant the expense, and a severe shortage exists. So if you are bitten by a coral snake, start saying your goodbyes. Fortunately, the Creator put a warning sign on the coral snake. It's not like a rattle, but it is easier to spot than a copperhead: bright colors—red, yellow, and black. It is easy to spot if it's moving. The coral snake has marks of identification.

God has stamped most things with marks of identification: the zebra has stripes; the leopard has spots; the camel has humps; the hyena has a laugh. Name most of God's creatures, and we can find its marks of identification either in how it looks, how it sounds, or how it acts. That is true of people, too. God has given us ways to identify different types of people. He says, "By their fruits you shall know them," in reference to false teachers and prophets. By the way, this does not refer to their lifestyle; it refers to the words that come out of their mouths. Apple trees produce apples; fig trees produce figs; grape vines produce grapes; and false prophets produce false prophecies.

Just as God tells us how to identify a false prophet, he also tells us how to spot a humble person. In James 4:6-10 we learned the importance of humility if we ever hope to solve the problems and conflicts in our lives. We solve those problems as God gives us more grace. The question was how to get more grace. The answer: humility. God resists the proud (God goes out to battle against the proud), but gives grace (undeserved kindness and favor) to the humble. We decided a humble attitude was the lowliness of mind that declares total dependency on God's grace for both the privilege and the power to live this life. Then we went through the steps toward **humility before God**.

In James 4:11-12 we want to examine **humility before men**. God can look into our hearts and see a humble attitude. However, men can only look at outer evidence to identify a humble person. If I tried to pick up a live coral snake to see *inside* its mouth as to whether the fangs were there or not, I would soon be dead. God has made the coral snake with bright colors like a flag on the *outside* to warn us of danger. The colors can be seen at a distance. So also can the true colors of a humble person be seen from a distance. He wears a badge that identifies him as humble before God. I am sure you have all heard about the minister who was given a badge by his congregation because he was so humble, but then they took it away because he wore it. Here is a badge that cannot be given by men, nor taken away. It is the outer evidence of the inward attitude of humility in James 4:11-12.

JAMES

"TRIUMPH THROUGH TRIALS"

Salutation (1:1)
Introduction (1:2-18)—The Value of Trials
Theme (1:19-20)—Qualities Needed
Body (1:21-5:6)—Qualities Developed

    I.   In Regard to Hearing (1:21-2:26)
    II. In Regard to Speaking (3:1-18)
    III. In Regard to Fighting (4:1-5:6)
        A. Cause of Conflict—Pride (4:1-5)
        B. Cure for Conflict—Humility (4:6-5:6)
           1. Humility before God (4:6-10)
           2. Humility before Men (4:11-12)

We suggested that humility is so important that James looks at it from three angles: before God (4:6-10), before men (4:11-12), and before the world (4:13-5:6). We have looked at humility before God. Now we are ready for humility before men. We will see the command (11a), the confusion (11b) and the clarification (12) regarding humility before men. Let's start with the command.

The Command (11a)

Do not speak evil of one another, brethren. He who speaks evil of a brother and judges his brother, . . .

The way this reads in the original makes speaking evil of one's brother the equivalent of judging one's brother. This is very helpful. Have you ever wondered what it means to judge a brother? Does it mean to talk about a brother behind his back? I threw a wet blanket on a gathering of pastors and their wives one time. We had been discussing the negative side of a sister in Christ for about ten minutes. So I asked, "I am going to be preaching on James 4:11-12 in a couple of weeks, and my question is whether we have been judging Sally for the last ten minutes by reviewing all the evil things in her life?" After a lot of throat clearing, they concluded that there is a difference between judging and discerning. The former is to put someone down, while the latter is with the hope of helping him or her.

That conclusion falls right in line with what James is saying. He equates judging with speaking evil of one's brother. Actually, the word used to begin verse 11 is another compound word: *kata* + *laleō* = down + to speak. The first word in this compound does not mean evil. *Kata* normally just means "down." We get our English words "cataclysm" or "catastrophe" from this word. However, speaking evil "puts down." You can speak someone down just like you can drag someone down or push someone down. Sitting around putting another person down or criticizing them can qualify for what the NKJ calls "speaking evil," which James identifies as a form of judging one another.

The goal of a put down is to lower the listener's estimate of the other person. We talk down the person in question in hopes of lowering the listener's opinion of that other person. Of course, we cover up our goal very creatively. We say things like, "Now stop me if I am wrong, but . . .." Or, "Now I don't mean to be critical, but . . .." Or, "Perhaps I shouldn't be saying this about him, but . . .." Or, "You know, John is such a wonderful person in so many ways, but . . .." The goal is to lower the listener's opinion of that person. You feel you have discovered some evil or negative aspect of that person and you want to share it with the world. This verbal maneuver can be spotted from the ubiquitous "but." Whatever follows the "but" usually expresses ten times more material than what was expressed before it.

William Barclay has this to say: "There are few sins which the Bible so unsparingly condemns as the sin of irresponsible and malicious gossip. To tell and to listen to the slanderous story—especially about a distinguished person—is for most people a fascinating activity."[22]

22 William Barclay, *The Letters of James and Peter,* (Philadelphia: The Westminster Press, 1976), 111.

If you want to get people's attention, just pick a name people look up to or anyone in the public eye, and then sprinkle it with bits of sordid information and you will captivate your audience. It is a power play by the tongue. James says, "Stop doing it." Sooner or later you will destroy everyone around you and ultimately yourself. People will label you a downer, like a drug. I like this bit of wisdom:

A little seed lay in the ground,
    And soon began to sprout,
"Now which of all the flowers around,"
    It mused, "shall I come out?
The lily's face is fair and proud,
    But just a trifle cold;
The rose, I think, is rather loud
    And, then, its fashion old.
The violet, it is very well,
    But not a flower I'd choose,
Nor yet the Canterbury bell—
    I never cared for blues."
And so it criticized each flower,
    This supercilious seed,
Until it woke one summer hour—
    And found itself a weed.

It is pathetically easy to find fault. One preacher advertised an open forum in his church in which he offered anyone a chance to air his objections to Christianity. Twelve hundred people filled the auditorium. The first objector said, "Church members are no better than other people." "The ministers are no good," shouted another. And so the objections were mentioned one after another, and the pastor wrote them down on paper: "Hypocrites in the church"; "The church is a rich man's club"; "Christians don't read the Bible anymore"— twenty-seven objections were offered. When they were through, the pastor read off the whole list, then tossed it aside and said, "Folks, you have objected to pastors, to church members, to the Bible, and to other things, but you have not said one word against Jesus." And in simple words he preached to them Christ as the faultless one. When he invited them to trust in him, forty-nine responded.

Yes, it is easy to find fault, to put down or speak down every Christian and every Christian institution, except the one who began it all, Jesus. No one is asking anyone to look up to preachers, Sunday School teachers, officers, or missionaries. Look up to the author and finisher of our faith, and the fault finding will stop. Stop putting each other down, brothers and sister. As someone rightly observed, "There is so much good in the worst of us, and so much bad in the best of us, it never behooves any of us, to talk about the rest of us."

The Confusion (4:11b-c)

He who speaks evil of a brother and judges his brother, speaks evil of the law and judges the law. But if you judge the law, you are not a doer of the law but a judge.

James has said, "Don't be a downer." Now in 11b, he ratchets the problem up a notch: Do not judge each other. This word "judge," *krinō*, means, "to pronounce condemnation on someone." This differs only slightly from speaking evil of a bother. It differs only in scope because when we speak evil of a brother we are judging him. Judging is wider in scope because to judge a brother no words need pass from my lips. In fact, probably most of the judgment between Christians is done in the heart. We come to some sort of mental assessment of a situation involving a person and then pass judgment in our hearts. Whether we verbalize our verdict of guilt does not alter the fact that judgment has taken place.

What are the biblical reasons we should not judge our brother? Here are some of the passages that warn us about this unhappy practice:

1. **A servant is only responsible to his master (Rom 14:4).** If you were working for a doctor at a hospital and you saw another employee loafing on the job, what would you do about it? Probably nothing. That person does not work for you, so he is not your responsibility. Even if you went

to your employer to complain, you would probably be told to mind your own business. The point is that we are fellow servants of Christ. He is our Lord and Master—our employer. Each of us is responsible to him, not each other. No other Christian is working for me. Therefore, he does not have to answer to me; he is not my responsibility. I have no right to judge him, for I have no authority over him.

2. **We probably do similar things (Rom 2:1-3).** Have you ever passed judgment on a brother and then been humbled by the Lord for making the same mistake? Often we are especially sensitive to certain weaknesses in others because we have the same weaknesses within ourselves. Sensitivity conceals guilt. We feel better when we can point a finger at those who are failing in the same areas in which we are weak.

I remember a particular professor I built up a dislike for in seminary. He had never hurt me in any way. In fact, he had gone out of his way to help me a couple of times. By the end of my third year I realized I had a real problem in my attitude toward him. It didn't make any sense whatsoever. So I took a deep, painful look inside myself and I realized the very things that caused me to dislike him were the negative traits in myself I disliked so much.

That is also when I realized that these negative attitudes in me would grow stronger and stronger as long as I dwelt on them. "As a man thinks in his heart, so is he" (Prov 23:7). Dwelling on the negative traits of others causes us to become just like them. We become what we think about. The very things we judge others for we will do, if not in action, then in thought. Or similar things. We may not commit physical adultery, but maybe we spend a lot of time with pornography. We may not steal money from our employer, but maybe we steal time. We may not kill people with guns, but maybe with stab them to death with our tongues.

3. **We may do worse things (Matt 7:3-5).** Jesus tells us not to talk about the splinter in our brother's eye while there is a log in our own. That is like a blind man walking around telling the world that people who wear glasses are inferior. If we are wrestling with problems more serious than the ones we judge our brother for, what right have we to judge at all? In fact, when you are around someone who is openly judgmental, it is a surefire symptom of his own guilt. Judgment conceals guilt. His conscience is hammering him hard for something. To compensate, he spears that guilt onto those around him.

4. **We shall be judged as we judge others (Matt 7:3-5; James 2:12-13).** Judgment will be harsh for those who judge harshly. That's a sobering thought, referring to the Judgment Seat of Christ. Perhaps I take my brother to court because he cusses a lot and then tries to teach high school students. I decide in my mind he is unfit as a teacher of young people and condemn him for so doing. Then at the JSC God will take that same harsh judgment I applied to my brother on earth, and will apply it to me in heaven. Many rewards will be washed away. He will have judgment without mercy on the person who has shown no mercy. Want to cancel out half your treasures in heaven? Judge your brother harshly. "With the measure you use, it will be measured back to you."

5. **We usually do not have all the facts (Prov 18:13, 17; 1 Sam 16:7).** You see, to judge accurately, we must know what is in the heart of a man. There is only one person who knows all about a person, all about his motives and circumstances. Sometimes we misinterpret a look or a glance from someone. We imagine she does not like us or that he is indifferent and cold. But we do not know

what is going on in anyone's mind or life at that moment. I remember a situation back in my seminary days. Every year we had Missionary Emphasis Week. Notoriously, the missionaries were weak in the pulpit, often just because of language shock—they had not been using English as their primary language for a long time. After one missionary had given a particularly bad message, a group of students was gathered in the foyer of the chapel cutting him down, wondering aloud why this missionary even bothered to take the podium when he was so ill prepared.

One of the best preachers in the senior class, in fact the fellow who won the preaching award that year, was in the center of this band of brow-beaters. A first-year man happened by and heard the discussion. When it was over, he went up to the senior ringleader and said, "Bill, you don't understand." "What do you mean, I don't understand? I understand that was a very slothful handling of God's Word," replied the senior indignantly. "Yes Bill, but you don't have all the facts. You see, just two hours before he gave that message, a long distance call from Nigeria informed him that his youngest son had just been killed. And just three months ago he and his wife received the news that she had terminal cancer. It was only God's grace and power that enabled this man to minister to us at all. He was trying to minister to us, when we probably should have been ministering to him. You didn't have all the facts, Bill."

We rarely do. That is the point of the rest of 4:11-12. Here James clarifies what he sees as the main problem with judging each other.

The Clarification (4:12)

There is one Lawgiver, who is able to save and to destroy. Who are you to judge another?

When I speak evil of a brother and condemn him, then I speak evil of the law and condemn it. And if I condemn or judge the law, then I have removed myself from under the law and have set myself above it as a judge. In fact, I have broken the law. I am no longer a doer of the law. For example, I remember a speed limit sign near where I used to live. It was at a "T intersection" leading away from a major six-lane highway. This particular road led to the entrance of the golf course where I was a member, so I took it as often as I played golf. The road was a mile long in a straight line away from the highway. The posted speed limit was twenty. It drove me nuts. I decided whoever made that law was also nuts. It was pretty much impossible for me to maintain twenty or less for a mile along that road.

What is going on here? I spoke evil of the law. More than that, I spoke evil of the lawmakers. In so doing, I lifted myself above them. I did not have the authority to do that. Because I deemed the law to be unjust, I felt justified in not obeying it. James says this is what is going on when we judge our brothers. The royal law of love is broken when we speak evil of and judge our brother. When we break the law of love, we are saying that it is not a good and necessary law. When we say that, we are saying that we know more than the lawmaker.

Now to say a lawmaker does not know what he is doing when he sets a speed limit law is one thing, but to say God does not know what He is doing is quite another. To judge the law, one must have authority over the law. He must be above the law. To speak evil of the law and to judge it no good is to say the law should be changed, but the only one who can change the law is a lawmaker. Again, to put myself on a level with the makers of human laws in one thing, but to put myself on the level with the maker of the laws of the Bible is an altogether different step.

This is exactly what 4:12 tells us. There is only one lawgiver who is able to save and destroy. In light of the context, I would have to say this refers to saving and destroying our works at the JSC. (See the discussion on James 2:14.) Of course, it is obvious the lawgiver is God. Only He has all the facts. Only He knows all the circumstances.

Only He knows what is in the heart of man. Only He is qualified to judge.

Men simply are not qualified to judge men. When people behave as we think they should, we judge them righteous, spiritual people. That may be a false judgment because they could have all the right words and works, but a selfish motive behind their good behavior. God, who knows all, will judge those works as unrighteous because they were not done in selfless love. On the other hand, a person may behave in a way that seems quite unbecoming to a Christian in our judgment, but God could exalt him highly for being faithful to all God asked of him. That is, he was faithful to all the light he had been given. Only God has all the facts.

We conclude, then, that judging a Christian brother is equivalent to saying, "I am God." It is another way of playing God, the most dangerous game Christians like to play as we saw in 4:6-10. These verses, 4:11-12, are closely connected to 4:6-10. How do I know if a man or woman is overcome with spiritual pride? How do I know if he is playing God? By his judgmental attitude toward other Christians, by his continual "put-downs" of other believers—always trying to lower our estimation of other people. One does not do that outwardly unless inwardly he has put himself on the level of God himself, usually unconsciously. Nothing is more detrimental to a healthy church atmosphere of love and freedom than Christians playing God.

By the same token, nothing is more detrimental to a healthy home atmosphere than one or both partners trying to play God, always putting each other down. Those judgmental attitudes are practically impossible to disguise, even if they are not verbally expressed. The poisonous vibrations can be felt and the negative thought waves can cripple. It is sad to say, this variation of PG is not limited to individuals. This same passage could easily be applied to "Group Judging." If I belong to a certain denomination, then my group is the in-group. If you give me half a chance, I will let you know with great detail what is wrong with all of the other groups. Soon my spiritual pride is barking like a dog and howling at the moon like a wolf.

The end of verse 12 twists a knife that has already sliced deeply into my heart. Just a little twist brings wrenching pain. The Greek word order puts a special emphasis on the word "you." It seems to be saying, "You then; who are you who judges another? "You, of all people. Just who do you think you are?"

I'd like to note that some Christians are bedecked in false badges of humility. The humble believer is not the fellow who is always putting himself down and telling you how the Lord did it all. He may be sincere or he may be camouflaging his true attitude of pride, especially if he is judgmental of other Christians.

What then is the badge of humility? Not too hard to figure out, is it? If putting other Christians down either mentally or verbally is a tip-off to pride, then building other Christians up either mentally or verbally is a sign of humility. I think we can turn 4:11-12 around. James says a sure-fire indication that someone is playing God is he is always judging other Christians. It follows that a sure-fire sign of a truly humble person is never putting other Christians down, either as groups or individuals. That is the badge of humility. A humble person doesn't put other people down. He knows his place. He knows only God has all the facts, so he defers judgment to him. In the final analysis, humility is not shown by what I say about myself as much as it is by what I say about others.

Ephesians 4:29 sums it up nicely: "Let no corrupt word proceed out of your mouth, but what is good for necessary edification, that it may impart grace to the hearers." That word "corrupt" actually means "that which tears down or destroys." Paul says that cutting, derogatory criticism and cynicism should never come out of the mouth of a Christian. Instead, only that which builds up and edifies a brother should be spoken. You might ask, "But what if he really deserves the ill treatment he is getting?" No matter—the words of edification minister grace to him. That is just the point, you see. He may not deserve the kind words, but we are treating him as Christ has treated us. It is our responsibility to hold each other up in love. We receive enough derogatory defamation from the world without giving it to each other.

A good example of what I am talking is a situation that happened years ago with the former Houston Oilers (now the Tennessee Titans). Houston was on a slide. In the middle of the season Sid Gillman took over. Their record at the time was 1-5. By the end of the season the record was 6-6. How did he turn the team around so drastically that he was up for NFL Coach of the Year? His answer: "We do not allow any negative or petty spirit on our team. None whatsoever. We build each other up; we love each other; we praise one another's abilities. We encourage one another in the game of football."

Gillman went on to say he spent his time with his men not pointing out all their flaws, but building into their minds, "You can play the game. You can win this game." As a result, they started wining. As you may know, when Gillman first assumed the helm, there was one player with whom there was immediate conflict. Big John Matuzak. He was the Number One Draft Choice in the whole NFL. Why the conflict? Matuzak was negative.

Matuzak wore red sweat pants to practice while everyone else wore grey.

So Coach Gillman said, "John, around here we wear grey."

"But, Coach, these are double knit."

"I don't care if they are triple knit, we wear grey."

Later on, the team was at a house together but Matuzak wanted to be alone in his own apartment. He said he rested better alone. Gillman said, "You'll rest with the team because we are going to be together." After another run-in, Gillman said there was nothing else to do but let Matuzak go. As soon as he was traded, the Oilers started winning. Not surprisingly, the team Matuzak went to began losing. Interesting, isn't it, how a petty and critical spirit from one person can corrupt and ruin a scene?

Do you allow that kind of spirit in your home, in your office, in your church? Sad that we have to turn to an NFL coach to find an example of what the Bible is trying to promote. I remember a time when someone on my staff was affecting our performance because of his critical attitude. I have supervised lots of employees through the years, but rarely fired anyone. I needed some wisdom. So I went to a church member who was a "turn-around" specialist. He had taken

Continental Airlines (now United) out of bankruptcy while a business consultant with Bain Consulting, the Boston based consulting company where Mitt Romney made his fortune. The Continental people were so impressed with him they tossed a bunch of stock options his way to lure him to Houston, the hub for Continental. If I remember right, he told me he fired 69 of the 75 managers at Continental during his first two weeks. "You can't save the ship with the people who are taking her down," he told me. I couldn't imagine firing that many people. But he was right. He took Continental's stock from six to sixty on the New York Stock Exchange in one year, the highest appreciation of any stock on the exchange that particular year.

So I asked for his wisdom in our situation. He said, "You can never solve a problem soon enough." What he was telling me was that if I let the problem fester, things would only get worse. Cut your losses. We did. And our organization "turned around" from that point. Amazing how a negative spirit from just one person can affect an entire organization.

What, then, are the colors of a humble person? He never puts down another Christian in a condemnatory way. Rather, he always accentuates the good and builds on the positive. That is the Badge of Humility.

Have you ever noticed that only the smaller birds sing? We have never heard a note from an eagle in all our lives, or from the turkey, or from the ostrich. But we have all heard the beautiful tones of the canary, the wren, and the lark. We can recognize the person who is a big bird in his own eyes because he crows, clucks, squawks, screeches, and gobbles. But the Christian who is a little bird in his own eyes can be recognized by the beautiful music he makes when he opens his mouth. When you open your mouth, my friend, what kind of sounds do you make?

Perhaps the best person at building others up without insincere flattery was one of my church members named Peggy Lesch. It didn't seem to matter what the situation was or the person in question, Peggy could find something positive to bring out. After awhile I began to wonder if this was real, but as the years went by and she never changed, I realized it was very genuine and a gift to the church body greatly to be prized. If you needed a pick-me-up, just rub shoulders with Peggy.

I remember one of my lowest moments as a pastor, when I fell on my motorcycle after thirteen years of accident-free riding. I broke twenty-six bones and had multiple surgeries. I had to sleep wedged in a recliner so as not to impede the setting of the bones by rolling at night. I had two casts, an external fixator, and a urinary catheter (fun, fun). Most of the church was not sympathetic. In fact, some were quite mad at their for pastor riding around on a motorcycle—the very idea of it!

There I was, laid up, feeling sorry for myself even though I knew the suffering was self-induced, and Peggy walked in with a friend.

"Oh, Dave Anderson, you just get right up and get back on that bike. Just get right up and get on that bike." Through my drug-induced stupor I wasn't sure I was hearing them right. But yes, there she stood, urging me on to do something she knew I enjoyed. "My, my," I thought, "Where do people like this come from?"

Later on I got to know Peggy's brother. He had visited our church a few times over the years and was always at the back after the service to say an encouraging word about the sermon. He lived in Midland, though, so I didn't really get to know him until I began teaching classes out there on behalf of our school. He was George Bush's campaign manager, his Secretary of Commerce, and one of the President's best friends in life. His name is Don Evans. He began coming to a Bible study I teach at the Petroleum Club in Midland, and we had dinner together several times with my brother-in-law, Charlie Younger. Despite his business success, political success, and other accolades too numerous to mention, Don is a completely humble person and, I am told, possibly the most respected businessman in Midland. But, like his sister, Don is something else: he is an encourager.

Don has had a number of difficult things occur in his life despite his success, but in all the times I have been with him, I have never heard a discouraging or disparaging word from him After my mother died this past December I received a note from him. It was handwritten and on his personal stationery. Among the things he said was this: "I am sorry for the loss of your mother. She must have been a great woman to have produced such a wonderful son and a great friend." I thought, "As busy as he is, where does he find the time to sit down a write something so encouraging to a person he barely knows? What a guy."

The disciples James and John were known as the "sons of thunder"; Don and Peggy could be called the "brother and sister of encouragement."

"THE MATERIAL MAN"

James 4:13-5:6

I have never been afraid of my wife until recently. We have been married forty-five years. She has always been a calm, steady, even phlegmatic soul who measures both her words and her actions with great forethought—until the last year. She came to me about a year ago and said the sky was falling and she had come to tell the king. I appreciated the compliment, but asked, "What's up?" She spouted off all these statistics about the world population reaching seven billion, the food shortages, the water shortages, the demise of the dollar—and all the other things she had heard on Christian radio.

"I want to buy gold . . . some silver . . . and some freeze-dried food. And I wished we hadn't filled in our swimming pool—good source of water." I said, "Well, my dad left me ten krugerrands. You can just have those and do whatever you wish." Next thing I know she has sold some of the coins for silver. Then she marches in and says she will not have to buy any freeze-dried food because she is becoming a consultant for a company that sells it. All of a sudden she has ten consultants under her. Then it happens. Boxes of freeze-dried food descend on the house. She has so much she is giving it away to people who can't afford it.

"Where will we keep all this, Betty?" I ask. "Under the bed." That's right, I sleep on about thirty five-gallon drums of food. One night I am lying there on our cache and I reflect, "You know, sweetheart, if people really get hungry, they are going to come for this food." Next

195

thing I know she wants a handgun for Christmas. Now she is a pistol-packing-mamma. And hers has a laser. I'm still OK. She needs to get a permit to carry a concealed handgun, so she heads down to Gander Mountain for lessons. I have to watch this. They start with virtual targets—ten, I believe. Betty never misses. Then they move to real targets, but not people. She never misses. Never shot a gun in her life, but never misses. That's when I got scared. She never misses. I come home late one night and see a red dot on my chest: "Don't shoot, don't shoot—it is just me." It wouldn't bother me if she missed now and then, but no, Betty never misses.

I know a lot of you gals out there are saying, "You go, girlfriend." And maybe you are right. Maybe getting a year's supply of food and some coins to barter with is a wise thing. There is some wisdom in being prepared for the future. On a grander scale, though, I wonder how much of our working lives we worry about whether we will have enough to retire. We are fortunate to live in a country and in an age where it is possible for a family to plan ahead for their retirement and not have to depend on anyone in their later years. But what did they do in biblical times? The NT talks about a retirement program. It's called children (1 Tim 5:4 and 8). I've always told my kids that my life goal is to live just long enough to be a burden to them. I'm almost there.

Solomon told us to study the ants and learn from them (Prov 6:6-7). They worked hard while they could to store up for a time when they could not work. On the other hand, Jesus told a parable about a man consumed with storing up goods to the neglect of the good he could do with his money today. The angel of death shows up without an appointment, saying, "You fool."

The French painter Bernaux tried to capture this parable on canvas. He painted a man who had his hands folded at his desk, brow furrowed. He had little bags of money on the shelf behind him. One bag of money sat alone, tied with a little sting. You could almost read his mind that he is saving it for something. He is looking out the window and there is a bumper crop. You can see the lush harvest materializing. His expression seems to ask, "What shall I do?" We know from the parable what his plan is. He accounted for everything but death. Every factor was included in his plans except for God. He went to work building bigger barns. He expands his operation. He calculates. He pulls out his iPad and works it all out. However, he forgets the possibility of death. And God comes and says to him, "You fool, this night your life will be required of you."

Bernaux read the last part of this passage in Luke 12 and flipped the canvas over to paint the other side. There he pictured a man at a desk. Same man, same desk, same crops. But this time he added something that was not there before: a thin layer of dust lay on the desk. And the angel of death is standing before the man at the desk with his lips parted, as though to say, "You fool."

The goal of the farmer was self-sufficiency. He doesn't seem too far off from the ants Solomon lauded. There must be a balance between the advice of Solomon and the advice of Jesus, between the ant and the farmer. What is it? Maybe James 4:13-5:6 can help.

James has been talking about the Cure for Conflict in our lives. He says the Cause for Conflict is worldliness (4:1-5), which is the offspring of the lusts that war in our flesh. Behind a lot of this worldliness is our pride. God resists the proud, but gives grace to the humble. We need more grace after becoming believers (freed from the penalty of sin) in order to overcome the lusts of our Sin Nature (freed from the power of sin). But this grace God only gives to the humble. Thus, the Cure for Conflict is humility. James tackles humility from three sides: Humility before God (4:6-10); Humility before Men (4:11-12); and Humility before the World (4:13-5:6). Only God knows our hearts, that is, whether we are humble before him. Before men and before the world there are two manifestations of our pride. In the church, our pride shows up when we judge our brothers and sisters by putting them down. Out in the world, there is another visible way to measure pride.

JAMES

"TRIUMPH THROUGH TRIALS"

Salutation (1:1)

Introduction (1:2-18)—The Value of Trials

Theme (1:19-20)—Qualities Needed

Body (1:21-5:6)—Qualities Developed

    I.   *In Regard to Hearing (1:21-2:26)*

   II. *In Regard to Speaking (3:1-18)*

  III. *In Regard to Fighting (4:1-5:6)*

       A. Cause of Conflict—Pride (4:1-6a)

       B. Cure for Conflict—Humility (4:6b-5:6)

          1. Humility before God (4:6b-10)

          2. Humility before Men (4:11-12)

          1. Humility before the World (4:13-5:6)

We have barometers to measure air pressure, thermometers to measure temperature, and speedometers to measure velocity. Is there anything to measure our pride before the world? A pridometer would be nice. Just as a thermometer can help us determine how sick we are, a pridometer could help us find out how proud we are. It wouldn't be the only test, but a helpful indicator to reveal our spiritual condition. So here it comes. This is James' big idea in this passage:

If pride is a declaration of independence from God, then the degree of my self-sufficiency is proportionate to my pride.

William Henley put the Pridometer to poetry in his inveterate "Invictus":

Out of the night that covers me,
Black as the Pit from pole to pole,
I thank whatever gods may be
For my unconquerable soul.

In the fell clutch of circumstance
I have not winced nor cried aloud.
Under the bludgeoning of chance
My head is bloody, but unbowed.
Beyond this place of wrath and tears
Looms but the Horror of the shade,
And yet the menace of the years
Finds and shall find me unafraid
It matters not how strait the gate,
How charged with punishments the scroll,
I am the master of my fate:
I am the captain of my soul.[23]

There you have it: self-sufficiency in a capsule. Our self-sufficiency is an accurate indicator of our pride.

True to form, James the Jabber knocks me out again in the third round with this passage, leaving me battered, bruised, and barely able to get up. Let's sit ringside and listen in, blow by blow. The bell rings in 4:13 and the first round begins. We are going to confront self-sufficiency in 4:13, correct self-sufficiency in verses 14-17, and condemn self-sufficiency in 5:1-6.

Confronting Self-Sufficiency (4:13)

Come now, you who say, "Today or tomorrow we will go to such and such a city, spend a year there, buy and sell, and make a profit."

We find a variation of PG being played in verse 13. Here the player imagines himself as final authority over his life and then he lives like it. If he thinks about God at all, he has Him locked in a little box and only lets Him out on Sunday. The object of his game is self-sufficiency. He is trying to make a profit so he can do what the people in chapter five have done. He wants to enter the class of the *nouveaux*

---

[23] William Ernest Henley, http://www.poemhunter.com/poem/invictus/.

riche addressed in James 5:1 who have heaped up treasures for the last days. We can assume 4:13-17 is connected to 5:1-6, since they begin with exactly the same words: "Come now."

We know the man in verse 13 wants to make a lot of money because he has oriented his entire life around his business. His goal is to make it on his own like Horatio Alger—the pull yourself up by your own bootstraps approach. Perhaps you will say, "Aren't you being a little harsh? All he wants is to be is a successful businessman. What do you think he should be, a failure?" A fair question. The answer is no, I don't think he should be a failure. But if he follows his own formula for success, he will be a failure, at least before God. Look at his rules for self-sufficiency:

1. **Choose my own time and schedule.** "Come now, you who say, 'Today or tomorrow.'" He is choosing his own schedule.

2. **Select my own location.** Today or tomorrow I will go to such and such a city. Got it? Selfishly plan my own life so I will have my own schedule and my own location.

3. **Limit my stay as it pleases me.** I will spend a year at such and such a place. Interesting, isn't it? I am not committing myself for the day, but for a year in advance. What am I saying to God? "Don't call me. I'll call you. I've got my year all laid out." And so I do.

4. **Arrange my activities for my benefit and pleasure.** I am going to spend a year there and engage in business as though to say, "This is the business I want." After all, it is all about me!

5. **Predict my profit and boast in it.** "I will buy and sell and get gain." Verse 16 says all such boasting is evil.

Do you see what this man has done? He has oriented his whole life around his business—his schedule, his location, his work are all of his own predetermination. Each of these is linked together to add up to his desired profit. There is no doubt about what is number one in his life. He has not taken God into account at all for either his life's work or where he will work or how long he should work. As usual, Satan has used the deceitfulness of riches to pervert this man's priorities.

A businessman came and said his spiritual life was on the rocks.

"How could I get closer to God?"
"Well, are you in the Scriptures at all?"
"Don't have time."
"Are you spending any time with your wife and kids?"
"Don't have time for that either."
"Are you serving anywhere?"
"Don't have time."

Turns out he was holding down two jobs to maintain the standard of living he wanted for his family and so that his wife could quit work someday. Wow! I am not condemning him. I just wonder what has happened in our affluent society that compels a family to put both husband and wife into the market place—and two jobs for the husband to boot—all to maintain a certain standard of living?

What are the priorities of the Material Man? They're pretty clear from the passage: Business > Pleasure > Family > God > Ministry. The Bible sets up our priorities differently. They could be looked at like a pie with God at the center. Everything revolves around him: family, business, pleasure, and ministry—all slices of pie revolving around God's will in each area. That is probably the best way to look at it. You could also make a case for: God > Family > Ministry > Business > Pleasure. Of course, there can be a connection between my business and my ministry, and there certainly is a connection between my business and my family (I need to provide for my family). However, when there is a conflict between God and family, God comes first for a disciple (Luke 14:26). When there is a conflict between family and ministry, family comes first (meaning I don't sacrifice my family for my ministry any more than I should sacrifice my family for my business). When there is a conflict between

ministry and business, Christ says ministry comes first (Matt 6:33—
Seek first the kingdom of God . . . and God will give you the material
things you need for life). Finally, when there is a conflict between
business and pleasure, business comes first (2 Thess 3:10), unless
you are a workaholic.

Why are we so busy "seeking all these (material) things first"? We
dress up in our material things to project what we think of ourselves.
All too often we use these material things to make ourselves look
better than others. This is pride on display for the entire world to
see.

Our Sin Nature is so twisted we can even get proud of our humility.
I had this passage in mind when I chose my current home to live in
as a pastor, a thirty-year-old foreclosure. I was very proud of living so
humbly. In fact, my daughter got caught up in it and liked to brag that
we lived in Humblism, TX. Twenty-one years later the house has so
many problems we are not sure we could sell it.

Then there is my car. I have been very proud of escaping the
clutches of the world by driving a fifteen-year-old car, a Buick no less.
One of my friends from college who goes to our church told me he
never thought he would see me driving a Buick. That just made me
more proud. But God has a sense of humor. Pretty much whatever
I get proud of He turns into a way to humble me. I was driving to
a church five hundred miles away in my old Buick, thinking how
spiritual they would think I am when I pulled into the church parking
lot in my old car.

Well, as I got on I-10 going from Houston to San Antonio, the
speed limit kicked up to seventy. I put it on cruise control and just
felt very smug as the newer cars whizzed by me. On the other side
of San Antonio, the speed limit went up to seventy-five. Wow, I
thought, let's set the cruise up five mph higher now. Of course, the
traffic continued to whiz by. But when I got to Junction, TX, the
speed limit went to eighty. Eighty—I'd never had the cruise control
set at eighty before. So here we go. I went about ten miles at eighty
and the car began slowing down. The power steering locked. The
brakes wouldn't work. I muscled it to the side of the road and sat in

103 degree heat while I waited three and a half hours for a wrecker to haul my beloved Buick all the way back to Houston. Of course, I had to laugh.

Some days I think God must wake the angels up in the morning and say, "What's up? Any of you guys bored? Let's go over and see what Anderson is up to today. It should be good for a couple of laughs."

By the way, we thought we were going to have to have a funeral service for my Buick because the engine had frozen, but it is being born again as we speak. Yes, there will be a new engine under the hood. The car had heard so many Christian tapes and CDs that it converted. I intend to drive it to heaven. If you see someone up there driving along the streets of gold in an old 1997 Buick, be sure to wave.

Pride has many disguises. Materialism is one of them. Ding, ding—that is the end of round one. Round two begins in verse 14. I hope we haven't had any early knockouts. In round one we got the confrontation. Now we get the counsel—how to correct this problem of self-sufficiency in 4:14-17. In verses 14-15 James explains the right attitude; then in verse 16 we see the wrong attitude. We will come back to verse 17 at the end.

Correcting Self-Sufficiency (4:14-17)

The Right Attitude (14-15)

> Whereas you do not know what *will happen* tomorrow. For what *is* your life? It is even a vapor that appears for a little time and then vanishes away. Instead you *ought* to say, "If the Lord wills, we shall live and do this or that."

The reason for the rebuke in verse 13 is because we have no knowledge of tomorrow. We don't know what our life will be like tomorrow. Most of us can look back a year and remember people who are no longer here because during the past twelve months they died unexpectedly—car wrecks, pancreatic cancer, heart attacks, and so on. A contemporary of mine was a football star in college and continued his workouts right into his 60's. He was still at his weight as a running back forty-some years prior. He weighed 230 lbs. A month later he weighed 200. A month later he weighed 170 and died of esophageal cancer. He didn't even know he had cancer until he started losing weight. Two months and it was over. We can all think of people who have died in the last year. How foolish to fly down the freeway of life and say, "I'll call my own shots. If I need you, God, I'll give you a call. I'm glad you are there, but I so enjoy this feeling of independence and self-sufficiency." Friend, you may need Him faster than you realize. Rather than ever-popular rugged individualism, here is the right attitude:

1. **"If he wills . . ."** James says since you don't know what tomorrow might bring, you had better remember the words of the psalmist from the Living Bible: "You speak, Lord, and man is turned back to dust. A thousand years are as yesterday to you. They are like a single hour. We glide along the tide of time as swiftly as a racing river. Then we vanish as quickly as a dream. We are like grass that is green in the morning but mowed down and withered before the evening shadows fall." Humility acknowledges the sovereignty of God over our lives. This includes our business lives.

2. **We don't know if tomorrow will come.** We simply do not know how long our lives will last. Every year names are deleted from church rolls because of death. Many, if not most, of these deaths were unexpected. Nonetheless, the death is entered into the record, "Deceased," and a date is placed by that name. You may not celebrate another Christmas. This year may be the last. You say, "But I am only twenty-three." Well, it may be your last birthday. My first funeral in my first pastorate was an eighteen year old killed in a car wreck. My second was a three year old accidentally shot. My third was three seventeen year olds

killed in a head-on collision. We just do not know what tomorrow may bring. The point is that God holds the keys to life and death. For us to assume sovereign control of our future by predicting our business successes or plans is the height of folly, because we have no knowledge of the future as far as our individual lives on earth are concerned.

3. **Life is a vapor—Psalm 90.** Even if we live a normal life span of around eighty years, our life is little more than a vapor, says James. Imagine we are sitting in a blizzard. It's thirty below zero. We all have our parkas and hats and long handles on when suddenly I go, "Poof." A small vapor would escape from my mouth and hang in that heavy, cold air. Then it would vanish. That's life. A vapor. A poof. Here for moment in the timelessness of eternity and then gone.

4. **Planning? Yes, but punctuated with, "If the Lord wills."** The skeptic will say, "But shouldn't we plan for the future? It is foolish not to plan." Right on. The Scriptures have much to say about not being slothful in business. A student who never thinks about tomorrow or plans ahead for a test is a foolish student. A father who never thinks about the financial outlay of his home is a foolish father. A mother who does not look over the affairs of her children with foresight is a foolish mother. God condones wise planning, but He wants us to take His desires into account in our planning. All of our plans should be filled with the parenthetical statement, "You may interrupt. You may step in. I welcome you to come in and change the whole scene, and I'll accept anything from your hand." What if verse 15 said, "If the Lord will, and if we live, we'll do this or that." That is the right attitude and in verse 16 James clarifies a symptom of the wrong attitude.

The Wrong Attitude (16)

But now you boast in your arrogance. All such boasting is evil.

You see, God is not against us being successful in business. God is not against us making a profit. I was once in the home of a man who was turned off by churches. Why? Because, according to him, churches thought it was a sin for him to make money. I hope I haven't given you that impression. God wants us to have material success, but not apart from Him, not with a goal of self-sufficiency. In Deuteronomy 8:11-20 God says He is the one who gives us power to make money, and if we forget it, watch out. The sin in verse 16 is boasting about what one is going to do or has already done. The evil is not success in business. The evil is bragging about how we will do this or how we did that.

The word "boast," *kauchasthe*, means "to bring glory to yourself." The word "arrogance," *tais alazoneiais* (plural), means "the things you have accomplished in this life" (remember "the pride of life" from 1 Jn 2:16). Boasting in our accomplishments brings glory to us instead of God and completely ignores His sovereignty and grace in our lives.

Ding, ding—end of round two. Round three is the knock-out punch. Here James turns into a prophet. It is one of the strongest passages in the NT. So far, in round one we saw self-sufficiency confronted; in round two self-sufficiency was corrected; and in round three self-sufficiency is condemned.

Condemning Self-Sufficiency (5:1-6)

Come now, *you* rich, weep and howl for your miseries that are coming upon *you!* Your riches are corrupted, and your garments are moth-eaten. Your gold and silver are corroded, and their corrosion will be a witness against you and will eat your flesh like fire. You have heaped up treasure in the last days. Indeed the wages of the laborers who mowed your fields, which you kept back by fraud, cry out; and the cries

of the reapers have reached the ears of the Lord of Sabaoth. You have lived on the earth in pleasure and luxury; you have fattened your hearts as in a day of slaughter. You have condemned, you have murdered the just; he does not resist you.

Like an OT prophet James cries out to rich men, "Weep and howl because of the trouble about to come upon you." James becomes a prophet in the mode of Zechariah 14:12-15. "Howl," is reminiscent of Joel 1:5, 13; Isaiah 13:6; and Jeremiah 4:8. It is an "end times" prophecy (notice the mention of the "latter days" here). At the end of the Tribulation Period (Zech 14:14) the wealth of the nations surrounding Israel will be gathered together and rendered useless. Silver and gold do not have "corrosion," but radioactive fallout could be the "poison" (*ios*) that renders them useless.

James addresses himself here to rich non-Christians. I think he is pointing to the Tribulation when the rich unbelievers are left on the earth after the Rapture. Christians are to be taken up in the clouds (1 Thess 4:17). There will have to be some obvious explanation for their disappearance. A nuclear holocaust would provide all the necessary conditions. America is not referred to in the Scriptures directly. Most of the professing Christians in the world are in Asia and Africa. However, most of the rich Christians in the world are in America. If the Rapture were to occur during a nuclear holocaust, not only would the American Christians be gone, the flesh of unbelievers left behind would be eaten by nuclear fallout. Their gold and silver coins would do them little good in that day.

I am not being dogmatic here by any means. Nor am I being sensational. It is just a possibility. Whatever is being described in James 5:1-6 is a time of judgment. The Lord of Hosts has heard the cry of the just men and deserving laborers who have been pillaged by the unethical business world. Enron executives, watch out. And lest my take here be deemed too far-fetched, just look at James 5:7-11, which follows. What are these verses about? The coming of the Lord. It is a prophetic utterance giving us a prophetic picture of the horrible holocaust hovering on the horizon of the unbelieving people who have trusted in uncertain riches.

What is James trying to tell us through all this? Certainly he is saying that self-sufficiency is not a legitimate goal for a Christian. In fact, it is an expression of pride. Is it wrong to enjoy material success? Obviously not. Is it wrong to have a five-year and a ten-year business plan? Obviously not. But we show our humility before the Lord when we punctuate our plans with, "If the Lord wills." We can all think of wealthy people who ran into trials from which their money could not deliver them. We need more grace in trials, but God only gives more grace to the humble.

This all sounds pretty negative, pretty much a downer passage. There is one bright verse here that is very positive. It is 4:17: **"Therefore, to him who knows to do good and does not do *it*, to him it is sin."** As we have already noted, the context here is what we do with our money. What we do with our money is an important way to stay humble. When we do good with our money, we are saying, "Lord, thank you for blessing me and my family. Instead of saving all of this for a tomorrow which may never come, I want to give some of it away today. I don't need this money to be self-sufficient. In fact, I never want to be **self**-sufficient. *You* are my sufficiency. *Your* grace is sufficient for my need. Giving this money today is my tangible way of proving what I am saying."

James is saying in verse 17, "Don't hoard for tomorrow what you can afford to give today." After all, since we don't know what the future holds, why should we hold onto the future?

I have a number of friends who are among the happiest Christians I know. One reason for their happiness is their victory over hoarding. These couples have earned more than they need over the years and have set up foundations into which they contribute most of their funds. They have chosen to give everything beyond what they consider their family needs to kingdom causes. Using this world's goods to further

His kingdom brings them great joy. It would embarrass them should I single any of them out. I will mention that they are not all wealthy. One is a middle-income banker, but he and his wife are sold out for what's coming in the next world. They set up their foundation to help keep their hearts pure in this world. They live modestly and give the rest to Christ's work.

One person who has made his giving very public is Rick Warren. The famous preacher became wealthy from the sales of his book *The Purpose Driven Life*. As the money rolled in, he and his wife decided to return his salary from twenty-five years of service to his church and to serve the church for free from then on. Out of the sales from his books, Warren and his wife are reverse tithing, that is, giving 90% and keeping 10%. This 90% was $13,000,000 in 2004. Some might say Warren already has his reward for his giving by making it so public. But he claims he did this because when he became both popular and wealthy, he knew the first thing the skeptical media would ask him was about using his religion to get wealthy. That's when he decided to give 90% away. He did not want his motives to be questioned.[24]

Like many popular and influential people, Warren has his naysayers. But it would be hard to impugn his giving. He is anything but a Material Man.

---

[24] Rick Warren, http://www.utsandiego.com/uniontrib/20060126/news_1c26warren.html.

"PATIENCE:
THE ART OF HOPING"

James 5:7-11

A French philosopher said, "Patience is the art of hoping." I like that. It is the best definition of biblical patience I know. When our pain threshold is reached, we need a hope to hang onto. The right hope can help us endure pain. What is your pain threshold? Mine is pretty low. When I get a cold, I mope around the house, and sometimes open the front door to yell at the neighbors, "I'm sick. Come feel my pain."

I learned something about my pain threshold when I had my first kidney stone. I'd heard about these things but never experienced it. When it happened, I knew exactly what it was. We live just a few blocks from the local hospital, so when it hit I didn't even wake Betty. I jumped in the car at about 1:30 AM and walked into the ER. As I ambled toward the check-in counter, the attending gal said, "You have a kidney stone, don't you?" I said, "I think so, but how do you know?" "Oh, all you men have the same expression on your faces when you have a kidney stone. Let's get some insurance information." I could hardly stand there and answer her questions and was glad to get to one of the pull-the-drapes-around cubicles.

Soon a nurse walked in and said, "The doctor will be here soon, but let's get an IV started." Fine with me. Well, she jabbed me in the right arm with no luck. She tried again, still no luck. She tried the left arm. Again, no luck and she said, "I'm having a bad night." I thought, "You're having a bad night?" Her jabs left bruises on my arms for several days. I have since learned about the wonderful world of phlebotomists, who specialize in drawing blood all day long. Now I always request a phlebotomist when the docs want some blood. People will sometimes ask me how I am doing after a recent illness. I usually reply, "Oh, much better after they gave me a phlebotomy."

Well, by this time the pain has raised from about a six to an eight. I ask about the doctor. She says, "Oh, I'm sure the doctor will be here any minute." An hour had gone by with no doctor. Meanwhile, the nurse says, "Are you Betty's husband?" Oh, my gosh. In my county I am known as "Betty's Husband" because she is better known than I am. But I really wasn't in the mood for it tonight. "Yes, I am Betty's husband." "Oh, I know Betty." "So do I," I am thinking, but WHERE IS THE DOCTOR? "Where is Betty? Does she know you're here?" "No, she's home asleep. I didn't want to bother her." "Well, I think it's good for men to have kidney stones." At this point the nurse is starting to feel like a second kidney stone. "And why is that?" "Because I have had babies and I have had kidney stones, and the kidney stones hurt worse. I think it helps men to empathize with a woman's pain in childbirth." Now I am getting delirious. Is this kidney stone going to be as big as a baby? WHERE IS THE DOCTOR?

Nurse Ratchet disappears. I am ready to fly over the cuckoo's nest. When you have a kidney stone, you don't want to lie down. You want to sit up or walk. It's now 3:30 AM. I have been in this ER for two hours without seeing a doctor. It would be an understatement to say I was losing my patience. In fact, I was close to losing my Christianity. So I started walking. Though she never got an IV started, she had me hooked up to the stand that holds the IV bags and other medical accoutrements. I didn't care; I took that with me. The cubicles were arranged in a rectangle with the nurses' station at one end. So, pushing the roller thingy and with the rear flaps open on my hospital "robe," I began to circle the nurses. Whenever

I got near them, I began to groan. I wanted them to know I had been there two hours without seeing a doctor with no relief in sight. I wanted them to know they were dealing with a very wimpy pastor who does not handle pain well. There was a gaggle of nurses. None paid me any attention. With each lap my groaning decibels increased.

Finally, Nurse Ratchet came out and said, "Mr. Anderson, we really can't help you. You need morphine, and only the doctor can give that to you." Ah, yes, the doctor. "This is an EMERGENCY ROOM, isn't it? You do have a doctor on duty, don't you? Please say YES." "Yes, we have a doctor, but she is on the second floor. You'll just have to wait for her to come down."

Okay, by now I am pretty well in the flesh. Why? Because I have lost hope. Just one broken promise after another and I am in pain. I went back to my little cubicle, put my head down, and just groaned quietly. The doctor finally came in at 5:30 AM, four hours after I had checked in. As far as I could tell, I was the only patient there. I had pretty well lost faith in the system. At least she got an IV in. My eyes were glazed over by the time the morphine hit. Nothing seemed to matter any more.

That is kind of where James' readers found themselves. Their trials had left them numb. They were in a spiritual stupor. They had lost hope in Christ's return. Every day was another broken promise. He said He would come back as He ascended into the clouds. He said when He came back He would set up His kingdom. But that was years ago. Persecution had set it. They were losing hope. Their faith was slipping—almost dead.

So James is trying to resuscitate their faith. Staying alive will take endurance (1:2-4) and patience (5:7-11). In the introduction, he taught how trials can produce endurance. Here in his conclusion he teaches them about patience and its connection to a vital hope. Remember the words of the French philosopher: "Patience is the art of hoping." As we enter the conclusion to this letter, we remember that James told us we needed three virtues to glean God's wisdom from our trials: Quick to Hear, Slow to Speak, and Slow to Wrath.

We finished his section on anger management in 5:6. As we start his conclusion we discover that a lack of patience was the cause of many of the problems James' readers faced.

Why did James spend all that time telling them to be slow to speak and slow to wrath? Precisely because they were quick to speak and quick to blow up. They had no patience. But if patience is the art of hoping, then we know they must have lost their hope. For where there is no patience, there is no hope; conversely, where there is no hope, there is no patience. That is exactly what we find when we look into James 5:7-11. These people were evidently having trouble with patience, primarily because they had lost their focus on the return of Christ. Their hope was in being delivered from their suffering when He returned. James wants to restore their patience and endurance by teaching them the art of hoping. In James 5:7-11, we will look at patience in three areas: Patience toward God (7-8); Patience toward Man (9); and Patience toward Life (10-11) in general.

Before we examine having patience with God, let's turn back to Matthew 24:48-49. "But if that evil servant says in his heart, 'My master is delaying his coming,' and begins to beat *his* fellow servants, and to eat and drink with the drunkards . . . ." It's an interesting parable about waiting for the Lord. The unfaithful servant does not believe Christ is coming soon, so he hits the servant nearest him and begins to live for self-gratification.

Look at the progression. First, he says the Lord delays His coming; second, he hits his fellow servant; third, he begins to live self-indulgently. It is exactly what James tries to correct in chapter four. Apparently, some sort of defection from the Lord's army has taken place among his readers. This he tries to correct in 4:7-10. Then there is the problem of smiting one's brother, even if it is verbally. This he tries to correct in 4:11-12. Finally there is self-indulgent living, which he attempts to correct in 4:13-17.

When the hope of the Lord's return is dimmed, these problems result. Although the imminent return of Christ is a new subject in the Book of James, he probably has had it in mind all along. With that in mind, let's look at 4:7-8, Patience toward God.

Patience Toward God (4:7-8)

> Therefore be patient, brethren, until the coming of the Lord. See *how* the farmer waits for the precious fruit of the earth, waiting patiently for it until it receives the early and latter rain. You also be patient. Establish your hearts, for the coming of the Lord is at hand.

How do you feel toward someone who continually breaks promises? I found myself dealing with these emotions some years ago when I was trying to get a dent in my car's fender fixed. The mechanic said it would take three days. When I checked back in three days it wasn't ready. A week later it still wasn't ready. When I finally went to pick it up, the supposedly fixed fender was a darker color than the rest of the car. I took it back and was told it would be ready in the morning. When I returned it hadn't even been moved from the spot I had parked it the day before. I was losing patience fast. Why? Because for one reason or another, this fellow kept breaking his promises. As I watched one promise after another break, I said in my heart, "I'll take my work somewhere else next time."

This is the disappointment these Christians were experiencing. Christ had made a promise to come back. Every new day was like a broken promise. Like the slothful servant, they were losing faith in His promises to return and with their loss of hope their patience was circling the drain, too.

"Patience" is made up of two Greek words that help us dissect its meaning. The first is *makro*, which means "far, distant, or long." The other is *thumos*. We get our word thermometer from it. It means "passion, heat, rage, or anger." Long-tempered is the thought. A colloquial term today is "short-tempered." Someone who is short-tempered has no patience. James says, "You need a long fuse." I am impressed by the word "patience" because of two things. First, it is the first word used in describing real love in 1 Corinthians 13:4. "Love is *makrothumei*." "Love is longsuffering," it says. This is the same word for patience. Love has a long fuse. Isn't it remarkable how much more patience you have with those you love than with those you don't?

Mothers work with their own children and another mother looking on says, "How can she possibly deal with that creature?" But the young mother of "that creature" pours all kinds of attention on her child because she loves her child.

Another thing about the word patience that impresses me is that we can't learn without it. The Greeks had a motto that said, "Learning is patience." Only the student who patiently pours time and attention into his work will really learn the subject. School today is often a lot of cramming. Cram it down the night before the test and make an A if you can. Then forget about it. The student who crams doesn't learn much. So it is with the lessons of life. We cannot learn the assignments God has for us without patience. We will never possess patience unless our hope in Christ's return is firmly fixed.

So James wants to reestablish their faith and hope in the Lord's return. He wants them to realize that Christ has not broken His promise. He uses the illustration of the farmer. The practical truth of the illustration seems obvious. A farmer must wait for rain before his crops will produce. Behind the simple imagery is a picture of Christ. The imagery of a harvest, a field, fruit, and a seed was so deeply imbedded in the thinking of the early church that NT believers would almost immediately see Christ as the farmer.

The field over which He is concerned is the world in which the gospel has been sown. The fruit is the result of that gospel. What then is meant by the expression "former and latter rain"? In Israel, the former rain comes around late October or early November, around seed-sowing time and is crucial in forming the right kind of environment for the seed to germinate. The latter rain comes in late April or early May and is crucial for a full harvest. Carrying the imagery through, what we have here are special periods of fruitfulness and blessing in the beginning and at the end of the gospel age. James seems to be saying that Jesus the farmer waits patiently for that special outpouring at the beginning of the age and at the end of the age.

Certainly we can see in Pentecost and in the Book of Acts the former rain, the special outpouring of the gospel at the beginning of the Church Age. It is quite possible that we are living today in the period of the latter rain. It is probably true that more people have heard the gospel in the last forty years (radio, TV, internet, printing press, thousands of missionaries) than in the prior nineteen hundred years. If that is anywhere near true, then this past generation has had a tremendous impact in sending out the gospel, possibly representing the latter rain. A tremendous harvest will come at the end of the gospel age. Behind the harvest is the patience of the farmer. He is patiently waiting for the harvest to come. It is the patience of the Lord Himself that becomes motivation for our own patience. James says, "Don't be impatient waiting for the Lord to come. After all, He is patiently waiting for you. The only reason He hasn't returned is that He is patiently waiting for the full harvest to come in."

We can hardly avoid the words of 2 Peter 3:9 at this point. He also was trying to explain why the promise of the second coming had not been kept. He said, "The Lord is not slack concerning *His* promise, as some count slackness, but is longsuffering [*makrothumei*—patient] toward us, not willing that any should perish but that all should come to repentance." Why hasn't the Lord come back? Because He is so patient with us. He is waiting for men to come to Him. Why then can't we wait for Him to come to us? That is exactly the logic of verse eight. Be patient and longsuffering as you wait for Him, just as He waits for us. "Be patient," says James, "because the coming of the Lord is near." I can wait patiently with hope knowing that unlike the mechanic, God has not forgotten His promise. Verses seven and eight help with patience toward God, but what about patience toward men?

Patience Toward Men (5:9)

Do not grumble against one another, brethren, lest you be condemned. Behold, the Judge is standing at the door!

Now if I can wait patiently for the Lord, this will influence my attitude toward my fellow servants. In verse nine James says not to "grumble" against our fellow servants. Interestingly enough, this word, *stenazō*, speaks of an internal feeling which is unexpressed. It is the idea of bearing a grudge. We remember an injustice and look for ways to get even. The most natural reaction in the world is to do unto others as they have done unto us—preferably worse than they have done unto us.

There are several words that describe our feelings at that point. One is revenge. Another is retaliation, returning evil for evil, getting back, or holding resentment. Men of literature have not overlooked this natural tendency in man. Nietzsche said, "Revenge is the greatest instinct in the human race." Byron called revenge "sweetness." Bacon said, "It is a sort of wild justice." Humans like to get back. Husbands and wives, businessmen, ministers, church members, athletes, everyone likes the sweet taste of revenge, even if it's against total strangers.

I have a pastor friend who told me about a strange experience he had. He drove into the parking lot of a supermarket. He had a little compact car and was able to squeeze it into a narrow space between some cars, which a larger car couldn't do. The only trouble was when he tried to get out he couldn't avoid nicking the car next to him with his door. Bending down, he wiped the spot and found there had not been any permanent damage done to the car next to him. But when he stood up, he noticed the owner had returned and was not smiling. The pastor smiled and said, "No damage." The owner of the other car still did not smile. So the pastor again said he was sorry and walked with his young son into the super market.

After he got inside, however, he had the strange feeling that he should look back. As he did, he saw the owner of the other car going wham, wham, wham against his car. His first reaction was to run out and separate this guy's head from his body. But the desire for revenge can be handled by applying James 5:9. "Behold, the judge stands at the door." What I am suggesting is that a bright and earnest focus on the any-moment-now return of the Lord can give us patience with other people when injustice occurs. Visualize the judge standing at the door, his hand resting on the doorknob, about to open the door and walk in. He will see that justice is done. If we avenge ourselves, judgment will fall upon us. "Vengeance is mine," says the Lord.

One of my favorite OT stories is in 2 Samuel 16. It is a story about Shimei and David. Shimei was a ding-a-ling. He stayed on the hill outside the court of the temple. David walks out a beaten man, overthrown by Absalom. Shimei was up on the hill throwing stones and cursing David. David had a bunch of buddies with him. And they said, "Want us to finish off Shimei? Let's take him out." David said, "No. God knows what He is doing. Let him shout. Let him go on. God is at work." Any individual in the flesh what would be up that hill in ten seconds if, in the midst of an embarrassing defeat, some ding-a-ling was cursing his name. He would cut Shimei's throat so fast you wouldn't know it until he sneezed. That is a natural reaction. But David said, "Oh, men, don't look up there; look up there," pointing to the heavens.

Let me share another helpful principle called the 50/20 principle. It is certainly not original with me, but it is helpful. It is based on the life of Joseph, in Genesis 50:20. His brothers had sold him down the river, left him for dead, and had even told his father he was dead. They said, "Look at the blood." And Jacob buried the boy in his mind. But Joseph was not dead and he went on to become prime minister of all of Egypt. His brothers came later begging for food.

Surely Joseph had to be thinking, "Oh, what a chance to get even." But did Joseph do it? No, he wept in their presence. And when they got it all out on the table, Joseph said, "Look guys, you meant it for evil, but God meant it for good." That is the 50/20 principle from Genesis 50:20. "Someone may mean it unto you for evil. But let me say, unless you can see beyond that someone, you are going to retaliate and return evil for evil. God meant it unto you for good. God is using that person to mold you and form you and shape you into a person you otherwise would never become. That is 50/20 vision. We don't need 20/20 vision when dealing with people. We need to be far-sighted. We need 50/20 vision.

What's the key to all this? How can we react patiently to injustices? Just remember. The Judge stands at the door. If you can only picture a courtroom where various people have gathered with their grievances. Some of them even have lawsuits against one another. While waiting for the judge to come in, there is a sort of arguing, a murmuring, a complaining among themselves as they discuss their grievances against one another.

In Roman times the pathway for the judge was made clear by a Roman lictor. The lictor was like an aid and bodyguard for Roman magistrates. And, if you can imagine the scene, the lictor walks in amidst all this clamor and complaining and says, "Quiet please, the judge is right at the door." Suddenly, an awesome hush falls over the entire audience. They all fix their eyes on the door, for any moment now, the judge in all his dignity and honor will stride in. I think this is the picture in James' mind.

We could almost look out over Christendom today, and there is a tremendous amount of grumbling amongst ourselves. James is serving here as God's lictor. He steps into the judgment hall and says, "Silence! Behold, the Judge stands at the door." The point is simple. If we once have the feeling that Christ is so near that He is about to step forth to try our case, we would not be so busy trying other people's cases and complaining one against the other. So we find that our hope in Christ's any-moment-now return not only gives us patience toward God, but also toward men. But what does patience add to life in general?

Patience Toward Life (5:10-11)

My brethren, take the prophets, who spoke in the name of the Lord, as an example of suffering and patience. Indeed we count them blessed who endure. You have heard of the perseverance of Job and seen the end *intended by* the Lord— that the Lord is very compassionate and merciful.

Finally, hope in Christ's imminent return is the key to patience toward life in general. Life is full of pain, especially for the spokesman of God. Great pain often comes from personal relationships that are broken and/or strained by misunderstandings, by unthinking, insensitive, but often unintentional words or deeds. What is your threshold of pain? Let's look at some real people who endured great pain in Hebrews 11:32-12:2.

And what more shall I say? For the time would fail me to tell of Gideon and Barak and Samson and Jephthah, also *of* David and Samuel and the prophets: who through faith subdued kingdoms, worked righteousness, obtained promises, stopped the mouths of lions, quenched the violence of fire, escaped the edge of the sword, out of weakness were made strong, became valiant in battle, turned to flight the armies of the aliens. Women received their dead raised to life again. Others were tortured, not accepting deliverance, that they might obtain a better resurrection. Still others had trial of mockings and scourgings, yes, and of chains and imprisonment. They were stoned, they were sawn in two, were tempted, were slain with the sword. They wandered about in sheepskins and goatskins, being destitute, afflicted, tormented—of whom the world was not worthy. They wandered in deserts and mountains, *in* dens and caves of the earth. And all these, having obtained a good testimony through faith, did not receive the promise, God having provided something better for us, that they should not be made perfect apart from us.

Therefore we also, since we are surrounded by so great a cloud of witnesses, let us lay aside every weight, and the sin which so easily ensnares *us,* and let us run with endurance the race that is set before us, looking unto Jesus, the author and finisher of *our* faith, who for the joy that was set before Him endured the cross, despising the shame, and has sat down at the right hand of the throne of God.

It is hard to me to imagine what these men and women endured. Oddly enough, the greatest physical pain I can remember did not come from kidney stones or motorcycle wrecks. It happened when I got a throat inflection so bad I couldn't swallow, if you can imagine that. If I did try to swallow, it felt like someone was jabbing the back of my throat with a flaming-hot fire poker. After one look my doctor said, "Into the hospital." I felt pretty dumb going into the hospital for a throat infection. When friends asked why I was admitting myself, I told them I was having my leg amputated—please pray.

Nevertheless, the hospital did have one thing to offer I really loved. And I learned a great spiritual lesson from this experience. It was Demerol, a pain-killing drug often used in place of morphine. It was the only time in my life I can remember looking forward to shots. Just one shot and for two or three hours I thought I was in the third heaven. I felt no pain. Then after those two or three hours, the effect began to wear off. The pain increased. Now, as I mentioned regarding the kidney stone, I have a very low threshold of pain. I mean I groan when a get a mosquito bite.

So when my shot started to wear off, my groaning began. Before long my groans had increased in such intensity that the nurses could hear them down the hall, so they would come and give me another shot. I would pass into euphoria once again. Now I was just getting used to the cycle after my first day, when without warning my groans did not bring a nurse. Over half an hour of groaning and no nurse.

Finally, when I was pushing buttons and groaning and kicking, a nurse came in. My sigh of relief melted into delirium when she said I had already reached my limit of shots and could not have any more. Suddenly, the intensity of pain increased seven-fold. The prospect of no more shots nearly caused me to faint. It was as though a hundred hot pokers were being crammed in my mouth all at once. I wasn't more than twenty groans in when I thought of a solution. I would call my doctor and get him to OK more shots. After all, he was my personal physician. He cared for me. We had a personal relationship.

I often thought how fast the ER doctor would have been down from the second floor to tend to my kidney stone if she had known me, or if it had been someone in her family, someone with a personal connection. I was on the third floor and my doctor was on the seventh floor. I called and explained my plight. Then came the most soothing words in the world. Hearing them was like dropping warm milk down the throat of a baby bird. He said, "I'll be down as soon as I can." These words were better than a half gallon of Homemade

Vanilla Blue Bell ice cream—that is the highest compliment I can give.

With those words—"I'll be down any minute"—in my mind I was able to sink back on my bed and rest. I focused on his promise. The physical pain was still there, but the mental pain was gone. The groans ceased. It was almost as though the shot of Demerol had already been administered. I could endure the pain patiently because I knew that any minute the doctor, my doctor, would be coming down to relieve my pain. I trusted his promise. What had been pure torture a moment before could be patiently endured because I knew relief was on the way. I drove the pain out of my mind by focusing on the relief. That is the art of hoping, and that is what James is trying to teach his readers.

In verse 11 James has come full circle. Remember 1:12. It contains the same thought—happiness, joy in the midst of pain. This is one step beyond merely enduring pain while groaning inwardly. This is inner joy and happiness. The example of Job is given. Now the interesting statement in this verse deals with these words: "the end of the Lord." Obviously, this refers to something that happened in Job's life. Job 42:10-12 shows us that this statement means "the end result," or "the way the Lord worked things out." What this is saying is that we go through trials and testing, which are often prolonged and extended. But somewhere down the road, God will put an end to that experience. In His end He will exhibit mercy and compassion.

I think the simple lesson is that whenever we are going through a trial, up ahead of us there is a very rich and abundant experience of the compassion and mercy of God. If we will endure in the midst of the trial, God will bring out of it the same kind of blessing he gave Job. It's possible he's hinting the blessing will correspond to the trial. Job was physically afflicted and Job was physically blessed. Sometimes our afflictions are spiritual and so too will the blessings be.

Matthew 19:27-30 indicates that the blessing will not always be in this life. The experience of one missionary couple illustrates this point. The missionary couple was returning home after serving the Lord in Africa for forty years. The return ship they were on happened to be the same ship that was bringing the Beatles to America for the first time. When they arrived in New York, a huge throng had gathered to welcome the Beatles—screaming, jumping up and down. No one had come to the dock to greet this aged couple. Suddenly the husband felt a great sense of resentment coming over him. "This isn't right," he thought. "We've given forty years of our lives in sacrificial service, and here comes a frivolous group of musicians, and the whole city has turned out for them. It is not right that we should be treated this way." He became quite bitter and resentful.

The couple went home to the barely adequate lodgings their missionary organization had arranged for them. The wife tried to encourage her husband, but he continued to be bitter and resentful. Finally, one day she said to him, "Honey why don't you go into our bedroom and tell God how you feel." So he did. He got down on his knees and said, "God, this just isn't right. We've come home after all these years and have received nothing!" He poured it all out. A few minutes later he came out of the bedroom and his wife knew by the look on his face that something was different. She asked, "Honey, what happened?" He said, "Well, I told God all about how I felt—how bitter I was that we came home and He didn't give us what was right. And He said to me, 'But, my child, you're not home yet.'"

You're not home yet. That is the glorious prospect that shines before us when we focus on the Lord's return. But remember what we learned about hope? The secret of patience? "Patience is the art of hoping." Our blessed hope is His any-moment-now return. Keeping that hope before us on a daily basis is an art that develops patience. The formula for patiently enduring any trial could be summarized from this passage this way: Look Up—to the Lord's coming; Look Back—take the example of the prophets who endured successfully; and Look Forward—to the end result the Lord shall bring out of the trial with His mercy and great compassion. The man who can look up, look back, and look forward—all at the same time—this is the man who endures trials with patience. Anybody need a shot of Demerol? Be patient. The Divine Doctor will be down any minute now with Demerol for all who wait on Him.

Zane Hodges was my "Baby" Greek teacher in seminary. Many guys coming to school already had Greek in Bible college, but about half of us had not. We had to start with beginning Greek. Prof Hodges, as we called him, was around six feet tall, light brown hair, and very slim. His speech was crisp and measured. Everything about him was buttoned-up and precise. Socially, he was very kind, very gracious, but a bit stiff. Little did I know the role he would play in my life.

Prof Hodges' primary influence began one summer when he offered to teach a couple of friends and me how to do exegesis, which is to bring out the meaning of a text. Greek was still pretty new to me, but I jumped at the chance anyway. We met every Friday evening for several hours as he poured his expertise into us. Zane was a genius of the first order: summa cum laude at Wheaton, an accomplished scholar of textual criticism before he even entered seminary. Ultimately Tübingen, a German university well known as a haven of NT scholars like Martin Hengel, offered Hodges a Ph.D. if he would turn over to them his trailblazing work on what is known as the Majority Text. He turned them down and, along with Art Farstad, had their work on the Majority Text published by Thomas Nelson. What a privilege it was to have this man pour into us.

Though I had done well in school, I never enjoyed it. It was just a means to an end. But when Prof Hodges taught me how to do exegesis the way I had never heard of before or since, I jumped in and began spending eight hours a day doing it. Seminary became an afterthought; I spent at the most two hours a day on homework for my seminary classes. Along the way, I learned more than just exegesis from Prof Hodges. I spent many a Saturday afternoon at his apartment (he never married) pumping him with what must have seemed very simple and sophomoric questions. Nevertheless, he was always patient with me, teaching me how to preach, how to teach, and last but not least, how to anticipate the Lord's return.

I have never known an academic as consumed by fervor for the imminent return of Jesus as Zane Hodges. For him, the pre-tribulational return of Christ (rapture before the tribulation) was not a peripheral doctrine. He taught me that anticipation of the Lord's imminent return and all that comes with it is fifty percent of the motivation for the Christian life. In fact, years later when he found out the other two friends of mine he had poured himself into had stopped believing in the "blessed hope," he said it hurt him deeply for they had "given up one of the most precious jewels of the NT."

When I asked Prof Hodges how he went about keeping the imminent return before him, he took me to a chest of drawers in a room of his apartment. Being extremely frugal with himself but generous toward missionaries, his chest of drawers was one of those where the shelves lacked rollers and practically fell out when pulled. But there it was. Each drawer was stuffed with clippings of contemporary events from newspapers and magazines by which he kept the hope alive and central to everything he did. He had been collecting these articles for years and would continue to do so until he died.

Truly, Zane Hodges was a man who could LOOK UP, LOOK BACK, and LOOK FORWARD at the same time.

"STILL SOVEREIGN, STILL OMNIPOTENT"

James 5:12-16a

A friend of mine has three boys, no girls. Two of his sons have a disease so rare the docs have never put a name to it. It is not MS, but it does involve a degeneration of the muscular control, and it is progressive. It began to show up when they hit puberty. It started with an awkward gait and some slurring in their speech. One of the boys is several years older than the other, so his disease is more advanced. He finally got to where he could not walk. He went up to almost four hundred pounds. They could no longer get him in a wheel chair. The brain also begins to go. I was with the dad visiting his son in the care center when the results of recent brain tests came out. It was not good. I remember the son looking at his dad and asking, "Am I retarded too, dad?"

I couldn't watch. I had to turn away. I was looking in on an exchange between father and son that was holy, set apart. It was as though the angels descended into the room and huddled around the father and son. There was an exchange of souls I can't explain. And pain. I didn't feel worthy to watch.

James grabs us by the gut. His dagger pierces my very core. He has been trying to help us tap into the vast stores of God's wisdom and grace in the midst of our trials. To tap into those stores we need to be quick to hear, slow to speak, and slow to wrath. We get that. But sometimes we need something more. I know He loves me, but sometimes I don't feel it and I can't make sense out of what has happened to me. I seem to be losing hope again. I need a word of encouragement to keep me going.

Some of our suffering does not end. Some of it will be with us for life. Whether or not it ends, there are times we need to be reminded that **GOD IS STILL SOVEREIGN, STILL OMNIPOTENT.** That is what James is doing in 5:12-16a. At first blush it appears that James is just tying up loose ends. Perhaps. But behind the loose ends lies a message about God's sovereignty and omnipotence that we need to hear.

Still Sovereign (5:12-13)

> **But above all, my brethren, do not swear, either by heaven or by earth or with any other oath. But let your "Yes" be "Yes," and *your* "No," "No," lest you fall into judgment. Is anyone among you suffering? Let him pray. Is anyone cheerful? Let him sing psalms.**

Don't Swear (12)

As we have already seen, James relies more heavily on the Sermon on the Mount than any other NT author and this is his most direct allusion. To better understand the meaning, let's turn back to Matthew 5:34-37:

> **But I say to you, do not swear at all: neither by heaven, for it is God's throne; nor by the earth, for it is His footstool; nor by Jerusalem, for it is the city of the great King. Nor shall you swear by your head, because you cannot make one hair white or black. But let your 'Yes' be 'Yes,' and your 'No,' 'No.' For whatever is more than these is from the evil one.**

Jesus makes it clear why we should not make vows. He says not to swear by heaven because *God* sits on the throne of heaven, not us. We have no right to invoke the powers of heaven when we do not control heaven. Nor should we swear by any earthly power or authority, for if heaven is God's throne room, earth is His footstool. This simply means God sets up earthly authorities. He is the authority behind all authority on earth. We have no right to stamp the authority of the earth on our vows. Neither can we swear by Jerusalem, for that is where Jesus will reign as king. Nor can we even presume the authority to swear by our own lives, for we have no final control over them either. The point is simple. There is not one single sphere by which we can undergird our vows, for God has sovereign control over every one of these spheres: heaven, earth, cities on the earth, and even our individual lives. To make a vow presumes that I have sovereign control over my life, which I do not. To make a vow upon something else presumes I have control over it, which I do not.

Vows are apt to emerge from the type of tricky situations envisioned in James. In 5:11 James urges us to have patient endurance in the midst of trials. As Zane Hodges remarks in his notes on this passage, "Oaths are frequently the expression of impatience and self-assertion. They rarely reflect a calm spirit in the hour of trial."[25] For example, I get in a scrape. I am not able to endure it. So I vow to the Lord, "Lord, if you get me out of this mess, I vow to read the Bible every day for the rest of my life." What happens? I get out of the scrape and remember my vow to the Lord. I faithfully read my Bible every day for six weeks. Then I miss a day for some reason. I feel guilty. Soon I miss another day. A year later I may miss an entire week. The vow has been broken and now just produces guilt in my life.

James says the danger of making vows is that we may fall into hypocrisy. The end of verse 12 requires a textual change. The majority of the Greek manuscripts read "into hypocrisy," instead of "into judgment." I feel rather certain James had his close friend Peter in mind when he wrote this. Turn back to Matthew 26:69-75. Earlier in the chapter Peter claimed allegiance to Christ unto death. He said, "Even if I must die with you, I will never deny you." Later we come to that famous denial by Peter. You are familiar with it, but note the wording. In his first denial Peter merely claims ignorance of Christ.

---

[25] Zane Hodges, unpublished class notes on James (Dallas, 1970).

But in his second denial he does it with an oath, a vow. In his third denial he curses and swears that he does not know Christ. Do you see the hypocrisy? The previous night Peter played one role in the presence of Christ. Now in the absence of Christ he plays another. It is pretense, hypocrisy. The man too ready to swear is the one most likely to use an oath hypocritically to cover his own weaknesses, faults, or cowardice.

Another interesting twist on the danger of oaths involves Herod Antipas in Mark 6:23. At one of his banquets Herod was pleased by the dancing of the daughter of Herodias, so he swore that he would give her anything she desired up to half his kingdom. When she asked for the head of John the Baptizer on a platter, Herod was very sorry he had made the oath. Yet verse 26 says he was bound by his oath. The sovereign king was proven not so sovereign after all. It was not his desire for John the Baptizer to die. Yet his own hasty, presumptuous oath caused him to go against his own will. The very same mistake caused Darius the Mede to throw Daniel into the lion den. What a rapier thrust God makes at human claims of sovereignty. If any human is sovereign, surely it is a king. Yet here are two kings, Darius and Herod, who are bound by their own will to act against their will. What irony!

Rather than swearing and taking oaths, our lives should reflect sincere truthfulness. A simple "Yes" or "No" is all that is needed. The Jews were fond of using oaths rather like Scout's Honor. "I really mean it." However, making these oaths implied that their other statements not backed up by oaths may lack sincerity or truthfulness. Jesus and James say, "Take oaths out of your life. Our word should always be sincere and truthful. Besides, to swear by heaven or earth or a city, *et cetera*, assumes an authority not yours. It presumes a future beyond your control. A simple yes or no should be good enough."

Jesus and James seem to say that oaths in times of trial only complicate matters. Decide what to do and let that decision be known with a simple yes or no. Our word should be good. We don't need to swear or take oaths. We should stick by our word as it is. When in a trial, I may face the temptation to get involved in a sinful deal or association. That is when I need the conviction to say no and mean it. Or perhaps when the sun was shining in my life, I said, "Yes," to the Lord. "Yes, I'll serve you in capacity a, b, or c." But a little storm cloud blows in and my "Yes" may not mean so much to me. That is exactly when I should be true to my word, lest it become empty and unreliable. I can think of no trait more desirable and more difficult to find than simple faithfulness to one's word. It is the third prerequisite for Christian service or discipleship: 1) Available; 2) Teachable; 3) Reliable. How can our Lord call upon us to do something until He is convinced our yes means yes? Say no when you need to and stick by it; say yes when you want to and stick by it. Losing the reliability of one's word can only make our ride rougher in times of trial. Instead of making vows, which implies a sovereignty we do not possess, we should pray to the One who is sovereign.

Do Pray (13a)

Is anyone among you in misery? The word here for suffering is another one of those compound words: suffering = *kako* +*patheō* = bad + to feel (or suffer) = to feel bad = misery. Some trials can make us feel absolutely miserable. I remember a wife of fifteen years who discovered her husband had been unfaithful to her for five years with many different women, including prostitutes. Not only did she cry day after day, but she felt so bad she could hardly eat. She lost about thirty pounds in two months (weighing only 130 lbs. before this trial).

We certainly don't want to get overly simplistic, but this is not the time for her to start making vows or bargaining with God. She should pray. Why? Because He is **STILL SOVEREIGN**. Though there is no guarantee God will save their marriage, there is the guarantee (Rom 8:28) that He can take even this sinful situation and work it around for her good and His glory. He also promises that the sufferings of this world are not worthy to be compared to the glory that shall be revealed (at the Judgment Seat of Christ) on behalf of these believers who choose to remain faithful in the midst of undeserved suffering.

Do Praise (13b)

Praying is a good thing; so is praising. E. M. Bounds' little book *Power through Prayer*[26] and Carothers' book *Power through Praise*[27] give evidence of the dynamic power of these practices to carry us through our storms. It's like a soldier going out on a mission with an AK-47 in one hand and a GTA missile in the other. Prayer and praise are some of the best weapons in the midst of trials.

Our feelings vacillate in trials. Sometimes we are up; sometimes we are down. I think James is telling us how we should respond to each feeling. We have seen that the word in 13a is *kakopatheō*, "to feel bad." The word in 13b is just the opposite: *eu* + *thumeō* = good + to feel = "to feel good or cheerful." If we feel bad we are to **pray**; if we feel good we should **praise**. The principle is this: suffer in silence, but praise in public. In our age of sophistication we so often do the opposite. We feel bad, so we vent our feelings to all with in earshot. It is the "Oh, my aching back" routine. But when we have something to feel good about, we so often keep it to ourselves.

No one likes to be around a sour grape kind of person. If things are not going our way, we shouldn't tell the world about it. Tell God about it. On the other hand, if things are going well, tell the world about it through a song of praise. Praise, uninhibited praise, seems so lacking in our Christian circles. I think we are afraid of being labeled as fanatics or charismatics. But to withhold and suppress these good feelings is unbiblical. James actually commands us to let it out. You may be feeling good precisely when another is feeling bad. Your song or words of praise may lift his spirits.

I can never forget the first time I preached in a church of African-Americans. I knew going in that they would be more expressive than my somewhat reserved culture. I was ready for a lot of "Amens," but that is really not what I heard. There were five black pastors sitting

---

[26] E. M. Bounds, *Power through Prayer*, (New York: Cosimo Classics, 1906, reprint 2007).

[27] Merlin R. Carothers, *Power through Praise*, published by Merlin R. Carothers, Escondido, CA, 1972.

behind me. Of course, the congregation was spread out in front of me. I felt like I was on an elevator sandwiched between praise teams. I would say something, and one of the guys behind me would say, "You got it now, Dave, run with it." Or, "Cross the goal line, now. Cross the goal line." Or, "Take it to the cross, take it to the cross." Some people even stood during the entire message.

It took me a couple of hours to come down after the service. They were such an encouragement. The whole sermon seemed like a team effort. Please don't take offense, but the thought crossed my mind that there are two things white men can't do: they can't jump and they can't worship. Some of you will take exception to that. You say, "I don't have to jump and scream to worship. My worship can be very calm and private." No doubt that is true, but that is not what James is getting at. He says there is a time to make a joyful noise unto the Lord. It may be in the midst of your trials.

If you are feeling down, don't take others down with you. Keep those feelings to yourself while praying to the Lord about your situation. I'm not suggesting there are not times when the body of believers needs to pray for you in your situation. This is primarily addressed to the whiner and complainer. And when you are feeling up, let it out. You may lift up others in the process. Yes, God is **STILL SOVEREIGN**.

Of course, whenever we emphasize the sovereignty of God, someone is sure to raise the question, "But what about human responsibility?" Properly understood, the two can work hand in hand. Take David and Goliath, for example. In 1 Samuel 17:40, David picked up five stones when he went against Goliath. Someone might say, "Well, if David had any faith he would have taken just one stone." Others have said, "No, not only did he think he would kill Goliath with the first stone, but he had four left over for the four giant brothers of Goliath" (2 Sam 21:15-22). Whatever David's reason for five stones, it was clear he believed the battle belonged to the Lord (1 Sam 17:34); God would give them the victory over the Philistines. Nevertheless, someone had to go out against Goliath. The Lord will bring the victories, but we still have to get on the battlefield.

So God is **STILL SOVEREIGN**. That is comforting in the midst of trials. There is something else we need to know, too. He is also **STILL OMNIPOTENT**.

Still Omnipotent (5:14-16a)

> Is anyone among you sick? Let him call for the elders of the church, and let them pray over him, anointing him with oil in the name of the Lord. And the prayer of faith will save the sick, and the Lord will raise him up. And if he has committed sins, he will be forgiven. Confess *your* trespasses to one another, and pray for one another, that you may be healed.

Our God is not only still sovereign; He is also still omnipotent. He did miracles in the day of James, and He can do miracles in our day as well. If our trial happens to be a severe illness, the sick person is encouraged to call upon the Lord through the elders of the church. The Sovereign, Omnipotent One may heal him.

Let's define the situation in these verses. The word for sick could refer to physical, moral, or even economic weaknesses. However, in this context it most likely is speaking of physical illness, but not just a headache or a cold. This is a probably a serious illness in which long term disability or even death is on the horizon of possibility. How can we help? Here are the instructions.

Faith Healing versus Faith Healers (14-15a)

1. **Sick Person Initiates.** He is to call for the elders of the church. This is very interesting. Let's observe exactly who is summoned. It is not the deacons. It is not a pastor. It is not a priest, even though the Roman Catholic teaching of "extreme unction" came from this passage. Although any serious illness could lead to the demise of the sick person, death is not mentioned. This passage isn't about imminent death. It is about sickness in life. He is not asking for someone to perform last rites before he dies. He is asking for a measure to raise him up. It is a passage on healing.

Again we must note, the passage does not call for the Apostles. Some who do not want to believe in miraculous healing today try to confine this passage to the Apostles who had the gift of healing. But nowhere do we find the word "apostle" in this chapter. It says call for the elders. It also does not say to call for a medical doctor. It may well be that there is a connection between the sickness and the spiritual life of the person. That is exactly what 5:15-16 implies. Unconfessed sin may be the cause of the sickness. In that case, the spiritual authorities in the church are called for. Perhaps they will be able to help dig out the spiritually malignant tumor that is eating up the life of the believer. How?

2. **Elder Functions.**

    a. **Anoint with Oil.** Perhaps your Bible has prayer first, then anointing. The Greek text can be read either way. The anointing itself can also go two different directions. Oil in NT times was a symbol of the Holy Spirit, so the anointing here is often seen as a ceremonial, religious ritual symbolic of the power and blessing of the Holy Spirit, a reminder that through His agency the healing might come. That may well be the proper interpretation, but let me give you another approach.

        There are two common words in Scripture for anointing. One is *krioō* and the other is *aleiphoō*. The first is that from which we get the name Christ. *Christos* means "anointed one." But generally speaking this word refers to ceremonial anointing. This is not the word used in James 5:14. Rather, the word *aleiphoō* has been selected. Its basic meaning is "to rub in." It is even used of plastering a wall where the plaster is smeared onto the wall. In NT times this word most frequently refers to the medicinal use of oil in which oil is rubbed into the body of the sick person. It helped heal.

We might remember that the Good Samaritan poured oil and wine into the wounds of the man robbed. One Bible scholar put it this way: "It is the use of consecrated, dedicated medicine. Instead of teaching faith-healing apart from medicine, the passage teaches just the opposite."[28] But why do the elders bring the oil instead of a doctor? Because the medical profession of today differs vastly from that of James' day. One physician might have been available for an entire region. Anyone could learn to rub on oil. Hence, medical treatment along with prayer are the instructions from James.

I can never get out of my memory bank a visit to a hospital to see a newborn. As I walked by the nursery, one little baby was especially upset. He was thrashing about spastically. I asked a nurse walking by what the problem was. She said the child's parents were Jehovah's Witnesses and did not allow blood transfusions. The child was dying. A transfusion could have saved his life. I think James would say to start with the best medicine available to you. Then pray.

b. **Pray for the Sick Person.** "In the name of the Lord" means according to His will. Elders are not omniscient. They don't necessarily know what God's will in a matter is. I read a book once called *Jesus Wants You Well.*[29] As I read the book, I kept saying,

---

[28] Zane Hodges, unpublished class notes on James (Dallas, 1970).

[29] C. S. Lovett, *Jesus Wants You Well*, (1979).

"Not necessarily." It simply is not God's will that everyone be healed. If it were, we would never die. Paul had the gift of healing. Yet he left Trophimus sick at Miletus (2 Tim 4:20). Nor did he heal Epaphroditus in Philippians 2:26-27. He could not even heal himself (2 Cor 12:7-9, where the same word for sickness is used and translated "weakness). Why? It simply was not God's will. Three times he tried. Three times God said, "No." Finally, Paul said, "I've learned to live with it." And in 1 Corinthians 11:30 Paul tells us God may actually cause our sickness as a form of divine discipline. So yes, pray for the healing of the sick person, but pray acknowledging that God in His sovereign plan may say, "No."

c. **Leave the Results to the Lord.** When it says the prayer of faith will save him, it does not mean that he becomes a Christian. We looked at this in connection with our study of 2:14. This is a sick Christian. We have learned that the word "saved" as James uses it never refers to going to heaven. Here it refers to a deliverance from the sickness and death that could have resulted. That is the first result of the prayer of faith. Next, the Lord will raise him up. The Lord restores him to health and usefulness again. Third, if sins have been committed, they will be confessed and forgiven.

Verse 16 urges us to confess our sins to these elders so we may be healed. This implies the possibility of a connection between sins committed and sickness. There is something therapeutic about such confession. However, I tend to think this verse is misapplied today. I see no virtue in standing before a congregation and dumping dirty laundry on them. Our confessions should almost always be to the Lord. The only exceptions I see are when I have hurt another human. Then I go to that person alone. Or, as in James 5, I make a confession to the elders in a case of serious sickness. Our mental institutions are filled with people who are simply running from guilt. James 5 would help some of them. When I was going to college, a Jewish doctor from Los Angeles told me he had given up his practice for a year to study religion. I asked him why. He said, "Because 20-25% of all my patients suffer from psychosomatic problems of guilt." He was a doctor of internal medicine.

The importance of 5:15-16 is to see that if healing takes place, it is the Lord who raises up. I believe in divine healing today, but not divine healers. I believe in faith healing today, but not faith healers. No faith healer today can do what the Apostles did. Here are the marks of the gift of healing seen in the NT:

1. **Instantaneous.** There was no time lapse.

2. **100%.** There were no partial healings.

3. **Everyone or no one.** If a city had faith, everyone was healed. If they did not have faith, no one was healed.

4. **Every disease.** They did not just specialize in backs and necks. Every disease: leprosy, paralysis, blindness, and so on.

5. **Raise someone from the dead** (Jesus, Peter, Paul) to prove one's power was from God and not the devil. Only Christ holds the keys to death (Rev 1:18). Satan can and will do all the other miracles through people (Rev 13).

How tragic was the story I read about a contemporary faith-healer who flew out to an Indian reservation, lined up over three hundred Indians who had come to be healed, and walked down the assembly line with one hand on their heads and the other hand in their pockets. When his collection was complete, he and his entourage got in their plane and flew away, leaving all the Indians standing there agape, just as debilitated as before the healing hawk swooped down. His take-- $6,000; his cures—0.

Who heals? The Lord heals. How does it work? The prayer of

faith, not some shyster laying hands on you. I still remember the little twelve-year-old boy who had diabetes. His parents took away his insulin when the faith-healer came to town. They buried that little boy three weeks later and went to trial for voluntary manslaughter. If I were seriously ill or incapacitated, I would have no hesitation at all about seeking the Lord's healing, but I wouldn't lie on a stretcher waiting for a faith-healer. I would call up the elders of my church and ask them to come over and pray for me.

When I was a Youth Pastor at Scofield Memorial Church in Dallas, the pastor's wife collapsed and fell into a coma around 5:30 PM Sunday evening. As a congregation we prayed for her at 7:10 PM, and at 7:10 PM she opened her eyes. I was leading in prayer and out of gratitude she wrote me a letter or two each year for the rest of her life. That was a divine healing. The Lord raised her up. It was a miracle. The prayers of faith saved her.

Years later the same woman had a stroke in the middle of the Sunday morning service. I prayed for her then just as I did years before. We visited her many times after that and prayed many times, and in 1971 I helped bury her. I buried her with absolute confidence that the Lord heard our prayers of faith. It is simply not His pleasure that everyone be healed. There is one healer . . . and that is God.

Yes, God is **STILL SOVEREIGN, STILL OMNIPOTENT.** His power is no less today than it was during the times of the Apostles. He can heal today and does. He is omnipotent. But He does not choose to heal everyone. We pray for healing according to His will—because He is still sovereign.

Sandra Westcott is an unusual woman in many ways. She was a brainiac at Georgia Tech and kept up with her love of math with a career in teaching calculus to high school students. She was also a great basketball player in her younger years. She married a handsome six foot five inch engineer from Georgia Tech, and they soon had three children, all boys. But these weren't just any boys. Her older son, Ben, was six foot eight inches and weighed three hundred pounds when he played on the line for Rice University. Her son Adam was six foot seven inches and played tight end for the University of Virginia. Her youngest, Dan, was six foot six inches and broke the Texas high school backstroke record when he was a freshman. He continued breaking his own record right through high school and went to Stanford on a swimming scholarship. He finished fourth in the Olympic tryouts for Beijing. Needless to say, Sandra was understandably proud of all the men in her family.

One day while vacuuming, Sandra fell and bruised her coccyx bone. When the doctor examined her he put her into a sling in the hospital to take the pressure off the bruise. She picked up a staff infection in the hospital, so they gave her some antibiotics to knock it out. Then they sent her to the Texas rehab center at the medical center downtown. Three days later she was back in a hospital with a roaring infection. Apparently, she had been given a double dose of the antibiotic. It killed the bad guys, but also killed all the good guys, leaving her defenseless. When the bad guys regrouped, there was nothing to stop them.

When I got down there, she had gained about thirty pounds of fluid. Her kidneys could not process the waste fast enough. Shortly thereafter she was in ICU and not expected to live. Dan was called in from Stanford. Adam was called in from Virginia. Ben and his wife were local. I went upstairs with Sandra's husband, Bill, to look at the situation. She was in an octagonal ICU unit on the top floor. By now she had gained nearly sixty pounds of fluid and was all but unrecognizable. She was in a drug-induced coma, strapped down because she was still writhing in pain. A doctor poked his head in and said, "We don't know why she's still alive."

Meanwhile, the prayer-a-troopers were on their way. At twelve midnight the medical shift changed. Another doctor looked in, saw Sandra fighting the straps and said to his assistant, "She's in pain; give her some morphine." Her husband jumped up and said, "Don't give her morphine; she's allergic to it. Read the chart. You'll kill her."

He was right. The doctor had been careless. Sandra's systolic blood pressure was 180. They expected her to die anytime.

I went downstairs and the prayer warriors were there, maybe ten or twelve. We surrounded a conference table and began to pray. Just like in the Bible, from the very minute we began to pray, Sandra's blood pressure began to drop—slowly, steadily. That was about ten years ago. I'm happy to say Sandra is alive and well today. I believe with all my heart that Sandra Westcott is a living example of the prayers of faith that God uses to heal the sick. Yes, God is still OMNIPOTENT.

God is still SOVEREIGN, too. The same people from the same church prayed for the healing of Paul Barrett from Lou Gehrig's disease. Did he have the power to heal Paul Barrett? Sure. But God is SOVEREIGN. **God's will is not limited by God's power, but by God's purposes.** For reasons we may not know until the next life or maybe ever, God in his OMNIPOTENCE chose to heal Sandra Westcott but in his SOVEREIGNTY did not choose to heal Paul Barrett.

"GOD'S MEDICINE"

James 5:16b-18

The story of modern medicine during the last hundred and forty years explodes with more wonder than a fireworks display on the Fourth of July. Louis Pasteur found the relationship between germs and disease. After that discovery, death-dealing diseases began to fall like ducks at a shooting gallery. Vaccinations for tuberculosis, diphtheria, tetanus, cholera, scarlet fever and others punctuated the story of modern medicine with one miracle cure after another. Lives were being saved—thousands of them, maybe millions.

Yet, despite all of the progress, more lives have been lost during the same time period than all the lives saved by modern medicine because of the persistent march of one little germ. The germ is sin. Once it gets into the bloodstream of a man or woman it slowly multiplies, yielding a wide variety of spiritual and even physical diseases. No vaccination has been discovered by man's medicine to halt the march of this insidious germ named sin. That is why James has so much to say about God's Medicine.

Spiritual diseases cannot be handled by man's medicine. But they can be the cause of physical disease. That is why God's medicine is so important. What is God's medicine? As presented to us in James 5, God's medicine is prayer. When we left off in James 5:16a, a man was lying sick on what could have been his deathbed. Man's medicine has been applied. Immediately following, God's medicine is put to use. Why? This man or woman may be in bed because of the evil work of the sin germ. If so, man's medicine may start the healing, but it won't finish it. God's medicine must kick in.

God's medicine is prayer. That is the cure for spiritual diseases caused by the many different strains of the sin germ. Prayer—pure and simple. Doesn't that sound trite? Sometimes a despondent Christian, held by the vice of some habitual sin, will explain his case history and wait for some exotic spiritual treatment to be prescribed to solve his problem. When I open my mouth and say, "Pray," he replies, "Huh? Maybe you didn't hear me. I said I have this sin problem worse than a poison ivy rash creeping all over my body and I can't make the itch go away." And again I say, "Pray." "But that sounds too easy."

More than likely the reverse is true. It is not easy. Simply trusting in God's medicine to cure disease is too hard for most people. Or the response may be, "But I've already tried that, and it didn't work." Such an answer indicates that the patient may have accepted the doctor's prescription, but failed to follow directions closely or stopped taking the medication too soon. More often than not, the defeated Christian walks away more despondent than when he entered. He was hoping for a new verse from Hezekiah he had never heard before. But instead of a new verse, he only receives an old adage—pray.

Why is it we hear so many messages on prayer? I don't know of too many books in the Bible one could teach from beginning to end without at least one message on prayer. This is our third prayer challenge in James. It has more to say about prayer than any other book in the NT. It is no wonder why James was nicknamed "Camel Knees" by those who knew him best. James spent so much time on his knees in prayer that they developed thick calluses and began to look like the knees of a camel. One commentator on James has remarked "James probably spent as much time on his knees as he did on his feet. It seems that every time he corners us, he gives us the escape route—on our knees—coming to God and waiting for him." In 1:5 he says if you lack wisdom as to what to do in a given situation, then pray. In 4:2 he says if you lack materially, it is probably because you have not prayed. You have not because you ask not. Now in 5:14 he says if you lack physical health, call the elders and let them pray for you. Problem after problem—spiritual, material, physical—the same, simple solution, the same, trite answer—pray.

The question then is obvious. Why aren't we satisfied with God's answer? Why do we complicate things by seeking a more sophisticated answer than prayer? A statement Howard Hendricks makes in his book, *Elijah*, impresses me. Hendricks writes:

> The older I become in the faith the more impressed I am with the subtlety of Satan. He always fogs in the area of the crucial, never the trivial. Satan does not mind your witnessing, as long as you don't pray. Because he knows that it is far more important to talk to God about men than to talk to men about God. Satan does not mind your studying the Scriptures, as long as you don't pray, for then the Word will never get into your life. You will simply develop a severe case of spiritual pride, and he loves that. Satan doesn't mind you becoming compulsively active in your local church or in some other form of Christian work, just so you do not pray. For then you will be active, but you will not accomplish anything.[30]

Prayer is the incubator in which God's miracles hatch. Prayer is the lever that unleashes God's power. Prayer is the handle that turns on God's loving kindness. Does this imply that prayer is magic or God a machine? Hardly. I suggest the reason our prayers are ineffective is simply that we don't know what effective prayer is. James 5:16b says, **"The effectual, fervent prayer of righteous man avails much."**

Let's concentrate on just those words from 5:16b, which 5:17-18 illustrate. James has mentioned prayer frequently, but now as he is about to sign off, he puts a couple of qualifications on prayer. He does not say just any kind of prayer avails much. He says there is prayer and then there is **prayer**. He is interested in prayer that really works. Aren't we all?

So let's stoop down on our knees to look at this verse at ground level. The primary focal point of our investigation involves one word

---

[30]   Howard Hendricks, *Elijah,* (Chicago: Moody Press, 1972), 51.

in the Greek text: *energoumenē*. It is literally a power-packed word. A derivative is the English word energetic, which gives us a feel for the trembling dynamism of *energoumenē*. We need to go deeper still, for only prayer qualified by *energoumenē* avails much.

Actually, commentators are divided as to which of two ways to take the word, so I will present both ways. The grammatical form has the option of going two ways (middle-passive). I think there is a fusing of both options in the word so that we get two sides of the same coin. But to give you a feel for the various approaches the translators use to translate this single Greek word: NKJ—effectual, fervent; ESV—has great power in its working; NIV—powerful and effective. Do you see how they are having trouble expressing what they understand to be the full meaning of the word with just one English word? We are going to look at the word from three angles, each one describing another aspect of prayer that avails much. This kind of prayer is earnest, energetic, and expectant.

EARNEST PRAYER

This prayer is earnest, sincere, and deep as opposed to dull, lifeless, or routine. Jesus taught the same idea by means of a couple of "do-nots" regarding prayer.

Do Not Be Insincere

Jesus said, "And when you pray, you shall not be like the hypocrites" (Matt 6:5). They were praying to impress men with their spirituality. If that is my goal, then I must pray where people can see and hear me. That is why "long prayers in private and short prayers in public" is a good maxim. Whenever a person gets lengthy in public prayer and sprinkles his prayer with a lot of neat, spiritual-sounding phrases, he is doing exactly what these hypocrites were guilty of doing. And when people slap him on the back and say, "My, what a wonderful prayer that was," then he is receiving his reward. His prayer won't make it through the cloud cover, but he received the praise and admiration of men.

People may walk around church corridors saying, "Oh, how I love to listen to Brother Jones pray. My, what beautiful prayers he gives." That is exactly why I try to keep my public prayers as short and simple as possible: KISS—keep it short and simple. I would far rather have men be unimpressed with my public prayers and have a prayer or two answered by God, than to impress people with unanswered prayers. The prayers of hypocrites are not earnest and sincere. They are for show and they are insincere.

Do Not Be Routine

Again, Jesus said, "And when you pray, do not use vain repetitions as the heathen *do*" (Matt 6:7). Unbelievers pray. Does that sound surprising? We usually don't think of those outside the family of God as being prayerful people, but indeed they are, many of them. They are like the Baal worshippers during Elijah's day who called upon their gods from morning until noon.

I made a trip to Nigeria some years ago and spent a few days in the company of a Muslim imam. You guessed it—five times a day. It really didn't matter where we were. We could be in the market place. He carried his prayer rug with him, and when the time came, down he went. He got on the rug and began his ritual. Even in my own home growing up we had a similar ritual. We were churchgoers, but we had never heard the gospel and were not born again. Yet, at every meal we prayed the same prayer. I respect my parents for respecting God, but all we were offering was a vain repetition to a God we did not know.

These two "do-nots" illustrate by contrast how we should pray. Rather than insincerely like the hypocrites, we should be sincere. Rather than being routine and ritualistic as unbelievers can be, we should put our heart into it. God knows the difference between a routine call and a cry for help. I was out at our local lake in a marina one day with my first two kids. My son was five and my daughter was three. At the ripe old age of three Christie did not know how to swim. We were there to have some family fun by fishing. I bought those little three-foot poles, and we were just dropping minnows straight down in the covered boat stalls. Fishing was amazing in those days. We could pull fifty crappie out in a couple of hours.

Well, my daughter grew bored. I wasn't paying a lot of attention to her. Being somewhat obsessive-compulsive, fishing has never been relaxing for me. It's me against the fish. So I concentrate on that line. Then I heard Christie call, "Hey, daddy, look at me." She was just six or seven feet away, but I was concentrating on my fishing so I didn't bother to look. Again she called, "Daddy, look at me." I thought I felt a nibble, so I said, "OK, just a second." Next thing I heard was a splash as she cried out, "Daddy!" I practically dropped my rod in the water and jumped over a boat stall to get to where I heard that splash. When I arrived, Christie was already under the dark, brown water. It was forty feet deep I learned later, and I was ready to jump in when the sinking feeling in the pit of my stomach turned to relief. The air in her lungs brought her to the surface and I nabbed her. The point is, daddy knew the difference between a routine call and an earnest cry for help. So does our Heavenly Father. In Isaiah 58:9 God promises: "You shall cry, and He shall say, 'Here I am.'"

It is the earnest prayer of a righteous man that avails much. There is another side to the adjective *energoumenē* James uses to describe prayer. It means earnest, yes; but also energetic. In fact, just look at the Greek word. It practically spells our English word energy.

ENERGETIC PRAYER

This kind of prayer takes it out of you. Takes what out? Energy. That is really the other side of the coin, isn't it? If you put a lot into something, that something will take a lot out of you. So it is with prayer. If you put a lot of energy into your prayers, they will take a lot of energy out of you. My point is simply this. Prayer that avails much is not a casual past time one engages in when there is nothing else to do or when one wants to redeem the time. The kind of prayer that avails much demands hard work, high energy, and long labor.

The Latin expression *laborare est orare* means "to work is to pray." The Bible teaches "to pray is to work." Colossians 4:12 mentions,

"Epaphras, . . . a servant of Christ, . . . always laboring fervently for you in prayer, that you might stand perfect and complete in all the will of God." It is like Bible study. Some people say they don't get much out of Bible study. Anyone who does get a lot out of it could easily respond, "Well, how much do you put into it?"

Surely Jesus told a parable like this one to drive this point home. I'll call it the Parable of the Peanut Machine. The Lord stood on the shore with his disciples and looking off afar, said, "Behold, a buyer went forth to buy. And upon entering the market place he saw a peanut machine standing by the tax collector's station. Straightway the buyer opened his purse and pulled out a penny. He placed the penny in the machine and pulled the lever. And, behold, forthwith came a penny's pile of peanuts into the hand of the buyer. And looking at the tax collector, he charged him saying. 'Tell no man.' But the tax collector published it abroad, speaking as only an eyewitness could, 'He put a penny in and got a penny's pile of peanuts out.' And they all marveled from that day forward."

Jesus' disciples spoke to him privately, asking, "What meaneth this parable?" He responded, "Are you dull of hearing? The parable is simple enough: you get out of it exactly what you put into it—no more, no less. Put a penny in, pull a penny's pile of peanuts out. He who has ears to hear, let him hear." Profound, isn't it? Paul says in 2 Tim 2:15, "Study to show yourself approved, a **workman** who does not need to be ashamed." Work. Bible study is work and so is prayer. Epaphras labored in prayer. How about you, my friend? Do your prayers avail little or much? Put a little in; get a little out. Put a lot in; get a lot out.

The only consistent way to do this is to set a time for regular prayer. I was reading a book by Watchman Nee called *The Prayer Ministry of the Church*.[31] In it he reminds us of what happened to the children of Israel when they began to plan for their exodus from Egypt. Pharaoh doubled their workload. He wanted them so preoccupied with work they would not have time to think about leaving Egypt. Satan will do

---

[31] Watchman Nee, *The Prayer Ministry of the Church*, (New York: Christian Fellowship Ministries, n.d.).

the same thing as soon as we decide to have a regular prayer time. He will more than likely increase our work schedule or things that must get done around the house so we will not have time to pray.

Many will say, "Yes, but I pray throughout the day as needs come to mind." Excellent. That is what it means to pray without ceasing (1 Thess 5:17). But the real work of prayer is done by appointment. Daniel, I am sure, prayed intermittently throughout the day. But for seventy years he kept a regularly scheduled appointment with God in his bedroom in the morning, at noon, and in the evening (Dan 6:10). Maybe his schedule would fit yours. I know one businessman who likes to spend the first and last ten minutes of the day kneeling by his bed in prayer. Then he spends ten minutes at lunch. Instead of going out, he brings a sack lunch and cloisters himself in his office. It is regular scheduled prayer time. In fact, he is a busy doctor, an ophthalmologist.

So the type of prayer that avails or accomplishes much is earnest prayer and energetic prayer. You put a lot into it, and it takes a lot out. *Energoumenē* adds one more angle to the kind of prayer that accomplishes much. It is expectant.

EXPECTANT PRAYER

The kind of prayer that accomplishes much expects much. How do I get this out of *energoumenē*? It comes from the tense of the word. It is a participle acting as an adjective. As a participle (a dependent verb), it has a tense (past, present, future). This word is in the present tense, which can speak of continuous action. I like that in connection with prayer because in the Sermon on the Mount, in the very context of teaching his disciples about prayer, Jesus says (Matt 7:7-11):

Ask, and it will be given to you; seek, and you will find; knock, and it will be opened to you. For everyone who asks receives, and he who seeks finds, and to him who knocks it will be opened. Or what man is there among you who, if his son asks for bread, will give him a stone? Or if he asks for a fish, will he give him a serpent? If you then, being evil, know

how to give good gifts to your children, how much more will your Father who is in heaven give good things to those who ask Him!

In this context of prayer, expositors will often translate that first verse as, "Keep on asking, and it will be given to you; keep on seeking, and you will find; keep on knocking, and it will be opened to you." All of these verbs are in the present tense. But because of the context some translators like to bring out a "continuous" aspect to the asking, seeking, finding. I think the context warrants that. Other passages about persistent prayer such as the parable of the widow who wore the judge out by her continual coming to him also bring out this continual aspect of certain kinds of praying. Jesus starts the parable of the widow this way (Luke 18:1): "Then He spoke a parable to them, that men always ought to pray and not lose heart." I don't think the point of the parable is that we can wear God down so He will answer our prayer to keep us from bothering Him. Rather, each time we make the same request without receiving a yes or no answer, it gets harder to ask the next time. This is one way God builds our faith. So I would suggest that the present tense of the participle that describes the prayer of a righteous man is repeated and persistent. It is a sign of **expectancy**.

A beautiful little book, *Expectation Corner*,[32] tells of a king who prepared a city for some of his poor subjects. Not far from them were large storehouses where everything they could need would be supplied if they but sent in their requests. There was only one condition. They should always be on the lookout for the answer, so that when the king's messengers came with the answers to their requests, they would be found waiting and ready to receive them. A sad story is told of one despondent citizen who never expected to get what he asked for because he was too unworthy. He would go to the mailbox and send in his request only once and then go back in and shut his door and feel sorry for himself because he never got what he

---

[32] E. S. Eliot, *Expectation Corner*, (Henry Altemus Company, 1987).

asked for. One day he was taken to the king's storehouses, and there to his amazement he saw with his address on them, all the packages that had been made up for him and sent. The king's messenger had been to his door, but found it closed. He was not on the lookout. From that time on he learned the lesson of expectancy that Jesus and James were teaching. As Micah 7:7 said, "I will continually look to the Lord; I will always wait for the God of my salvation; my God will hear me."

Prayer that avails much will be sincere and earnest. There will be an energy transfer: energy out of the prayer warrior and into the prayer. It will also be persistent because it is expectant. Earnest, energetic, expectant prayer avails much. These are the three observations I would make regarding the word *energoumenē*. But how about an illustration? James obliges in 5:17-18.

> **Elijah was a man with a nature like ours, and he prayed earnestly that it would not rain; and it did not rain on the land for three years and six months. And he prayed again, and the heaven gave rain, and the earth produced its fruit.**

Elijah illustrates these three prayer principles. But as we look at him, it is encouraging to remember that he was a man subject to the same feelings, the same passions, and the same nature to which we are subject. The Greek word here (*homio* + *pathēs* = same + feelings = the same feelings) really refers to our feelings. We even get the pathos from the second word in this compound. Great men of history always appear to us as larger than life, especially biblical heroes. But James reminds us that Elijah was cut out of the same bolt of cloth as the rest of us. He had times when feelings of doubt, discouragement, and depression made his ministry seem futile and worthless.

In fact, I have noticed it is not uncommon for ministers to wrestle with depression. It does not make them defeated Christians. Often it is due to their make-up, plus the nature of their work. As we shall see, Elijah was subject to depression even after the greatest victory we know about in his life. His great victory over Ahab and his serpentine wife, Jezebel, with all their false gods and prophets, came on Elijah's knees. The victory did not come through theological debates with the heretics or through the preaching of a mighty sermon. Elijah pinned the enemy by wrestling on his knees.

James tells us Elijah prayed that it would not rain for three and a half years and then that it would rain, and that is exactly what happened. It was an amazing miracle. We stand back in awe and say, "Oh, I could never have faith so great. That is like saying to a mountain: 'Be removed into the sea.' I just don't have that much faith." Well, hold on a minute. Look where Elijah got his boldness to pray such a prayer. Look at 1 Kings 17:1. God told Elijah that it was not going to rain for several years. Then in 18:1, after three years and some months God again spoke to Elijah and told him it was about to rain. After God's Word in 17:1 about a drought, Elijah fell to his knees and began praying and it did not rain on the earth for three and a half years. Then after His Word in 18:1 Elijah again began praying, and sure enough, rain came. Some will say, "Well, Elijah did not need so much faith after all. God told him what was going to happen. That is not so spectacular after all."

In a way, that would be correct. Elijah merely took what God had promised and began to pray for it. He claimed God's promises in prayer. Not so spectacular. Or is it? Can you name the last promise given by God in His word that you claimed in prayer? Some soul counted the promises given by God in His Word. It came to almost 7,500 promises. I wonder how many of those promises we can name. Could our success in prayer be related to our knowledge of His promises? No wonder we don't have the victories Elijah had. We don't pray as Elijah prayed. Before we can claim God's promises, we must know them.

Let's peek into Elijah's prayer closet to see just how he illustrates prayer that is *energoumenē*. Howard Hendricks has a beautiful analysis of this prayer in his book *Elijah*.[33] In verse 41 Elijah announces to Ahab that he hears the sound of a great storm in his ears. That is the ear of faith because two verses later we learn there wasn't a cloud in

---

[33]   Hendricks, op. cit.

the sky. Elijah runs up to Mt. Carmel to watch, wait, and pray for the storm. There is not a cloud in the sky. He throws himself down on the ground and bows his head between his knees. This posture of prayer is not a spiritual callisthenic to impress God; it is an indication of inner attitude. Elijah was casting himself at the Lord's feet for the earth is His footstool. His posture was an indication of the earnestness of his prayer. Therefore, Elijah illustrates prayer that is sincere and **EARNEST**. James, too, says Elijah prayed earnestly.

We also see that Elijah's prayer was **EXPECTANT**. After praying in verse 42, he sends his servant to the cliff that would give him a view of the horizon out over the sea. What was he looking for? Storm clouds, obviously. Elijah expected an answer to his prayer. But there was a clear sky. So what did Elijah do? Pack up and go home? "Well, Lord, I prayed once. I gave you a chance to perform." No, because he expected an answer, Elijah kept praying. He sent his servant to the edge of the cliff to see if the answer was on its way seven times! Elijah prayed continuously until the answer came.

When it was all over, what did Elijah do? 1 Kings 19:4 says he fled from Jezebel into the wilderness. He was worn out. He showed he was truly a man of passions as we are. He prayed a stupid prayer he probably didn't mean. He said, "Lord, I've had enough. Take my life." If he really wanted to die, he would not have run from Jezebel. This only proves how much energy had gone out of him. There had been great energy output. Elijah was tired and needed to renew his strength. So Elijah's prayer was earnest; it was also **ENERGETIC**; and finally, it was expectant—he kept praying until the answer came. This is the kind of prayer that avails much.

James gives one more qualification, doesn't he? It is not enough to offer a prayer that is earnest, energetic, and expectant. That prayer must also come from a righteous man. What does that refer to? Do you have to be a preacher like Billy Graham or a prophet like Elijah? Scripture says (Rom 3:10), "There is none righteous, no, not one." No one is righteous because of the work he is doing for the Lord. God's righteousness comes by faith in Jesus Christ upon all those who believe. Until a man is declared righteous by God by putting his faith in the cross, his prayers will never be answered. If you are a child of the King, then come boldly unto the throne of grace. Don't leave all those gifts wrapped up in one of heaven's storage bins with your name and address on it. We have not because we ask not.

James got a nickname because of his prayer life—"Camel Knees." If people looked in at your prayer life, what might your nickname be? Doubter; Now and Then; You Owe Me; Mayday, Mayday; Snowjob; Only When Called Upon; Never? Prayer is God's medicine. It will cure the spiritual and physical problems that man's medicine will never touch. Much kneeling keeps us in good standing with God. We cannot stumble when we are on our knees. Remember the words of Jesus Christ when he said (Jn 16:23), "Verily, verily, I say unto you, Whatever you shall ask the father in my name, He will give it to you. Hitherto you have asked nothing in My name; ask and you shall receive, that your joy may be full."

In May of 1980, retired Col. Heath Bottomly gave the commencement address at Dallas Seminary. He wanted to talk about something that happened to him in WWII, so he brought out two journals in which he had written day by day during the war, one from 1944 and the other from 1945. He read several excerpts. The first one was dated Nov 7, 1944. He said, "Two men joined our squadron today, one of them a handsome aristocratic dude from New York, the Tyrone Power of the army, I decided to call him. He seemed to be a nice fella, but I couldn't talk with him. He spoke Long Gisland, and I couldn't understand a word. I was assigned to him as his check-out officer, and I thought, "Wow, will this ever be a disaster. We won't be able to communicate."

Bottomly's next entry was from a week later, Nov 14, 1944. "I really like this guy from New York. His name is Marshall Edward Kyle, III. He carries a Bible with him and he prays, if you can believe this, before he takes off each time. He says God has a plan for our lives, and some day he wants to share that plan with me." At that time,

Bottomly was not a Christian. The next entry is from January 1945. They were stationed in Hilandia, New Guinea. The entry read:

> We lost two pilots today. One of those pilots was my friend Marsh Kyle. He got separated from the others somehow, and we could see him coming in. There was a long, white plume of smoke streaming after his plane. As he got nearer, we could hear him say something about smoke in the cockpit and, "I can't see." The next thing we knew he had plunged straight into the cliff just short of the overrun of the runway.

Bottomly grabbed a piece of guy rope and lowered himself down the cliff. It was an avalanche of torn metal, split rubber, with 100-octane gas spread all over the cliff side, torching off everywhere. He looked and looked for Marsh's body, but couldn't find it. Sliding down the hillside were broken wings, pieces of metal, the broken canopy—everything was a mess.

Then a little further down the cliff, Bottomly saw a green piece of cloth that he thought might have been part of Marsh's overalls. He walked over to it and sure enough, looking down, he saw what was left of Marsh's body. Each of his four limbs was missing parts. He was burned so badly he looked like an enormous, blackened marshmallow. He was worse than dead.

They took a rope, tied it around the gory mess and hauled it to the top. They placed his body in a cardboard box, put him on one of those gooney birds, and watched it take off for Brisbane, Australia, sending him to the graves quarters at the quarter masters station in Brisbane. And that was the end of it.

Bottomly watched as his friends drove back from the airstrip in a Jeep, but he walked back. And as he did so, he was screaming. "Why him, God? Why Marshall? Why him. Of all the men in this squadron, he is the only one who knew you and acted like it. Why him?" He said as he got back to his bunk, he decided to write Marshall's mother a letter. He described what happened, but when he got to the part about "why," he left it blank, because he didn't know why.

Several years later, through various circumstances, Heath

Bottomly became a Christian. He retired from the military and opened a retreat center in Colorado for young people. He had a son he named Rock. He traveled 250,000 miles a year around the nation raising funds for his retreat center. He wrote books and journaled compulsively. On October 20, 1980, on a Tuesday night, he was in Greenville, South Carolina, finishing a mini-revival. At the end they invited everyone who had made a decision during the four days to come forward.

The pastor went to the foyer and Col. Bottomly was there signing autographs on his books and shaking hands. He said there was always some elderly woman there who wanted to know if he had known her son during the war. One lady was just hanging on to him, assuring him that he must certainly remember her son as he was signing a book. Then, out of his peripheral vision, he could tell there was a gap in the line after this woman. He kept signing, and all of a sudden he noticed the gap had been filled, but by someone rather short, not walking normally. As the person drew closer, Bottomly noticed the person's pant legs were awfully thin. Then he heard the click, click of metal knees. The on-comer then bent forward and lunged toward Bottomly, grabbing him about the neck with metal pinchers. It hurt. Bottomly asked himself, "What have I here?"

Bottomly finally looked up, straight into the angular, handsome face and warm, grey eyes of Marshall Edward Kyle, III. You see, because of bad weather, the gooney bird was not able to land at Brisbane. They went on to Sydney, Australia, where the hospital for the casualties of war for American forces was centered. When they opened the cardboard box, it was a requirement to do a mirror test. They had to pass a mirror in front of the deceased's nose to make sure it did not fog. It fogged. Kyle was still alive. There was a Jewish doctor there who took him on as a challenge. For three months he tried to straighten out the twisted torso, sewing, grafting, doing everything he possibly could to keep him alive. Marshall was not conscious.

Then they sent him to the great burn hospital in San Antonio, Brooks General Hospital, and for four years he was in a coma, kept alive only by tubes and machines. One day a passing nurse saw his eyes flicker and open. She cried out for the doctors. They worked with him for five more years before he could move along in a wheel chair. But Marshall Kyle persisted. He wanted to walk. He worked for another five years before he was able to walk with the aid of prosthetics. Unfortunately, he had yet another problem to overcome. He couldn't talk. After ten more years with the work of a specialist, he learned to speak with the aid of a special device in his throat.

On October 20, 1980, in Greenville, South Carolina, when these two war buddies grasped each other for the first time since the accident, Marshall Kyle was 60 years old, and he had just graduated from Furman University in that city. But he didn't stop there. He was headed to Duke Medical School to receive training in how to help accident victims. He told Bottomly in his raspy, electronic clatter, he was sorry he had never been able to explain God's special plan for Bottomly's life before the crash. But as he was going down, his last thought and last prayer were that Bottomly would become a Christian. That was even his first thought and his first prayer when he came out of his coma four years later. He continued praying for Bottomly when he had no proof that Bottomly himself had not been killed in the war.

Those prayers were answered. Does that tell you anything about the persistent, expectant, fervent prayer of a righteous man? Even more, does that tell you anything about the persistence of God? He did have a plan for Heath Bottomly's life. Heath's son Rock went to seminary, pastored several churches and is presently a senior fellow for Marriage and Leadership Studies at the Focus on the Family Institute. Generations of Christians and thousands of young people have been touched by the ripple effect of one prayer warrior who would not quit—Marshall Edward Kyle, III.

"GOD'S REHABILITATION PROGRAM"

James 5:19-20

It used to be said, "A man's home is his castle." Now, at least in America, it is becoming his fortress. Private spending on self-protection is growing. Smith & Wesson (January, 2013) can't fill all the orders for their guns, 54% of which are hand guns. People are pouring millions of dollars into weapons, and not just guns. Security includes alarm systems, special locks, watchdogs, and on it goes. Why? Because the hand of fear has tightened its grip on our country. It's little wonder why. According to an article in U. S. News and World Report, during one fifteen-year span (after prayer had been taken out of our public schools in 1962) murder increased 116%. Robbery tripled. Auto theft was up 256%. Crimes of violence—the kind that terrify people most—leaped 204%.

Why the sudden increase in crime? To be sure, the increase in broken homes adds to the spiral since 90% of all juvenile delinquents come from broken homes. Civil strife with its riots and "pig hunters" has helped inflate the crime balloon. But according to crime authorities themselves, the greatest single cause of this tidal wave of crime crashing across our nation has been the failure of our courts, prisons, and rehabilitation programs to deal with the criminals.

Official records show that almost two thirds of all crimes in this country are committed by repeat offenders, that is, people with records of previous arrests. One man in Washington, D.C., was arrested fifty-seven times in five years before he was convicted. Up to 35% of all persons awaiting trial are likely to be arrested for a second offense while out on bail. Because the court process is so slow and lenient, for these career criminals, crime *does* pay.

Even after conviction and sentencing, our penal institutions seem totally incapable of rehabilitating the criminal for an honest, productive life in society. *Confronting Confinement,* a June 2006 U.S. prison study by the bipartisan Commission on Safety and Abuse in America's Prisons, reports than on any given day more than 2 million people are incarcerated in the United States, and that over the course of a year, 13.5 million spend time in prison or jail. Within three years of their release, 67% of former prisoners are rearrested and 52% are re-incarcerated, a recidivism rate that calls into question the effectiveness of America's corrections system, which costs taxpayers $60 billion a year.[34] Recidivism, the tendency to relapse into prior behavior, is not only a problem in our prisons; it is also a problem in our churches.

It would be nice if we the church could sit back in our easy chairs and congratulate each other for not playing a direct role in our national failure to deter violations of state law. However, it may come as a shock for some of us to learn that we are directly responsible for deterring violations of *divine* law. God has appointed the church to be His task force to confront and correct serious violators of His laws. The church, through both its individuals and its body, make up a judicial, a correctional, and a rehabilitation system all in one. Yet our track record of failure is far more appalling than those of our nation's penal system.

Peter does not give percentages, but he addresses the problem in 2 Peter 2:18-22 where he says, "It has happened to them according to the true proverb: 'A dog returns to his own vomit,' and, 'a sow, having washed, to her wallowing in the mire.'" These repeaters

---

[34]   U.S. Prisons Overcrowded and Violent, Recidivism High—Infoplease. comhttp://www.infoplease.com/ipa/A0933722.html#ixzz2CQmZ3Qxf.

offenders either enter a life of hypocrisy or leave the church completely. Something is missing in our approach to those who have fallen—both in our nation and in the church. Undoubtedly, much of our failure stems simply from a state of ignorance—ignorance of both our responsibility and God's program for rehabilitation of the brother or sister in Christ who has strayed from the truth. In our final lesson on the book of James we will discuss God's Program for Rehabilitation. I want to establish **the missing link** that keeps us from restoring God's children to usefulness in James 5:19-20. In these verses we come to the end of our journey through James. Here is where we have been.

JAMES

"TRIUMPH THROUGH TRIALS"

Salutation (1:1)

Introduction (1:2-18)—The Value of Trials

Theme (1:19-20)—Qualities Needed

Body (1:21-5:6)—Qualities Developed

    I. *In Regard to Hearing (1:21-2:26)*

    II. *In Regard to Speaking (3:1-18)*

    III. *In Regard to Fighting (4:1-5:6)*

Conclusion (5:7-11)—Be Patient!

Final Thoughts (5:12-20)

This is where we are going:

Brethren, if anyone among you wanders from the truth, and someone turns him back, let him know that he who turns a sinner from the error of his way will save a soul from death and cover a multitude of sins.

Interpreting these final two verses of James has been notoriously difficult and so has the application. We will look at both, beginning with the interpretation.

THE INTERPRETATION: DIFFICULT

What It Does Not Mean

1. Not How to be "Born Again"

At first blush these verses surely talk about evangelism. After all, when we "save a soul," aren't we evangelizing? Not necessarily. In our discussion of 2:14 we decided evangelism could not be the subject because James is addressing the "brethren." We also showed from 1:16-18 that the word brother or brethren refers to people who have the new birth. Therefore, unless we believe a brother can lose his salvation, these verses are not about evangelism. We proposed that of the five uses of the word "save" (*sōzō*) in James, none refers to evangelism or going to heaven when we die.

If not "save," what about the word "soul"? Surely that means we are looking at evangelism. We discussed this word, *psyche*, in 1:21. There we saw that of the 105 uses of this word in the NT, only five or six refer to the immaterial part of man that goes to heaven or hell in the next life. About half of the rest refer to our inner psyche, and the other half to our time on earth, our "life." We suggested that both occurrences in James (1:21 and here) refer to our "life," our time on earth. Thus, 5:20 is not about evangelism.

2. Not How to be "Born-Again, Again"

In Hebrews 6:4-6 we read:

> For *it is* impossible for those who were once enlightened, and have tasted the heavenly gift, and have become partakers of the Holy Spirit, and have tasted the good word of God and the powers of the age to come, if they fall away, to renew them again to repentance, since they crucify again for themselves the Son of God, and put *Him* to an open shame.

Regardless of how we interpret this controversial passage, at least one thing is clear: you cannot be renewed to repentance. I do not think this passage means you can lose your salvation, but if it does, it also means you cannot get it back. I don't know anyone who thinks you can lose it, who doesn't also think you can get it back. But that cannot be done, at least not according to this passage. You can't be born-again, again.

What It Does Mean

1. A Christian brother or sister has strayed from his or her walk with the Lord.

The word for "wander" here is *planeō*, the word from which we get "planet." What is a planet but a physical body that orbits around a star? The implication is that this brother is in orbit. James is talking about someone "among you," and he addresses brethren. This brother wandered away from his orbit around the Son. He wandered from the truth, meaning he was once walking according to the truth.

2. Another brother helps to turn him or her back to the straight and narrow path.

The old KJV had the word "convert" in its translation since its translators assumed evangelism was in view. Someone got a convert. The NKJV says "turns" because the Greek word *epistrephō* means just that: turn or turn around. We have a picture of a brother walking with the Lord. He steps off the path of truth. Another brother comes along and turns him around, that is, brings him back to the fellowship, brings him back to walking according to the truth.

What about the word sinner? Isn't a sinner an unbeliever? Not according to its use in James. Remember James 4:8? James was urging the beloved brethren to deal with their sins after drawing near to God. You wouldn't tell an unbeliever to draw near to God. Nowhere in all of Scripture is such terminology used for unbelievers and God. Repent, believe—but not "draw near." James is calling the believers who step off the path double-minded, spiritual adulterers, and sinners.

3. The sinning brother may have been kept from a premature physical death.

The text says the sinner is saved from death. If this death does not refer to eternal separation from God, then what is it? There are two viable options. One would be a premature physical death. My father-in-law drank himself to death. He died of many diseases, but they were triggered by alcoholism. He was fifty-six. If someone had been able to reach him along the way, he might have been turned around and saved from a premature physical death.

Another possibility could be the living death of 1 Timothy 5:6. This probably is not as likely since it is primarily Paul that uses death to mean the misery of a defeated Christian life. It is a possibility though.

4. **The loving brother who reaches out to turn his sinning brother around certainly helps prevent a bunch of sins the sinning saint might have committed had he not been turned around.**

Here we must determine the meaning of to "cover a multitude of sins." The OT is helpful in that the word "cover" means to "prevent." Proverbs 10:12 says, "Hatred stirs up strife, but love covers all sins." Whatever "covers" means here, it must be the opposite of "stirs up," since we have what exegetes call antithetical parallelism. In Hebrew poetry sometimes the second line says the same thing as the first line, just in different words. That is called synonymous parallelism, since the second line is like a synonym for the first line. Based on that you can figure out what antithetical parallelism is. The second line is saying the opposite of the first line. If hatred stirs up strife love does the opposite. The opposite of stirring up would be something like suppresses or prevents.

I am suggesting that if this sinning brother had not been turned around, he would have committed many more sins on the way to his early demise. Yet from the time he is turned around, all the potential sins between his turn around and his early demise have been prevented. That is surely an encouragement to those who get involved in this type of ministry.

We are looking at God's rehabilitation program. It is just a couple of short verses. As we saw in 1:16-18, in the midst of trials, there are temptations. Nestled within every trial is an inherent temptation. Our brothers and sisters are just as susceptible to those temptations as we are. The devil waited until Jesus was weak physically to tempt him. He may wait until you are weak from your trials to tempt you. But when we fall, God encourages our brothers and sisters to reach out and help restore us, to help us up and turn back in the right direction. Fortunately, James was not the only one to write about this intra-body ministry. Having established our interpretation, let's spend some time on application. It is not easy.

THE APPLICATION: DIFFICULT

This kind of ministry is difficult for a number of reasons. One is because of the sensitivity of the sinner. He is already riddled with guilt, if he is normal. So approaching him about his sin is a little like jabbing around an infected wound on someone's arm. It is going to be sensitive and they will most likely recoil.

I mentioned an ophthalmologist friend and his routine for prayer. One day I saw a strange instrument in his office and asked him about it. He said it's what he uses to remove small objects from an eye. Some objects you can't just wash out or use a pair of tweezers to get out. He has to be very careful. The eye is one of the body's most sensitive parts. So he sets the patient's chin down as we have all experienced in an eye exam. Then he brings this instrument close to the eye and begins flicking. By that I mean there is a flexible metal prong that the doctor pulls back and lets go. It may take many flicks before he gets close enough to the eye to hit the object. With each attempt, the doctor moves the instrument a little closer to the eye. Obviously, this instrument is not handheld. The eye is extremely sensitive. So is the sinner. This is delicate, sensitive work. God is not ignorant of that, so he tells us how to rehabilitate our brothers carefully.

Restoration—Galatians 6:1

Brethren, if a man is overtaken in any trespass, you who *are* spiritual restore such a one in a spirit of gentleness, considering yourself lest you also be tempted.

1. "Overtaken"

The word here, *prolambanō*, means to get caught red-handed, meaning there is a lot of evidence. This is more than a rumor. Guilt is not a question.

2. "You"

Plural. This is not apparent from English, but the Greek (*humeis*) is very clear here. DO NOT GO ALONE. When we go alone, which is a different issue (Matt 18:15), the offender is more likely to react to you personally. It's harder for him to do that if there are several coming. After years of doing this kind of work with elder boards, we discovered that the key to success is sending someone who has a close relationship with the offender. It is the difference between being disciplined by a loving parent versus a maximum security prison guard. If the offender knows those approaching him love him, he will react one way. Without love, the reaction usually goes another direction. It is not always possible to send someone who has a close relationship, but it is certainly preferable.

3. "Spiritual"

This could mean anyone in the church who is walking with the Lord, but that is unlikely. It probably means those who have spiritual authority over the sinning brother. Although it is hard to prove that church membership existed in the early churches, there certainly isn't anything in Scripture disproving it. We have found it wise to have it, if for no other reason than it gives the elders a basis for church discipline. When someone joins the church we ask him if he is involved in any gross, moral sin (1 Cor 5:11-13). If he is, he is not allowed to join the church. It's not a country club where you pay your dues once a month and live however you wish. We also ask prospective members if they are willing to be in submission to the elders. If all systems are go and they join the church, there is a basis to come to them if they get involved in the kind of sin(s) that require confrontation.

"Spiritual" probably means something beyond having spiritual authority in the church. A surgeon is careful to cleanse his hands before invading someone else's body. Similarly, anyone doing this kind of work needs to be germ free. When I go to visit someone in the ICU, I am required to wash my hands and wear a gown and gloves. It would be detrimental for someone with a serious disease to import his own germs into the situation. Bottom line: the people doing this kind of work need to be walking in the light.

4. "Restore"

The word *katartizō* was used in regard to mending bones, restoring them to their former usefulness. This highlights an important aspect of God's Rehabilitation Program. The goal is always reconciliation and restoration. As long as someone is still alive, God has a place for him or her in the body. They can be used. Sometimes we may do things that will disqualify us for usefulness in certain capacities, but we are never incapacitated completely. After David's horrendous train wreck with Bathsheba and her husband, he prayed that God would restore the joy of his salvation. If God would do that, David promised that he would teach transgressors God's ways (Ps 51:13). The primary record we have of David doing just that is his song, (Ps 51) which was sung by the temple choir. How would you like to write a song about your most grievous sin and have the church choir sing it on Sunday morning? After the Bathsheba affair, I do not think David ever returned to his former "glory." Many of our sins carry consequences we cannot reverse, but David certainly was restored to usefulness.

5. "Gentleness"

Proverbs 18:19 says, "A brother offended is harder to win than a strong city. Their contentions are like the bars of a castle." This work takes sensitivity; it takes gentleness. Gentleness is a fruit of the Holy Spirit (Gal 5:22). Again, it is those who are Spirit-controlled that should be involved. This word also carries the idea of humility and meekness. We need to go with the attitude of, "But for the grace of God I would be in your shoes." It helps if you can remember a time when you strayed away yourself. There should never be a feeling of delight when correcting a brother like, "Oh, boy, won't this be fun! I have been waiting for this a long time." If you have it, stay home.

6. "Tempted"

Pride goes before a fall. If anyone is tempted to spiritual pride in the church, it is usually the spiritual leaders. Pastors and elders (often the same group) face this temptation more than most. They are also the ones who are usually called to facilitate rehab most often. But watch out! Going with the attitude of how much more righteous you are than the fallen sinner is an ominous prelude to your own fall.

Rehabilitation—2 Corinthians 2:5-11

> But if anyone has caused grief, he has not grieved me, but all of you to some extent—not to be too severe. This punishment which *was inflicted* by the majority *is* sufficient for such a man, so that, on the contrary, you *ought* rather to forgive and comfort *him,* lest perhaps such a one be swallowed up with too much sorrow. Therefore I urge you to reaffirm *your* love to him. For to this end I also wrote, that I might put you to the test, whether you are obedient in all things. Now whom you forgive anything, I also *forgive.* For if indeed I have forgiven anything, I have forgiven that one for your sakes in the presence of Christ, lest Satan should take advantage of us; for we are not ignorant of his devices.

This passage is a follow-up to 1 Corinthians 5, in which the incestuous brother was to be put out of the church if he would not repent of his sin. Again, there are important principles here that complement Galatians 6:1.

1. "Forgive"

The word to "forgive" here is *charizō,* the same word from which we get "grace." Of course, the idea behind this is Ephesians 4:32. We are to forgive one another just **as** Christ has forgiven us. One important aspect of His forgiveness is, "I will forgive their iniquity, and their sins I will remember no more" (Jer 31:34b). What is going on here? Has the omniscient God had a memory glitch? No, "to remember no more" does not mean in God's omniscience He *cannot* dredge up our sinfulness. It means He *will not* dredge it up as a barrier to fellowship. He will not throw it in our faces ever again. Confession and repentance took care of it. So, in God's rehab program for the church, once a brother is forgiven, we are to let it go. Don't bring it up anymore. Allow the forgiven sinner to enjoy fellowship.

In verse 10 we get an interesting angle on this forgiveness, which comes from the tense of the verb "forgive." Twice it refers to Paul's forgiveness of the offender. It is translated "have forgiven." The "have" is bringing out the perfect tense, which usually signifies completed, past action with present results. The point is that this is not partial forgiveness. Paul is not holding anything back. He has completely forgiven this brother in the past and the forgiveness still holds in the present.

2. "Comfort"

The word *parakaleō* here is the same word used for the Holy Spirit in its noun form. The *para* part of the word is just like our word parallel—alongside. It suggests coming alongside the forgiven person and putting our arms around him to welcome him home. It is the father running out to meet his prodigal son. It also means to encourage. The offender will feel sorrowful and discouraged because of his failure; he will need encouragement.

3. "Reaffirm"

The word here is *kurioō*, which means to validate. Here it means to reaffirm your love. The one who has strayed will feel unworthy of being loved. You need to do something tangible, if possible, to validate your words. Words are one thing. James is big on actions.

4. "Take Advantage"

The word *pleonekteō* means to "defraud, cheat, or outwit." Because "devices" comes from the word *voemata* for "thoughts or designs," the word *pleonekteō* probably means "to outwit." Satan is always trying to outwit us. He has a plethora of "designs or devices" to do that. He hit the early church from the outside (the Sanhedrin), then the inside (Ananias and Saphira); then the outside (the Sanhedrin), then the inside (the widows); then the outside (killing of Stephen), and on and on. He is always looking for an angle from which to destroy the church or an individual. In this scenario in James, Satan already has a strong hold on the sinning brother because of his sexual sins. When he repents and seeks forgiveness from the church, if not handled carefully, Satan will take advantage of the situation and destroy the one repenting.

Tim Keller wrote an awesome book about the prodigal son called *The Prodigal God*.[35] In it he remarks that most of the sermons on this passage in Luke 15 are directed at prodigal sons and are about the forgiving father. He argues that preachers are speaking to the wrong crowd. Keller says there aren't any prodigal sons sitting in church. That is why they are prodigals. He claims churches are full of "older brothers." These are the people who "have never sinned." Of course they have sinned, but not to the extent of the prodigal. But these people are not happy when the prodigal returns. The father was happy; the prodigal was happy; it says the people were happy. There was only one unhappy person at the reunion—the older brother. Why? Because he was a legalist and had always been faithful to his father. His younger brother was getting something he didn't deserve (called grace), and he was not getting what he did deserve. He was angry. Be wary of legalism. It is one of Satan's ways to outwit us. It is one of his devices. If he wins, we lose the prodigal. He will go right back to the slop.

Philip Yancy wrote about what turned him off about church when he was young in his book *Church: Why Bother?* He said:

> Grace, I concluded, was the factor most glaringly absent from my childhood church. If only our churches could communicate grace to a world of competition, judgment, and ranking—a world of ungrace—then church would become a place where people gather eagerly, without coercion, like desert nomads around an oasis. Now, when I attend church, I look inward and ask God to purge from me the poisons of

---

35   Timothy Keller, *The Prodigal God*, (New York: Penguin Group, 2008).

rivalry and criticism and to fill me with grace. And I seek out churches characterized by a state of grace.[36]

Why is it that there is so much recidivism in the church? It could simply be because rehabilitation is a forgotten function in so many of our churches. Even when it is attempted, it often backfires. I wonder why. What is the missing link in our attempt to put God's Rehabilitation Program to work? Perhaps John Wesley's mother put her finger on the missing link when she was asked which of her children she loved the best. She said, "Which child of mine do I love best? I love the sick one until he is well, the one away from home until she's back."

Right there, Mrs. Wesley captures the missing link in most rehabilitation programs. Love. Henri Nouwen described lonely, abandoned people who have no one to love them in his book *The Wounded Healer*. "No man can stay alive when nobody is waiting for him," he writes. "Everyone who returns from a long and difficult trip is looking for someone waiting for him at the station or the airport. Everyone wants to tell his story and share his moments of pain and exhilaration with someone who stayed home, waiting for him to come back."[37] Love will reduce recidivism in the church. As Proverbs says, "Love covers (prevents) all sins."

---

[36] Philip Yancy, *The Church: Why Bother?*, (Grand Rapids: Zondervan, 1998), 23.

[37] Henri J. M. Nouwen, *The Wounded Healer*, (New York: Doubleday, 1979), 66.

POSTSCRIPT

It is an understatement to say that life keeps a sloppy appointment book when it comes to trials. You never know when they'll drop in. The most unexpected visitors knock on the front door of our lives, many of them unfriendly. Just this week as I was landing from my weekly trip to Midland, TX, I got a text that a parade honoring veterans stopped with one of the floats on a railroad track, and yes, that float full of veterans was hit by a train, killing four and injuring many. Go figure.

This past month the Children's Director at our church went into the emergency room because of a persistent cough. He lives and breathes children and has so for the ten years I have known him. He and his wife, Kelly, have two children of their own and adopted three more of various races. They have been foster parents with over twenty kids who have gone through their home in the last decade. Adam is forty-six. The cough led to pericarditis, which led to cardiomyopathy, which led to a 15% ejection fraction for expelling blood from his heart (55-85% is normal, I am told). At midnight on Sunday his organs began to shut down. By divine intervention (we believe) he was taken to the medical center in downtown Houston where they saved his life—so far. Adam walks around with a big clot that they are trying to thin out with Coumadin and other blood thinners. He is on a list for a transplant. He may or may not make it long enough to get one.

We all know cases like this. Do they make sense? Not in this life.

Neither did my son's death, but then, neither did the death of Stephen, the first Christian martyr, or Jesus Himself. The Book of James points us to a world where we will not miss this old world, which is passing away. It encourages us to park our cars and our cares in another lot. It encourages us to look for our help in and anchor our hopes in the One who is sovereign over this world and is great enough to ultimately make something glorious out of something calamitous.

Most of all James calls for endurance. Someday we will see the "end *intended by* the Lord—that the Lord is very compassionate and merciful." My wife and I look forward to the day when our firstborn son, our beloved Jimmy, welcomes us into that world.

DAVE ANDERSON graduated from Rice University in 1967. He received his Th.M. from Dallas Theological Seminary in 1972 and his Ph.D. from Dallas Seminary in the Greek New Testament and Early Christian Literature in 1998. He and his wife Betty have served as church planters in the Houston area for over thirty years. He has served as Adjunct Professor for Dallas Seminary in Greek NT, Systematic Theology, and Bible Exposition and is currently President and Professor of Biblical Languages and Systematic Theology at Grace School of Theology.

CPSIA information can be obtained at www.ICGtesting.com
Printed in the USA
LVOW13s0111300913

354595LV00006B/15/P

9 780988 411234